A SOCIOLOGICAL HISTORY OF
CHRISTIAN WORSHIP

In this book the 2,000-year history of Christian worship is viewed
from a sociological perspective. Martin Stringer develops the idea of
discourse as a way of understanding the place of Christian worship
within its many and diverse social contexts. Beginning with the
biblical material the author provides a broad survey of changes over
2,000 years of the Christian church, together with a series of case
studies that highlight particular elements of the worship, or specific
theoretical applications. Stringer does not simply examine the mainstream traditions of Christian worship in Europe and Byzantium, but
also gives space to lesser-known traditions in Armenia, India,
Ethiopia and elsewhere. Offering a contribution to the ongoing
debate that breaks away from a purely textual or theological study
of Christian worship, this book provides a greater understanding of
the place of worship in its social and cultural context.

MARTIN D. STRINGER is lecturer in the Sociology and Anthropology
of Religion and Head of the Department of Theology and Religion
at the University of Birmingham.

A SOCIOLOGICAL HISTORY OF CHRISTIAN WORSHIP

MARTIN D. STRINGER

CAMBRIDGE
UNIVERSITY PRESS

PUBLISHED BY THE PRESS SYNDICATE OF THE UNIVERSITY OF CAMBRIDGE
The Pitt Building, Trumpington Street, Cambridge, United Kingdom

CAMBRIDGE UNIVERSITY PRESS
The Edinburgh Building, Cambridge, CB2 2RU, UK
40 West 20th Street, New York NY 10011–4211, USA
10 Stamford Road, Oakleigh, VIC 3166, Australia
Ruiz de Alarcón 13, 28014 Madrid, Spain
Dock House, The Waterfront, Cape Town 8001, South Africa

http://www.cambridge.org/9780521525596
©Martin D. Stringer 2005

First published 2005

Printed in the United Kingdom at the University Press, Cambridge

Typeface Adobe Garamond, 11/12.5 pt.   *System* Advent 3B2 8.07f [PND]

A catalogue record for this book is available from the British Library

Library of Congress Cataloguing in Publication data

Stringer, Martin D.
A sociological history of Christian worship / Martin D. Stringer.
p.   cm.
Includes bibliographical references and index.
ISBN 0 521 81955 5 (hardback) – ISBN 0 521 52559 4 (paperback)
1. Worship–History. 2. Worship–Sociological aspects. 3. Religion and sociology.
I. Title.
BV5.S77 2005
264'.009–dc22   2004057069

ISBN 0 521 81955 5 hardback
ISBN 0 521 52559 4 paperback
ISBN 13: 978052181955 8 hardback
ISBN 13: 978052152559 6 paperback

Contents

Preface and acknowledgements

The origins of this book go back to my final year at University in Manchester when I sat through a course on the History of Liturgy delivered by Richard Buxton and Kenneth Stevenson. I remember sitting, even then, thinking that one day I would really love to deliver a course of this kind. My own course, however, would look nothing like that offered by Richard and Kenneth. This is not to say anything against the course itself; I learnt a great deal from it, and it inspired many different thoughts that have ultimately led to this book. I am very grateful for all that they taught me. It was simply that at the time I was taking a degree in Social Anthropology and the approach to liturgy taken by Richard and Kenneth was basically textual. I could see so many possible connections between the work that I was doing in anthropology and the material I was being presented with in the course on liturgy. I was just dying to bring the two together.

Twelve years later, having been appointed as a Lecturer in the Sociology and Anthropology of Religion at Birmingham University, I was invited by the then Head of Department, Frances Young, to offer a course on the History of Liturgy for the B.A. in Theology. This was my chance to bring together all the reading and reflection that I had done in the previous twelve years and to create the kind of course that I wanted to teach. The response of the students was very positive, and I have taught that course a number of times since that first attempt. I have also changed it over time through further reading and in response to the questions and comments from the students themselves. Without the contribution from those students this book would never have been written.

This book, therefore, derives from that course, although in a very indirect way. It is not a textbook as such. It does not aim to bring together all that we need to know about Christian worship or all that should be taught in any course on the subject. In this book I am aiming to present something of the thinking behind the course, the way in which anthropological and sociological ideas and concepts can be applied to the history of Christian worship. In writing the book, however, I have been conscious of aiming at students of liturgy as well as established scholars in the field, and at all those worshippers who are keen to explore their practice further. I have aimed, therefore, to be comprehensive in my scope while focusing on specific situations that I feel could be of interest to the general reader, or that relate to specific elements of the theoretical discussion. I have not tried to enter into all the intricacies or sophistication of the theories themselves; this is not a book on social theory. However, I have tried to present as much of the theoretical material as would be necessary to understand its application. I have also tried to focus on recent work in social history and liturgical study rather than going back over older arguments in the discipline. My bibliography, therefore, concentrates primarily on works in English that have been produced in the last thirty years.

In writing this book I have, of course, to recognise my debt of gratitude to Richard Buxton and Kenneth Stevenson, who set me on this road back in Manchester over twenty years ago. I also have to thank many different colleagues in the field of liturgical study and sociology that I have learnt from over the years, especially those who have attended the conferences of the Society for Liturgical Study and the BSA Sociology of Religion Study Group where elements of this work have been presented. I also have to thank my colleagues at Birmingham who have encouraged me in this work and with whom I have had many useful conversations on various aspects of the task. In particular I wish to recognise the support of David Taylor and Christine Alison, who have provided between them many stimulating hours of conversation on the minutiae of situation and theory. I also wish to thank Katharina Brett and the editors and readers of Cambridge University Press who, through careful and thoughtful engagement with the text, have contributed so much to the finished book. Finally, I wish to thank David Salt without whom, it is fair to say, the text would never have been completed. In particular I wish to thank him for his continuing support and for the contribution of his knowledge, expertise and invaluable book collections in the fields of Armenian, Georgian, Ethiopian and Byzantine history. Needless to say, despite the contributions of so many other scholars, all the remaining errors and mistakes in the book are entirely my own.

Discourse, devotion and embodiment

HISTORIES OF WORSHIP

For almost as long as we have records of specifically Christian worship there has been a sense of the history of that worship. In his letter to the Corinthians, written twenty to thirty years after the death and resurrection of Jesus, Paul talks about what 'I received from the Lord' and 'passed on to you'.[1] This sense of tradition is also central to many of the earliest commentators. The compilers of what were to become known as the 'church orders' in the third and fourth centuries made a feature both of the supposed apostolic origin of these orders and of their collecting together of elements of the tradition.[2] 'Tradition' dominated Christian thinking on the history of worship for much of the first fifteen hundred years, with the explicit assumption that all Christians continued the practices instituted by Jesus and his Apostles. Beginning in the seventeenth century, however, new ideas began to develop and the understanding of a 'history' of Christian worship began to take root.

With printing and the development of scholarship Benedictine monks such as J. Mabillon (1632–1707) and E. Martène (1654–1739) began to collect together, and print, the various manuscripts relating to their own specific 'tradition'.[3] It was in studying these manuscripts, noting their differences and developments, and in tracing these through time that the origins of 'liturgical' study can be seen. The study of the 'liturgy', that is of the texts of Christian worship, continued to develop over the centuries. At

---

[1] 1 Corinthians 11:23. All quotations are taken from the New International Version.
[2] P. Bradshaw, *The Search for the Origins of Christian Worship, Sources and Methods for the Study of Early Liturgy*. London: SPCK, 2002, 73–97.
[3] Mabillon's *De Liturgica Gallicana Libri Tres* was first published in Paris in 1685 and Martène's *De Antiquis Ecclesiae Ritibus* was published in Rouen in 1700–2. E. Palazzo, *A History of Liturgical Books from the Beginning to the Thirteenth Century*. Collegeville: Liturgical Press, 1998, 7–8.

first things developed relatively slowly with an emphasis on the collection and publication of texts. However, with the development of historiography in the nineteenth century, the collection and cataloguing of texts was transformed into the 'science of liturgiology'.[4] Drawing on contemporary scholarly models of comparative linguistics, texts were compared and laws developed that were seen to determine the development of liturgical practice. The earliest attempts simply set out principles for the dating and comparisons of texts, such as William Palmer's *Origines Liturgicae*.[5] Later work tried to develop principles that could place any prayer into a family type or historical period based on its language and style.[6] Towards the end of the century this came together in Anton Baumstark's classic work on *Comparative Liturgy* that still stands today as one of the very few works of theory as applied to liturgical history.[7]

At the same time a more narrative approach to the history of Christian worship was also developing, reaching its classic form in L. Duchesne's *Christian Worship*.[8] These two traditions, the theoretical and the narrative, combined in what have become the definitive volumes in the study of Christian worship, Gregory Dix's *Shape of the Liturgy*, and Joseph Jungmann's *Missarum Sollemnia*.[9] In the *Shape*, Dix presents a narrative account of the history of the eucharist, concentrating particularly on the first four centuries (with subsequent chapters on medieval developments and the English Reformation), while also applying a structuralist style of analysis that leads him to define a common shape for all eucharistic liturgies across time and space.[10] Jungmann focuses specifically on the Western, Catholic tradition and begins with a narrative account of the development of the rite. This is followed by a detailed exploration of each element of the mass, producing what might be called an 'archaeological'

---

[4] J. M. Neale, *Essays on Liturgiology and Church History*. London: Saunders, Otley & Co., 1863.

[5] W. Palmer, *Origines Liturgicae, or Antiquities of the English Ritual, and A Dissertation on Primitive Liturgies*. Oxford: Oxford University Press, 1832. See M. D. Stringer, 'Antiquities of an English Liturgist: William Palmer's Use of Origins in the Study of the English Liturgy', *Ephemerides Liturgicae*, 108 (1994), 146–56.

[6] M. D. Stringer, 'Style against Structure: The Legacy of John Mason Neale for Liturgical Scholarship' *Studia Liturgica*, 27:2 (1997), 235–45.

[7] A. Baumstark, *Comparative Liturgy*. London: Mowbray, 1958.

[8] L. Duchesne, *Christian Worship: Its Origin and Evolution, A Study of the Latin Liturgy up to the Time of Charlemagne*. London: SPCK, 1904.

[9] G. Dix, *The Shape of the Liturgy*. London: Adam & Charles Black, 1945, and J. A. Jungmann, *The Mass of the Roman Rite, Its Origins and Development (Missarum Sollemnia)*. New York, Benziger Brothers, 1959.

[10] Dix's 'shape' is more closely related to the early structuralism of Arnold Van Gennep's work on *The Rites of Passage* (London: Routledge & Kegan Paul, 1960) than the later structuralism of Claude Lévi-Strauss and his colleagues.

approach to liturgical history.[11] Structuralism and other theoretical traditions have been applied to liturgical history through the remaining years of the twentieth century but never in such a systematic fashion.[12]

Throughout this tradition of historical writings a number of principles became established as defining features of all 'liturgical' history. These were determined largely by the kind of data that the authors had to work with. The first principle was inherited from the earliest pioneers and has been retained to the present day. This is an emphasis on texts. The most complete evidence that we have from the past exists in the form of texts. These texts have been collected over the centuries, edited, published and made available to scholars, and, while they raised many interesting questions about dating and interpretation, it is easy to assume that the texts are all that we possess. It is only in recent years, with the growth of social history and the application of other kinds of evidence, that the idea of a history of liturgical practice or of personal responses to worship, rather than liturgical texts, has become possible.[13] This is not to deny the value of textual analysis. Great strides have been made in the understanding of texts, and without this work the broader project of a history of practice or responses would have been all but impossible. However, it is still the case that the analysis of texts and the tracing of elements of rite through the texts remains one of the principal tasks of those who call themselves 'liturgists'. It is for this reason that I have titled this work a history of 'Christian worship', and for the most part avoided the word 'liturgy' in what follows. I am by training an anthropologist with an interest in the practice of worship, not a textual scholar interested in the minutiae of words and phrases.

The other consequence of the particular historical tradition associated with the study of 'liturgy' is also related to the textual nature of the analysis, and concerns the time frame covered by the histories that have been written. The Benedictine origins of liturgical scholarship have been

---

[11] By 'archaeological' I refer to the process of discovering the origins, or even pre-history, of various elements of the rite in the different strata of the textual record. See M. Foucault, *The Archaeology of Knowledge*. London: Routledge, 1972.

[12] See R. Taft, 'The Structural Analysis of Liturgical Units: An Essay in Methodology', in R. Taft (ed.), *Beyond East and West, Problems in Liturgical Understanding*. Washington: Pastoral Press, 1984, 151–66.

[13] Although even in a detailed and comprehensive work of social history as applied to Christian worship, such as Miri Rubin's *Corpus Christi, The Eucharist in Late Medieval Culture* (Cambridge: Cambridge University Press, 1991) or Susan White's *A History of Women in Christian Worship* (London: SPCK, 2003), the emphasis is still primarily on texts, albeit a very wide range of texts, and the ideas they express.

developed in mainland Europe, and have led to a great tradition of scholar-ship on medieval liturgy exploring and elucidating the amazing diversity, variety and intricacy of the medieval traditions of Western Europe. This tradition is best summarised in Cyrille Vogel's great work on the sources of medieval liturgy.[14] Another tradition is seen more clearly in Dix's book on the *Shape of the Liturgy*.[15] This focuses on the first four centuries and then jumps through to the Reformation and ends with a few relevant comments about the present day. For almost as long as scholars have been working on the history of Christian worship, one of the principal concerns has been the question of origins.[16] Many scholars, even up to the end of the nineteenth century, assumed that we could get back to the very words that Jesus, or at least his immediate disciples, used. Others, recognising the incredible diversity of texts within the earliest traditions, began to look for other kinds of origin. Dix reconstructed the 'origin' of Christian worship as a structure or 'shape' rather than a text. Others have looked to the Jewish traditions to try and identify sources for a different kind of origin.[17] Increasingly, today, scholars recognise that to talk of a single 'origin' does not equate with the data that we have.[18] However, even in the most recent studies there is still a tendency to place undue weight on the first few centuries of liturgical history at the expense of the following sixteen.

Whether the liturgical history is written from the tradition of medieval scholarship or from that focused on origins, and the first four cent-uries, even if it is written from the perspective of the Reformation churches,[19] there has been an almost universal neglect of the period from the end of the sixteenth century to the middle of the twentieth cent-ury when, in textual terms, very little is thought to have happened.[20] Linked with this has been an emphasis, seen most clearly in Jungmann's work,[21] on the Western tradition, whether that of Latin Christianity or, more recently, the Reformation churches that grew out of this tradition. An increasing number of scholars have been working on the Eastern tradition, particularly that of the Byzantine Rite (which again for obvious textual reasons concentrates on early and medieval

---

[14] C. Vogel, *Medieval Liturgy, An Introduction to the Sources*. Washington: The Pastoral Press, 1986.
[15] Dix, *The Shape*. [16] See Bradshaw, *Search*, for a recent review of this tradition.
[17] See pp. 32–41 below for a wider discussion of this body of work. [18] Bradshaw, *Search*, 20.
[19] See, for example, G. S. Wakefield, *An Outline of Christian Worship*. Edinburgh: T. & T. Clark, 1998 or J. F. White, *A Brief History of Christian Worship*. Nashville: Abingdon Press, 1993.
[20] There are a few notable exceptions to this, including Kenneth Stevenson's *Covenant of Grace Renewed, A Vision of the Eucharist in the Seventeenth Century*. London: DLT, 1994.
[21] Jungmann, *Missarum Sollemnia*.

traditions).[22] A few notable scholars have also worked on other Eastern traditions, but often as examples of obscure, exotic and interesting variations on the Latin or Byzantine traditions, rather than with any wish to explore how these traditions were used in and of themselves.[23]

All of this leaves us with a very partial view of the history of Christian worship. It is a view that is dominated by an understanding of the texts rather than that of practice. It is a view that is focused on certain times and places at the expense of others. Finally it is a view that is often written from within the tradition itself, for purposes that are closely related to the needs of the church. Walter Frere's classic work on the *Anaphora*, for example, in which he outlines the early history of the Eucharistic Prayer, is written specifically to rebut those who questioned his ideas about liturgical revision in England in the 1920s and 1930s.[24] Much of the history of Christian worship has been written with half an eye on the needs of the revisers and renewers of contemporary worship. Practically all the rest has been written by those with a theological as well as a historical interest. Alongside the textual emphasis in the liturgical tradition, therefore, there has been a constant theological emphasis. This is not surprising, or necessarily a problem. Theology and worship are intimately connected and it would be impossible to discuss one without exploring the other, as many contemporary theologians are discovering.[25] To tell the story, however, with a pre-determined theological perspective may not be helpful to the wider development of scholarship. We must also recognise that there are other ways of telling the story that can, within reason, put the theological to one side. This is the approach that I intend to take in this particular text.

Recent histories of Christian worship, therefore, tend to fall into three types. There have in the last twenty years of the twentieth century been a series of excellent studies of specific forms of Christian worship. Kenneth Stevenson's work on marriage,[26] or Robert Taft's work on the Office[27] are good examples of histories that focus on one specific rite.

[22] See R. F. Taft, *The Byzantine Rite, A Short History.* Collegeville: Liturgical Press, 1992 and H. Wybrew, *The Orthodox Liturgy: The Development of the Eucharistic Liturgy in the Byzantine Rite.* New York: St Vladimir's Seminary Press, 1989.

[23] A recent exception to this is the work of Gabriele Winkler on Armenian and other Eastern rites. See the essays in G. Winkler, *Studies in Early Christian Liturgy and Its Context.* Aldershot: Ashgate, 1997.

[24] W. H. Frere, *The Anaphora or Great Eucharistic Prayer, An Eirenical Study in Liturgical History.* London: SPCK, 1938.

[25] See, for example, A. Kavanagh, *On Liturgical Theology.* New York: Pueblo, 1984 and C. Pickstock, *After Writing: On the Liturgical Consummation of Philosophy.* Oxford: Blackwell, 1998.

[26] K. Stevenson, *Nuptial Blessing, A Study of Christian Marriage Rites.* London: SPCK, 1982.

[27] R. Taft, *The Liturgy of the Hours in East and West, The Origins of the Divine Office and its Meaning for Today.* Collegeville: The Liturgical Press, 1986.

Graham Woolfenden's work on early Spanish worship is just one of the latest in a long line of specific historical and regional studies.[28] A second type of history is being written primarily by historians in the social or 'cultural' history tradition. These writers have aimed to explore personal narratives, court records or other texts that focus on real people, to explore the way in which individuals at different times and places have responded to worship. Susan White's *History of Women in Christian Worship* is an excellent example of this kind of writing and quotes many similar texts that focus on more specific times and places.[29] The final type of history that is common today is that which is aimed at the student, either those studying the tradition as part of a wider study of Christian history,[30] or those who are training for ministry in the church. These studies tend to be partial and, as James White's title illustrates, are in practice only *Brief Histor[ies] of Christian Worship.*[31]

This text probably falls into the final type. It would be impossible for me to draw on all the work that has been written about every single element of Christian worship and to combine this into a single volume, or even into many volumes. Every history has to make choices and to set limitations. This, therefore, is inevitably a 'brief history'. However, as I hope I have already suggested, it is a brief history with a specific agenda. It is not a history of texts. It is not a history of theologies. It is not a history of personal responses to worship. It is a history written by a social scientist with an interest in the practice of worship. It therefore both draws on, and in many ways distinguishes itself from, many of the traditions of liturgical history that I have just outlined.

CULTURE, RELIGION AND DISCOURSE

If I am not going to construct my history in terms of texts or theologies then I need to find an alternative organising principle, something that I can say that this is a history of. For an anthropologist one obvious alternative may be 'culture', a history of Christian worship in its cultural context, or perhaps a cultural history of Christian worship. This would certainly be a

---

[28] G. Woolfenden, *Daily Prayer in Christian Spain, A Study of the Mozarabic Office.* London: SPCK, 2000.
[29] S. J. White, *Women.*
[30] See, for example, J. Harper, *The Forms and Orders of Western Liturgy from the Tenth to the Eighteenth Century, A Historical Introduction and Guide for Students and Musicians.* Oxford: Oxford University Press, 1991.
[31] White, *Brief History.*

possibility, and to some extent what follows could be described in both these ways. However, I remain very uneasy about the concept of 'culture'. As used by anthropologists, culture developed as a way of describing and analysing contemporary societies. It is therefore a synchronic rather than a diachronic concept, it captures a snapshot of society rather than providing a dynamic, changing picture.[32] Certainly Edward Tylor, in his famous definition of 'culture', uses the term to discuss evolutionary history.[33] However, the discipline moved on from this, rejected evolution and began to use the term synchronically. In later anthropological writings we see the possibility of the world being divided into a mosaic of self-contained and unique cultures, each one of which needed to be investigated and described by an anthropologist.[34] Later writing still has challenged the essentially static nature of this model and talks in terms of the dynamics of culture, both across time and in terms of the boundaries between cultures.[35] However, for all this, there is still, associated with the word itself, a sense of 'culture' as something all-encompassing, essentially coherent and fundamentally static.[36] This does not help us, I would suggest, to engage in a historical account of Christian worship over two thousand years.

At the very least we need to ask whether we can talk in any meaningful sense about a single 'Christian culture' that can cover such a span of time. If not, then we need to explore Christian cultures, or perhaps the presence of Christianity with other, perhaps pagan or humanist 'cultures'. Where does one 'culture' finish and another begin? At which point does the late Roman culture of Gaul become the early medieval culture of France? What about the possibility that in any one region we can talk about layers of culture; an aristocratic culture alongside a popular or peasant culture, or perhaps an urban culture contrasted with a rural culture? Questions may also be raised about the existence of 'subcultures'. Was Christianity a distinct 'subculture' within first-century Corinth, or in thirteenth-century Kerala? More importantly, what would it actually mean to suggest that it was, and what impact would that have on the understanding of worship? Finally, at

---

[32] See for example Roy Wagner's discussion in *The Invention of Culture.* Chicago: University of Chicago Press, 1981.

[33] E. Tylor, *Primitive Culture: Researches into the Development of Mythology, Philosophy, Religion, Art and Custom.* London: John Murray, 1871, I, I.

[34] J. Beattie, *Other Cultures: Aims, Methods and Achievements in Social Anthropology.* London: Routledge & Kegan Paul, 1964, 22.

[35] A. Rosman and P. G. Rubel, *The Tapestry of Culture: An Introduction to Cultural Anthropology.* New York: McGraw-Hill, 1995.

[36] See Tim Ingold's *Evolution and Social Life.* Cambridge: Cambridge University Press, 1986 for a wider discussion of these trends.

what point in the third or fourth century does Christianity cease to be a 'subculture' and then become the 'culture' of the later Roman Empire?

'Culture' has also been claimed as a term by disciplines outside of anthropology, particularly those that trace their roots back to 'cultural studies'. In this context the understanding of culture is far less static than the traditional anthropological use of the term. However, it is very difficult to define exactly what it is that these disciplines actually mean by 'culture'. In part the term is used to refer to 'popular culture', the product of the ordinary people of a society, rather than the art, music and literature of the elite. This expectation goes back to the work of the Centre for Contemporary Cultural Studies in the University of Birmingham where this use of the term was first publicised.[37] In a similar way 'material culture', as used by many historians and archaeologists, also refers more to the everyday objects of a society rather than the grand, defining set pieces. In these terms, much of my own approach in this book is 'cultural'. I am trying to get beyond the textual and the elite understandings of worship to take account of everyday behaviour, the use of space, material artefacts and the practices of ordinary people. In another sense, however, I am not perhaps going as far as many 'cultural historians'.

I am not, for example, going to be giving as much space to the domestic or private context of worship as I could have done. As such I am conscious of missing out on much of what is currently being uncovered about women's understanding of and roles within worship, despite the exciting nature of this work.[38] This book deliberately offers a study of the social, or public, practice of worship and the impact that Christian worship has had on societies as a whole. It must always be recognised, however, that the boundaries between the public and the private, the domestic and the social, are always porous and constantly shifting over time, even to the extent that some authors deny such a boundary exists at all in some periods of Christian history.[39] I simply do not have the space in this book to cover everything, and that perhaps is my main concern with the concept of 'culture'; it has come to suggest that it does cover everything with no real discrimination between what is cultural and what is not. I have chosen, therefore, to use the word 'sociological' in the title of the book in a

---

[37] S. Hall, 'Cultural Studies and the Centre: Some Problematics and Problems', in S. Hall, D. Hobson, A. Lowe and P. Willis (eds.), *Culture, Media, Language*. London: Unwin Hyman, 1980, 15–47.

[38] See White, *Women*, and T. Berger, *Women's Ways of Worship, Gender Analysis and Liturgical History*. Collegeville, Liturgical Press, 1999.

[39] White, *Women*, 201–5.

deliberate attempt to narrow my own focus. This is particularly true in relation to the wider possibilities of the so-called 'cultural'.

As an anthropologist, therefore, I find the concept of 'culture' far too vague and much too slippery for the kind of purposes that I am trying to engage with in this text. Perhaps equally problematic is the relationship between 'culture' and 'religion'. Religion, like culture, is a wide, catch-all kind of concept that is almost impossible to define. Like culture it also carries associations of continuity and coherence that make it difficult to use in a historical context. Any author writing on the history of religion in a specific period of time has to hedge their discussion round with so many qualifications that it becomes difficult to see exactly what they may mean by 'religion' in that specific context.[40] Effectively, religion is one of those terms whose meaning we assume that we know and which we can apply to any particular context, but when we come to try to define it, in anything but a very specific sense, it begins to elude our grasp.[41] There will always be elements of religion that are considered to be 'on the edge': superstition perhaps, or even magic. There will always be questions about the relationship between 'religion' and other spheres of life such as 'economics' or 'politics'; a discussion of one can never fully avoid a discussion of the others. In most societies, certainly those unaffected by the modern separation of religion from other aspects of society, religion cannot easily be distinguished as one thing among many and studied as a separate entity. If we then turn the discussion to focus on the perspective of the individual, rather than the global perspective of society, we can see individuals describing religion more as a 'way of life' encompassing everything that they do, rather than a series of distinct activities or ideas confined to a time or place of their own. Such a 'way of life' is very close to traditional understandings of 'culture' and it can, therefore, be argued that for many – if not the vast majority of – societies throughout history and across the world, 'religion' and 'culture' are one and the same thing.

If this is true then a study of the history of worship within a religious context raises the same questions about boundaries and definitions that I have already raised for 'culture'. Neither of these terms, I would suggest, actually has lasting value as an organising principle for a study such as this.

[40] See, for example, Robert Swanson's discussion in *Religion and Devotion in Europe, c. 1215–c. 1515.* Cambridge: Cambridge University Press, 1995, 311–42.
[41] There is a long anthropological tradition behind this kind of definition of religion. See, for example, G. Lewis, *Day of Shining Red, An Essay on Understanding Ritual.* Cambridge: Cambridge University Press, 1980 and more recently C. Humphrey and J. Laidlaw, *The Archetypal Actions of Ritual, A Theory of Ritual Illustrated by the Jain Rite of Worship.* Oxford: Oxford University Press, 1994.

Neither has the analytical robustness to allow us to see what might actually be going on over time and in different parts of the world. We need to look elsewhere for such a tool.

In order to try to make some sense of this history I wish to turn to a concept that I have used before, that of 'discourse'.[42] Discourse has some advantages over culture and religion in that it is not too familiar, and therefore does not come with quite the same amount of baggage as these other terms. That said, discourse has been used very widely in recent years by a range of authors, each of whom tends to use the concept for their own purposes and with their own definition.[43] I therefore need to be more precise about the exact meaning that I am giving to the word in this context. In order to create a usable concept that allows for detailed analysis and explanatory value it makes sense to focus on the use made of the word by one particular author. The most helpful for my purposes is that of Michel Foucault in *The Archaeology of Knowledge*.[44] In this text Foucault is trying to understand history and to place particular ideas, and bodies of ideas, into a historical context. It is within this context that he introduces the ideas of 'discourse' and 'discursive fields'. It is through a development of his use of these terms that I wish to try to understand the history of Christian worship.

The Archaeology of Knowledge is a complex text that relies on concepts of discontinuity, difference and rupture in history. There are, however, a number of criteria and principles that come out of Foucault's writings that are worth drawing attention to as these will help us to understand more clearly what I am talking about when I am using discourse in relation to Christian worship. The first point that Foucault makes is the relationship between discourse and 'discursive fields' or 'discursive formations'. Each discursive field has its own set of discourses and this is the primary use of

---

[42] M. D. Stringer, *On the Perception of Worship, The Ethnography of Worship in Four Christian Congregations in Manchester*. Birmingham: Birmingham University Press, 1999, 61–79, and 'Discourse and the Ethnographic Study of Sufi Worship: Some Practical Suggestions', in A. Zhelyazkova and J. Nielsen (eds.), *Ethnology of Sufi Orders: Theory and Practice*. Sofia: International Centre for Minority Studies and Intercultural Relations, 2001, 412–32.

[43] Those who use discourse as an organising principle tend to make a virtue of its lack of precision. Foucault, for example, says 'As I see it, two series of problems arise at the outset: the first, which I shall leave to one side for the time being and shall return to later, concerns the indiscriminate use that I have made of the terms statement, event and discourse.' M. Foucault, *The Archaeology of Knowledge*. London: Routledge, 1972. Lutz and Abu-Lughod go even further. They suggest that 'rather than being alarmed by its spread . . . it might be better to ask . . . what theoretical work . . . [we] want the term to do'. C. Lutz and L. Abu-Lughod (eds.), *Language and the Politics of Emotion*. Cambridge: Cambridge University Press, 1990, 7.

[44] London: Routledge, 1972.

the term. So, for example, there is a discourse associated with medicine. This discourse consists of a series of statements that are used within the discursive field in question. Foucault says: 'We shall call discourse a group of statements in so far as they belong to the same discursive formation; it does not form a rhetorical or formal unity, endlessly repeatable, whose appearance of use in history might be indicated (and, if necessary, explained); it is made up of a limited number of statements for which a group of conditions of existence can be defined.'[45] He goes on to describe discourse not as 'an ideal, timeless form that also possesses a history', but rather as 'a fragment of history, a unity and discontinuity in history itself'.[46]

For Foucault a discourse is made up not of an ideal set of possible statements, but rather of real utterances and actual events. At one level the statements of a discourse contain the vocabulary of, for example, medicine: its jargon, words that would be known only to those within the discipline, specific usages of more common words that take on a specific meaning within the discursive field, and so on. Secondly, there are ways of saying things, formulas and phrases that are distinctive to the field. These can exist within a written discourse, such as the academic writing on medicine, or they can be used more widely within society, such as the language and phraseology that is used within the doctor's surgery or within the operating theatre. What is important for Foucault is that they have been said, that they are stated rather than existing in any kind of ideal form.

The statements that make up discourse, however, do not just refer to words and to language. If they did then they would be of little more use to me than the concept of 'text'. Foucault distinguishes the word 'statement' from the common use of the word 'sentence' and wishes to include partial sentences and even graphs and illustrations as statements within discourse.[47] I would want to develop this possibility further and incorporate actions, images and environments as further statements within my own understanding of discourse. So, for example, within medicine there are a series of actions, diagnostic techniques for example, that are distinctive to a medical discourse. There are also certain images (a particular form of anatomical poster or even the ubiquitous white coat) that also form a central part of the discourse. Finally there are particular settings that are traditionally associated with the discourse, the surgery or the operating theatre, and we feel somewhat uneasy when we identify distinctive parts of the discourse in other non-appropriate settings. For Foucault this is

[45] Foucault, *Archaeology*, 117. [46] Ibid. [47] Ibid., 82.

implicit rather than explicit,[48] but for my purposes it is the whole package that makes up the 'discursive field' of medicine, not just the language or the words. It is this sense of a complete, and complex, whole that makes the concept usable in the context of religion and worship.

There are, however, a number of other features of discourse in Foucault's analysis that can also be useful in my own work. First we have the understanding of change and development. Discourses do not stand still; they develop, sometimes in surprising and unpredictable ways. Within this development, however, the kind of change that is possible is never entirely arbitrary. Certainly it is possible for one discourse to interact with others, to borrow statements and other elements from other discourses, and to make them its own in the process. In principle, however, the development of a particular discourse is tightly controlled by the internal dynamics of the discourse itself. This leads us on to another of Foucault's central points. The distinguishing feature of any discourse is that it is restrictive; it controls and in many ways even determines what can and cannot be said within it.[49] No discourse can develop and change randomly. The discourse itself sets limits as to what is, and what is not, sayable, as well as limiting in many cases who can say it and in what context it is appropriate to be said. If we go back to the discourses of medicine, for example, we can see this very clearly. When a patient enters a surgery and says to the doctor that they have a headache, there are only a limited number of responses that the doctor can make. If the doctor suggests, for example, that the headache is caused by the anger of an ancestor and that what the patient needs to do is to sacrifice a cockerel and scatter the blood to the four corners of their house, then we would think that something very odd is going on. The discursive field of Western contemporary medicine does not allow for this kind of development. This scenario represents a different discourse imposing itself upon the situation. Most incongruities and inconsistencies are actually much more subtle, and far more difficult to detect, than this example, but the principle remains. There are elements of any discourse that restrict and constrict what can and cannot be said, and these change gradually but distinctively over time. What is more it is often when people do introduce new and incongruous elements into the discourse, or if somebody speaks out of turn or in the wrong place, that the discourses change and develop.

The other significant advantage that the concept of 'discourse' has over those of 'culture' or 'religion' is that it does not contain the sense of being unitary and all-encompassing. In fact, for Foucault this is the very

---

[48] See Foucault's discussion of the sites of discourse in ibid., 51.   [49] Ibid., 50–5.

starting point of his analysis.[50] We can see immediately the possibility of there being many different discourses within any one society, some of which begin to cross boundaries between societies. It is also possible to break larger discourses, such as medicine, down into smaller discourses such as dentistry, neuropsychology or whatever. Taken at this lowest, most specific level, we can also introduce the concept of the 'discourse community', the community of those who use and work within the confines of a specific discourse. This, however, is also partial, as we have to recognise that any one individual must have access to a wide variety of different discourses, each with their own specific context and community. This leads to the possibility of what Gerd Baumann defines as 'dual discursive competence',[51] trying to define the situation where members of sub-groups within a society can switch easily between the discourse of the in-group and that of the wider society, each of which may work by entirely different rules and assumptions. Finally, and following on again from Baumann's particular use of the concept, we can distinguish between 'dominant' and 'demotic' discourses in any one society.[52] The 'dominant' discourses are those held and used by those in authority, and inevitably have an element of 'power' within them. 'Demotic' discourses are used within everyday conversation and among small sub-groups within a society. All discourses, inevitably, have some element of 'power' associated with them, either excluding individuals or imposing a particular way of thinking throughout a discourse community. This is explicit in Foucault's initial treatment of the term and is an element that I will continue to return to throughout this book.

It is in relation to 'discourse', therefore, as outlined above, that I intend to study the practice of Christian worship through two thousand years. I will be using discourse to relate to texts, to language, to actions and to settings. I will aim to show the constraints and limitations that certain forms of Christian discourse have placed on worship at different times and how these constraints have changed over time. I will aim to show how the interaction between specifically Christian discourses and other kinds of discourse within different societies has impacted on worship and how Christianity has changed its status over time from a demotic to a dominant discourse, and back again. Finally, I will be exploring power relations between discourses

---

[50] Ibid., 21.
[51] G. Baumann, *Contesting Culture, Discourses of Identity in Multi-Ethnic London.* Cambridge: Cambridge University Press, 1996, 34.
[52] Ibid., 10.

and those who use these discourses, and the role of worship within this process in many different contexts and situations. Within all this I will be tracking the specific histories of individual Christian discourses of worship across time and space throughout the last two thousand years. Before doing this, however, I need to explore a little further the relationship between discourse and worship, and the specific nature of Christian discourses before we can get on to the details of the history.

DISCOURSE AND WORSHIP

In order to explore in more detail the relationship between discourse and worship we need to address ourselves to the question of what it is that captures and expresses discourse within society. What is it that fixes discourse in the lives of individuals? At one level this is a question about the kind of evidence that we have for discourses of the past. Where are we to find evidence for such discourses? At another level, and more importantly for my current purposes, it is a question of how discourses work. What impact do they have on the people that use them? So, where do we find discourses in society, what is it that fully captures and expresses such discourses? If we are to take Foucault seriously then there is unlikely to be any one object or class of objects that fully expresses a discourse. If discourse includes words, images, texts, settings, actions and so on then these are not going to be encapsulated in any one place or any single phenomenon. If we wish to look, for example, towards images or art then we may find expressions of discourses within the frame, but this will always be partial. The same is true of texts, whether of literature or theology or of a more practical nature. These texts will only ever capture certain elements of the overall discourse. Even if we find a collection of texts, spreading over many years, that demonstrate the development of thinking and of language in relation to a specific discipline, this cannot of itself provide a source for the complete discourse associated with that discipline. It will only ever be partial. What is more, in societies where the production of images or texts is relatively expensive then the range of discourses, and the sources of the discourses that become expressed in these images or texts will inevitably be limited to those of the elite within the society. This is useful in many ways, but once again it is partial.

In order to answer my original question it is perhaps worth going back to Foucault's own original example, that of medicine. Where do we find, most typically, the discourse of medicine expressed? Where do we need to focus our attention to gain the greatest insight into the content and use of the medical discourse? The answer has to be the surgery, or perhaps the operating theatre, or the hospital ward. Each of these is an environment conditioned to the discourse. The environment itself, according to Foucault, is a part of the discourse. It is also the environment in which the constraints of the discourse are most compelling; a doctor can be freer in her language and explanations on a home visit than she can in the surgery. What is more it is not just the environment that matters in seeking the core of the discourse, it is the observation of what takes place within that environment that gives us the greatest insight into the essentials of the medical discourse. It is in observing a consultation, or an operation, or some other form of medical practice that we will see the discourse in action, that we will be able to note the structure of the discourse, its limitations, its cadences, its subtleties, and, I would suggest, its most essential form. In other words it is in praxis that the discourse exists in its most complete form and it is in the observation of praxis that we must distil the discourse for analysis.

If this is the case for medicine, then is it possible to argue that the equivalent form of praxis for religious discourses is worship? Worship in this sense is not confined to public events, although these are, of course, essential. It can also include private devotions, momentary reflections or minor ritualistic activities. I do not want to restrict the term too closely. We may also wish to include acts of charity or other kinds of praxis that are considered by the actors to be of a religious nature. In principle, however, it is the corporate acts of worship that I am most concerned with and it is these, I would argue, that have most in common with the 'ritual' of the surgery or the operating theatre in terms of their relationship with the discourses of Christianity in its various shapes and forms. Once again, however, I need to stress that it is not the text of the worship alone, or the space of worship, or any other single aspect of that worship, which will express the discourses under discussion. It is the performance of the worship, the praxis of people actually involved in the process of worship that really gets to the heart of the issue. It is this level of actual practice, of performance, of liturgical praxis, that I am aiming to uncover and analyse within this book.

One of the central reasons why I wish to place such an important emphasis on praxis brings me to another central concept of the book, that of 'embodiment'. David Torevell uses the concept of 'embodiment' in his book, *Losing the Sacred*, to encapsulate the difference between pre- and post-Vatican II Catholic worship.[53] Torevell relates embodiment to ritual

[53] D. Torevell, *Losing the Sacred: Ritual, Modernity and Liturgical Reform*. Edinburgh: T. & T. Clark, 2000, 48.

and to a way of understanding the liturgy that is essentially captured in movement rather than intellectual ideas. This, he argues, has changed, through the work of the liturgical movement and the recent revisions, to a situation in which contemporary worship is to be understood primarily by the mind as opposed to the body. I will take up this particular argument again in Chapter 7; for now I want to focus specifically on the concept of embodiment itself. I also want to challenge Torevell's implicit assumption that embodiment is only associated with ritual. It is not just in obvious and deliberate ritual action that the body is used within worship. Even in the most intellectual and interior of worship there is still some level of embodiment; it is simply different from that of the highly ritualised worship of other times and periods.

In order to explore the concept more closely I want to draw on the work of Pierre Bourdieu, more specifically his concept of 'habitus'.[54] Bourdieu is concerned with the kinds of issues that I was raising earlier, about the way in which culture is practised and made real to people. He was reluctant to see this entirely in intellectual terms as would be assumed if we take a Tylorian view of culture. Rather, Bourdieu argues, culture is played out in practice. It is what people do as well as what they say that they do. It is written onto and into the body, in the way in which bodies are used and function within any specific society. This is what he calls the 'habitus' of the society. Habitus is, in Bourdieu's view, something akin to common sense. It is that which functions in all the unthought actions of people that, in its full collective expression, is defined as 'culture'.[55] Habitus is socialised into each individual and consists in part in the unique and defining ways in which the body moves and acts within all social activity. Habitus, for Bourdieu, is always embodied.[56] The assumption, which is born out of empirical evidence, is that the use made of the body, say in the way people walk or react to other bodies, is distinct to a specific society or social group (although as with 'culture' there are serious questions to be raised about boundaries and the dynamics of change over time). It is this distinctive, unthought 'practice' that Bourdieu defines as habitus.

Habitus is, of course, learnt behaviour. It is behaviour that is learnt within the normal processes of socialisation within the family and in the wider society. Among the many contexts in which this behaviour is learnt must be the various contexts of ritual. In ritual, for example, the habitus is perhaps

[54] P. Bourdieu, *Outline of a Theory of Practice.* Cambridge: Cambridge University Press, 1977.
[55] Ibid., 78.   [56] Ibid., 87–95.

more explicit, more pronounced. It is, however, there and the particular use that is made of the body within the ritual, the range of bodily postures and actions employed, inevitably spills out into the rest of society. Where that ritual is an integral part of the dominant discourse of a society, say where Christianity is the dominant discourse, then the actions and postures of the ritual are an essential and very powerful part of that wider dominant discourse. The fact that these postures and actions are internalised subconsciously and inform the general habitus of the society in question makes this embodiment in ritual an important arena for the presentation and encapsulation of the discourse itself. If, on the other hand, the ritual is part of a demotic or sub-dominant discourse then it may only be practised by a few and may not inform the full habitus of the society, but it will clearly function as an important element in the specific habitus of those who partake. The expectations of Charismatic worship, for example, as opposed to that of most contemporary Western Catholicism make a very clear comparison, and the fact that people from one environment find the habitus, and subsequent bodily practices, of the other not only alien but disconcerting, goes some way to prove the value of the concept.[57]

It is in embodiment within the ritual context, therefore, that the discourses of society are most explicitly expressed and transferred from generation to generation. It is in this arena, also, as Torevell implicitly makes clear, that the changes in embodiment and in habitus become most noticeable. It is within worship, therefore, that we can track the play of Christian discourses through the centuries and across the world. This is what I aim to do within the context of this work. I will come back to embodiment and habitus on a number of occasions throughout the book; I now need to move on and ask what, if anything, forms the common theme or structure for all so-called 'Christian' discourses?

UNDERSTANDING CHRISTIAN DISCOURSES

In order to identify the core or common elements of the wide variety of Christian discourses that have existed over the last two thousand years it might make sense to compare Christian discourses with those of other dominant traditions. If we take the wider view, and look specifically at Western Europe, we can see Christian discourses in relation to two other

---

[57] See, for example, the discussion of habitus in Thomas Csordas's work on Catholic Charismatics in *Language, Charisma and Creativity, The Ritual Life of a Religious Movement.* Berkeley: University of California Press, 1997.

kinds of dominant discourse. In the first three centuries Christianity existed within a society whose dominant discourses were various forms of paganism. It is not possible to be precise about what we mean by 'paganism' in this context, and the variety of pagan discourses is clearly one of the defining elements of 'paganism'. However, attempts have been made to define the core elements of pagan discourses.[58] It is also clear that, from the beginning of the fourth century, Christian discourses slowly, and in varying degrees across Europe, began to replace pagan discourses as the dominant discourses of the region. From the fourteenth century onwards, however, a new series of discourses, with different underlying principles, began to emerge and eventually to begin to be the dominant discourses of most Western societies. We may want to call these new discourses 'modernism', or 'science' or 'rationalism'. All of these terms have been used within the literature. The term I wish to use, however, is 'humanism'. I recognise that this has some problems, as this term is used for very specific forms of discourse at different periods and is perhaps not used widely of the dominant discourses of contemporary Europe. However, as I will explain in Chapter 6, the term 'humanism' appears to capture the essence of this new dominant discourse more completely than any of its alternatives. Once again, however, as with Christianity and paganism, we must recognise that there are a considerable variety of humanist discourses and it is the essence of these, or rather the points of difference from Christian discourses, that are most significant for the current purposes. Finally, we must also recognise that many of the discourses of different societies are actually formed by combinations and syntheses of pagan and Christian, or Christian and humanist, elements and so a 'pure' Christian, pagan, or humanist discourse is almost impossible to identify.

Before going on to look at the core of the Christian discourses in relation to that of pagan or humanist discourses, I do need to recognise that in other parts of the world other discourses have been dominant and the relationship between Christian discourses and these other dominant discourses is equally significant. The dominance of the Islamic discourses across much of the Middle East and North Africa cannot be ignored and the relationship between Christian and Islamic discourses is a fascinating topic in itself.[59] The ever-present Jewish discourses, both within and outside

[58] See, for example, K. Dowden, *European Paganism, The Realities of Cult from Antiquity to the Middle Ages*. London: Routledge, 2000.
[59] See, for example, D. Thomas (ed.), *Syrian Christians under Islam: The First Thousand Years*. Leiden: Brill, 2001.

Christian-dominated areas, have also been significant at many different times and places throughout the history of Christianity and these will be looked at wherever relevant in the text below. Finally, beyond the European and Mediterranean core of Christian discourses we need to take account of the discourses of pre-Islamic Persia, of India, China, Ethiopia and many other areas of the world in their relationship with generally non-dominant Christian discourses in understanding the full impact of Christian worship in these societies. For our current purposes, however, the comparison between Christian, pagan and humanist discourses will be enough to identify what I want to claim are the core elements of all Christian discourses.

When we look at core or common elements of any series of discourses we need to work on a number of different levels. At one level, these will focus on elements of content, vocabulary, images or concepts that are shared by all those who claim allegiance to a particular discourse. Perhaps the centrality of the figure of Jesus would be a good example within the range of Christian discourses. Unfortunately this does not really get us very far. Many Islamic and other discourses also relate to Jesus as a person or as an idea, and these cannot easily be defined as Christian (nor can we say that it is simply attitudes to Jesus that matter, as a number of Christian discourses have a view of Jesus very similar to that of some Islamic discourses). The other element we need to take into account is that of the structure, or we might want to say the grammar, of the discourse. It is in the combination of structure and content, the particular limits that are set to the fundamental understanding of the world, that ultimately define the core of a series of discourses. In order to explain this further I would like to identify four elements of Christian discourses that I think are central, especially in comparison with the discourses of paganism and humanism that pre- and post-dated Christianity as the dominant discourses of Western Europe.

The first element of the Christian discourse relates to cosmology, or more specifically to time. Understandings of space, and the related understandings of heaven, hell, the nature of the earth and so on, have changed very dramatically over the centuries.[60] The central sense of time, however, has, I would argue, remained constant. In many pagan discourses time was understood as being cyclical, moving with the seasons or with the cycle of life, death and rebirth.[61] These cycles may be short or of considerable

---

[60] See the discussion in R. Markus, *The End of Ancient Christianity*. Cambridge: Cambridge University Press, 1990, 85–135.
[61] Dowden: *European Paganism*, 192–212.

length, but the basic understanding was of return and renewal. Within Christianity, however, time becomes linear, with a clear beginning and a very distinctive end (although it never fully lost the idea of cyclical time in, for example, the seasons of the liturgical year). What is more, Christian discourses talk not only of the beginning and the end, but also of the middle, the central event around which the whole of history is understood to be pivoted. The specific understandings of the incarnation, or the cross, may vary from discourse to discourse, but the idea of history being divided into two distinct eras, before and after Christ, is central to all Christian understandings of the world. This also has its impact on the understanding of the life, death and afterlife of the individual. Again this is linear rather than cyclical and, despite considerable variation on the nature of life after death, the idea that life goes on beyond the physical death is central. This is most commonly associated with notions of judgement and of resurrection. It is also closely linked to an understanding of the end of history. However, once again, the specifics of the ways in which these elements relate chronologically or conceptually may change. It is the linearity of time and the common knowledge of an end that is essential. Humanist understandings have retained some of this sense of linear history but tend to work in terms of geological time (with a far longer timescale than most traditional Christian histories) and with mechanical time, that is time measured by mechanical devices rather than the seasons and the movement of the sun and the moon. Finally, humanist understandings of human life often fail to see the potential for life after death, unless it remains in the memory of the living. Thus Christian discourses have a distinctive understanding of time that distinguishes them from other dominant discourses.

The second element of the Christian discourses, that is central to the way they function, relates to the relationship between the human and the divine. It is not the fact that Christian discourses have an understanding of the divine that makes them distinctive; many religious discourses share this feature. It is, I would argue, the particular nature of the relationship between the human and the divine that is specific to most, if not all, Christian discourses. The word I want to use here is 'intimacy' and I want to relate that to the second word of my title for this chapter, 'devotion'. These two concepts are, I would argue, closely related in all Christian discourses. There is a body of literature that argues that intimacy is a particular feature of late twentieth-century Western society and in a certain way this may be true, especially in relation to the prominence of the discourses of intimacy in human–human relationships.[62] James Stevens argues that this late twentieth-century public discourse on intimacy is seen pre-eminently in contemporary Charismatic worship.[63] Again this is clear, and we will explore this more fully in the final chapter. I would want to argue, however, that this relationship of intimacy can be seen in all Christian discourses to a greater or lesser extent. The roots of this understanding of the relationship between the human and divine are, of course, understandings of Jesus, relationships with Jesus and the specific relationship that Jesus is understood to have with his Father in heaven. At the heart of the Christian understanding of God is a relationship between the Father and the Son, a relationship of intimacy so close that the two cannot be divided. This is seen especially in the traditions that derive from the Gospel of John. This does not mean, however, that at certain times in Christian history God is not perceived as distant, terrible and unapproachable. That element is clearly part of many Christian discourses and is inherited from certain forms of earlier Jewish and pagan discourses. What always exists in Christian discourses, however, is an alternative source of intimacy. If God is unapproachable, we can turn to Jesus, our friend, our brother, or our lover. If Jesus is constructed as beyond human reach, then other alternatives move in to take his place, be that Mary, his mother, the saints, the Spirit or occasionally some other less definable element. At all times some aspect of the discourse of intimacy is present. In terms of worship this element of intimacy is seen in what is generally referred to as 'devotion'. This may be full-blown mysticism, a particularly close relationship with a patron saint, or a series of charismatic experiences. Devotion expresses, not the form, or even the content, of a particular activity; rather it denotes an attitude, a relationship with the divine, a relationship that is rooted in intimacy. This, I would argue, is central to any understanding of Christian worship and the discourses that surround it.

Thirdly, I want to focus on the concept of 'charity'. 'Love' in its various forms, based on the range of Greek words that can express what we think of as love, has been an essential part of all Christian discourses, both positive and negative. 'God is Love' is a core statement. In part this relates back to

---

[62] See for example, R. Sennett, *The Fall of Public Man*. New York: Knopf, 1977 and the wider discussion in A. Giddens, *Modernity and Self Identity; Self and Society in the Late Modern Age*. Cambridge: Polity Press, 1991.

[63] J. H. S. Stevens, *Worship in the Spirit, Charismatic Worship in the Church of England*. Carlisle: Paternoster Press, 2002, following the lead of M. F. Mannion, 'Liturgy and the Present Crisis of Culture', *Worship*, 62:2 (1988), 98–123.

the centrality of intimacy in our relationship with the divine, but it also relates to the specific way in which Christian discourses interpret human–human relations. I am not at this point concerned with the more intimate elements of human relations, although there is arguably a common set of Christian discourses on this. I am more concerned with the way in which Jesus' command to 'love thy neighbour' is played out in all the different discourses that make up Christianity. We only have to look at the way in which Ancient Rome was able to dismiss large sections of its society as in many ways sub-human, and the importance of kinship and family to its discourses of human relationships, to see how Christianity transformed these older pagan discourses.[64] Of course, as Christian discourses became dominant in the empires of the Middle Ages, an open conflict arose between those who centred their discourses on the idea of charity and those who ruled. This was inevitable. It is noteworthy, however, that even among the ruling elite, the concept of charity never fully disappeared, even if it was only something to be done after death rather than in life. It remained as a pang of conscience in the discourses of society that allowed those who centred on the concept to remain fundamentally disruptive. We must also recognise that the Christian discourses of charity are fundamentally different from the humanist discourses of 'rights'. We cannot talk of the poor, the widowed and the sick etc. as having 'rights' within a Christian discourse. To say this effectively negates the very concept of charity, which is seen as a self-giving love to those who probably do not deserve it as of right. Charity, however, underpins most Christian discourses in some shape or form.

The final aspect of specifically Christian discourses that I wish to explore relates to the core of the discourse, or rather to its roots. This concerns the specific relationship set up within Christian discourses between 'truth' and the 'text'. The root of all Christian discourses is a text, or rather a series of texts. Once again the exact content of these texts has changed to a certain extent over time and place. The specific nature of the relationship with the text has also changed.[65] The texts, however, must always be central as they contain the only witness Christian discourses can offer to God's self-revelation and hence to 'truth'. The first distinctive feature of the texts is that they are generally seen to be witnesses to revelation, and not, as with Islam, the core of the revelation itself. The second distinctive feature is that

[64] M. Kuefler, *The Manly Eunuch: Masculinity, Gender Ambiguity and Christian Ideology in Late Antiquity.* Chicago: University of Chicago Press, 2001.
[65] D. C. Parker, *The Living Text of the Gospel.* Cambridge: Cambridge University Press, 1997.

they are, by any reckoning, partial. These texts cannot answer all the questions that Christians may have. They are not written to provide such answers, and when they do give answers these are often wrapped up in a high level of ambiguity. The texts, therefore, always need some level of interpretation. One consequence of this is that it is always possible to go back to the text and to begin again. As the social context illustrated in those texts is minimalist in sociological terms, whether of Jesus wandering in Judea and Galilee with his disciples, or of the small house churches suggested by Paul's letters, there is always the potential for Christians, when looking at these texts, to 'go back', to 'reform', to 'simplify', to get back to the purity of the 'Gospel message'. We can see this element of Christian discourses over and over again throughout Christian history, not only in the big 'reformations' but also in many smaller reforms and revisions. The history of monasticism is one of constantly aiming to get back to 'apostolic simplicity', however that is defined. Theology also, however complex it has become in association with various philosophical traditions, has always been brought back to basics when brought into juxtaposition with the texts. The potential for reform, with its essentially backward gaze, is, I would suggest, built into the fundamental structure of all Christian discourses and will always be present to a greater or lesser extent, even in the history of Christian worship.

These four elements, therefore, are, I would argue, that which sets Christian discourses apart from those of paganism, humanism or other religious discourses. These elements do not, in practice, offer that many limits to the sheer diversity of Christian discourses that are possible, as we shall see. It is also clear that these specific elements of the Christian discourses are always intertwined with elements of other discourses, be they social, cultural or those of other religious traditions. This is only to be expected. There never can be a 'pure form' of Christian discourse. These four elements, however, define a discourse as 'Christian' and therefore underpin the many different discourses that function within the history of Christian worship.

THEMES AND STRUCTURES OF THE BOOK

Before embarking on that history I need to conclude this introduction with a few words on the way in which the text itself is structured. It would be impossible, not to say foolish, to try to encompass every different aspect of the Christian discourses as they are expressed in worship over two thousand years. Choices have to be made and decisions taken in order to construct a definable narrative through the mass of material that is now available. I have therefore decided to follow a fairly rigid structure that enables me to tell a broader story while also illustrating the points that I wish to make in relation to the details of specific examples.

Within the book I have divided my history into chapters that focus on three-hundred-year periods. This division is not intended to have any inner logic or to form any kind of straitjacket and I have on a number of occasions drifted at the edges and failed to maintain rigid boundaries. Having seven chapters of roughly three hundred years each, however, did seem to make some sense, especially as many of the most significant events in Christian history appear to happen at either the early fourth century, the early tenth century or the early sixteenth century and so on.

Taking each three-hundred-year unit, I have then chosen to focus specifically on some aspect of the theoretical discussion concerning worship and discourse that appears to be most appropriate to that particular space of time. This has enabled me to spread the theoretical debate throughout the text and to develop my argument from chapter to chapter. It has also enabled me to concentrate on diversity in the argument rather than trying to tie everything up neatly and to apply the same principles to every possible time and place, something that would have been impossible. By developing the argument over the seven chapters I have also been able to tell a stronger narrative about the development of Christian discourses in relation to other discourses with which they have had to interact. Lastly, this more extended theoretical discussion has enabled me to look more closely at questions of change and development that are often lacking in other theoretical discussions of discourses but which are essential to any understanding of discourse as I am choosing to use it.

Alongside the theoretical questions themselves, I have also tried to explore, in far more detail, specific case studies that illustrate and develop the theoretical questions I am raising. In each chapter, therefore, following a theoretical introduction, I have introduced three specific case studies (or in a couple of cases a series of related case studies). These cases are chosen both to highlight important aspects of the development of worship within the three-hundred-year period under consideration, and to illustrate elements of the theoretical discussion. They should be understood, therefore, as snapshots, attempts to encapsulate a particular time and place, or a particular issue in relation to worship. The case studies allow me to explore a specific situation in more detail and they also allow me to draw on a far wider range of times and spaces than would be possible if I was telling a single coherent story. In each chapter there is one main case that usually draws on the principal Christian traditions of Eastern or Western Europe. The other two cases, however, allow me to develop the ideas, or the theoretical issues, in relation to regions where Christianity is not the dominant discourse or where that discourse has undergone a significantly different trajectory. In other words, I have attempted to draw on the margins of the Christian world as well as on its core.

This element of margins and core should also be apparent in the way in which I have approached all the case studies. In each case, as well as illustrating a specific theoretical development, I have attempted to show how we can begin to explore worship in performance, how we can illuminate the different ways in which worship has been understood and practised by those who used it, not only the elites (whether clerical or political) but also, and perhaps more specifically, the ordinary members of ordinary congregations. This is not always easy, as we do not always have access to the kind of data that would make this possible. However, by combining a range of historical methods associated with the discipline of social history, and the insights of anthropologists and others who have studied ritual in performance across the world, I have attempted to bring to light as much as we can of each situation as I have developed it.

Finally, each chapter will end by a recapitulation of the theoretical ideas, drawing specifically on the case studies developed, and will aim to draw some kind of provisional conclusion. This is not, therefore, in any sense, a completed work. My sole purpose is to try to encourage others to become excited by the ideas and studies that I am presenting, to disagree with me about their interpretation if they so wish, to engage in dialogue and discussion, and so to develop yet further our understanding of the history of Christian worship, beyond the texts and into the realm of performance and devotion. We begin, however, with the Bible and the earliest accounts we have of specifically Christian worship in Chapter 1.

CHAPTER I

Early Christian worship, texts and contexts to AD 300

In my Introduction I explored the way in which we have to understand worship as a form of discourse. I argued that a purely textual or theological approach to worship was not adequate. I said that in this book I would be exploring the practice of worship, trying to understand the way in which ordinary people approached their worship. This still remains my focus. However, when we go back to the very beginnings of Christian worship, it is only texts that we have to work with. What is more, these texts are partial and limited. They emerge from many different places and over considerable periods of time. It is difficult to see any coherent narrative within or between them. While in the Foucaultian sense all these texts act as 'statements' within an emerging Christian discourse,[1] it is not easy to see that discourse in anything other than an entirely fragmentary form. We have to recognise this, therefore, as we begin to sift through and explore the evidence that we have.

One of the biggest obstacles facing scholars in understanding the nature of Christianity in the first few centuries after the death of Jesus is the temptation to read back presuppositions drawn from the subsequent two thousand years of Christian history. This has been particularly true in the area of worship. It has been suggested, for example, that the debate about the origins of Christian worship has been little more than a battleground on which Catholics and Protestants have conducted their own liturgical disputes.[2] Both groups have tended to reinterpret what little evidence there is in a way that supports their own particular understandings. One reason why this has been possible, I would suggest, is that many of the earliest

---

[1] See pp. 10–14 above for a wider discussion of Foucault.
[2] Kurt Niederwimmer makes this point explicit in his commentary on *The Didache*. Minneapolis: Fortress Press, 1998.

Christian writings use words and phrases that, over the centuries, have developed very technical or highly contested meanings. Such words would include *ekklesia* (church or assembly), *episkopos* (bishop or overseer), *diakonos* (deacon or servant) and even terms that do not have contested meaning but are equally weighed down with Christian interpretation such as 'baptism', 'Lord's supper', or 'speaking in tongues'. None of these words, when used by early Christian authors, can be treated in an entirely neutral way by contemporary commentators. When these commentators come to the texts, therefore, with particular ecclesial positions to defend, then it is easy to see how the use of such terms can be the starting point for a serious misreading of the evidence.

Even without the burden of ecclesial presuppositions many of the specific actions or rituals that we encounter within the text, what we might call the 'grammar' of the worship, have a very familiar ring. Communities gathered to share songs and prayers, they broke bread, they blessed wine, they baptised in water and they laid hands in acts of healing and dedication. This familiarity of action exists because these texts have in many cases come to form the definitive scriptures of Christianity and have therefore set the agenda, and formed the vocabulary, for all subsequent discourses on worship. This familiarity, however, often obscures significant differences in worldview, in thought processes and in the meanings that may have been attached to the actions and rituals discussed.

One of the most significant developments in biblical scholarship over the last twenty to thirty years, therefore, has been the attempt to try to get beyond such ambiguity and assumed familiarity. This has been achieved by trying, so far as it is possible, to situate the language of the texts within the culture and structures of the societies that produced them. In order to do this biblical scholars have drawn on the insights of social historians, sociologists and social theorists.[3] Biblical scholarship has tried to contextualise the texts, either within the kinds of communities that may have produced them, or within the wider social milieu of first-century Judaism, Hellenism or the Roman Empire.[4] We cannot enter such a world, it is suggested, with all our presuppositions intact and expect to find values,

---

[3] For a good summary of this material see S. C. Barton, 'The Communal Dimensions of Earliest Christianity', in S. C. Barton, *Life Together, Family, Sexuality and Community in the New Testament and Today*. Edinburgh: T. & T. Clark, 2001, 85–116.

[4] See for example the recent essays in Troels Engberg-Pederson's edited volume *Paul Beyond the Judaism/Hellenism Divide*. Louisville: Westminster John Knox, 2001 and Bruce Malina's discussion on the role of anthropology in the study of the New Testament in *The New Testament World, Insights from Cultural Anthropology*. Louisville: Westminster John Knox, 2001.

institutions and practices that are necessarily similar to, let alone identical with, those we know today. This is particularly true of worship.

The evidence that we have is scattered in texts whose purpose was not primarily to inform posterity about the practice of worship and the meanings this worship had for its practitioners. These texts are letters, or apologies, or treatises on many issues other than worship. Even those texts that claim to contain examples of worship may not reflect contemporary practice.[5] What we need to do, therefore, is first to recognise the limited nature of the evidence that we do have: what Paul Bradshaw refers to as 'little more than a series of dots of varying size and density on a large sheet of plain paper'.[6] Secondly, we need to treat all the apparent technical terminology of worship within these texts with a considerable level of scepticism, asking, so far as it is possible, what the communities that produced the texts may have understood by such terms. Thirdly, we need to draw on as much information as we can from studies of other aspects of the society within which the texts were produced in order to learn something of the values, institutions and practices that surround them. It is only after we have done all this that we can begin to comment critically on the possible practices referred to in the texts themselves. Even having gone through this process, however, we must still recognise that what we may learn from such texts will still only apply to the time, the place, the community and perhaps even the individual who produced the text itself.

Throughout most of the first three hundred years of Christian history there is often fifty years or so between one text and the next, and the texts, while mostly written in Greek, are written as far apart as Antioch in Syria, Lyons in Gaul and Carthage on the North African coast. We have no evidence that the practice of the Christian community in each of these different locations (or times) is going to be consistent. How can we know that the way in which Christians in Corinth in the middle of the first century thought about their worshipping life was the same as those in Alexandria towards the end of the third century? We cannot begin with such assumptions and the evidence itself is not entirely clear. What we can say, however, is that there is a clear relationship between the texts. Tertullian, for example, writing in Carthage in the first half of the third century, was certainly aware of, and in some cases quotes verbatim, texts written by Paul

---

[5] This is part of the continuing debate about the Didache and other Church Orders. See P. Bradshaw, *The Search for the Origins of Christian Worship, Sources and Methods for the Study of Early Liturgy.* London: SPCK, 2002, 73–97.

[6] P. Bradshaw, *The Search for the Origins of Christian Worship, Sources and Methods for the Study of Early Liturgy.* 1st edn. London: SPCK, 1992, 56.

(written in Ephesus in the mid first century), Ignatius (Antioch, early second century) and Irenaeus (Lyons, later in the second century).[7] Such a relationship between the texts, however, cannot assure us that there is a similar relationship between the practices, and more specifically between the meanings associated with these practices, among the communities from which these individual authors emerged. It is vitally important, therefore, that we first contextualise each of the texts on an individual basis, and only then move on to try to explore links and connections between the ideas and practices that they contain. While such a task is clearly the ideal, there is not enough space within a book such as this to undertake a complete study of all the relevant texts. Within this chapter, therefore, I can only begin to scratch the surface. On the basis of the considerable work of others in the field, I simply want to show what may be possible and to illustrate the kind of questions that such a procedure may force us to address.

PAUL'S LETTER TO THE CORINTHIAN COMMUNITY

I wish to begin with Paul's first letter to the Corinthians, as a detailed analysis of this text will illustrate a number of the points that I would want to make about contextualisation in general.[8] I have chosen this particular text partly because it is the earliest first-hand account of Christian worship that has survived, and partly because the Corinthian community has been one of the most widely studied of all the early Christian communities from the perspective of social history and sociology.[9] Like almost all the other texts of the first three hundred years, Paul's letter is not primarily about worship. However, within the context of the letter as a whole Paul does make some significant comments about the worship of a particular Christian community in Corinth. As this is by far the earliest reference we have to any form of specifically Christian worship it would seem to be a good place to begin.

---

[7] See E. Evans, 'Introduction', in E. Evans, *Tertullian's Homily on Baptism: The Text Edited with an Introduction, Translation and Commentary.* London: SPCK, 1964, ix–xl.

[8] In the following analysis I am making certain assumptions about 1 Corinthians that are generally agreed upon in the scholarly literature. In particular I am assuming that Paul is the author, that the letter was written in about 50–55, and that it forms one complete whole and is not made up of different texts. See J. D. G. Dunn, *1 Corinthians.* Sheffield: Sheffield Academic Press, 1999, 13–26.

[9] See the classic texts of Gerd Theissen (*The Social Setting of Pauline Christianity: Essays on Corinth.* Philadelphia: Fortress Press, 1982) and Wayne Meeks (*The First Urban Christians: The Social World of the Apostle Paul.* New Haven: Yale University Press, 1983). For a more recent summary of the sociological work on Corinthian Christianity see S. C. Barton, 'Christian Community in the Light of 1 Corinthians', in Barton, *Life Together*, 187–206.

In the first letter to the Corinthians, Paul discusses at least two distinct gatherings or assemblies at which worship takes place.[10] The account of the 'Lord's supper' is self-contained in Chapter 11 (17–34). This event consists primarily of a meal. There must have been some actions involving bread and wine, and something to define this meal as 'worship', but beyond this there is very little we can say with certainty. The second account of worship, in Chapter 14 (26–40), is an informal gathering, a 'coming together',[11] at which different members of the community bring their own gifts: prophecies, hymns, revelations etc. and join together in an act of praise, possibly with some kind of teaching. Within the text, Paul makes no direct link between the meal and the act of open worship. However, because later eucharistic worship came to contain both praise (combined with readings etc.) and the sharing of bread and wine, most scholars have assumed that these two accounts refer to two parts of the same event.[12] If we try not to read later practice back into earlier writings, then we have to recognise that there is no direct evidence to support this unitary form within the text itself.[13]

What does link the two accounts is the obvious sense of disorder or chaos that Paul is trying to counter in his letter. In the case of the meal this disorder is seen as a consequence of status differences, a lack of sharing and a possible atmosphere of drunkenness (11:21). In the case of the gathering for worship, it relates to ecstatic utterances and a general sense of free-for-all within the worship. We cannot be entirely sure whether the comments Paul is making in these accounts refer to actual practice among the Corinthians or whether he is engaging in some kind of rhetorical gesture.[14] Either way, the fact that Paul is trying to encourage some kind of order does nothing to detract from either the chaotic reality of the situation he is describing, or his general approval of this enthusiastic, Spirit-filled, event. Paul clearly took the role of the ecstatic in worship as normal for the

---

[10] The assembly called to eject a member of the community who has sinned in Chapter 4 may or may not be seen as an act of worship. My view would be that this probably occurred within the context of a wider meeting. Whether that was a meeting for worship is difficult to determine (see Meeks, *First Urban Christians*, 143).

[11] Meeks notes the importance of the phrase 'coming together' to define assemblies within the Corinthian community (ibid., 142).

[12] D. E. Smith, *From Symposium to Eucharist, The Banquet in the Early Christian World*. Minneapolis: Fortress Press, 2003, 200–16.

[13] Dennis Smith uses the uniform structure of the classical banquet, the meal followed by conversation with wine, to suggest that the two parts obviously go together. The link is not, however, clear in the text. See Smith, *Symposium*, 200.

[14] The reference to drunkenness in the account of the meal is a good example of this. See V. K. Robbins, *The Tapestry of Early Christian Discourse, Rhetoric, Society and Ideology*. London: Routledge, 1996, 116.

Christian community.[15] He even boasts of his own spiritual gifts, including tongues, visions and prophecy (14:18). His concern for the Corinthians appears to relate primarily to the impact this form of worship might have on casual visitors from outside (14:23). Paul is also concerned that all parts of the worship should encourage, or 'build up', the community (14:12). Ecstatic worship, therefore, was clearly a central element of the practice of the Christian community in Corinth and was clearly something that Paul approved of in principle even if he wished to see a greater sense of order or direction in its performance.

This text also includes Paul's statement that women should not speak in worship (14:34). Apart from the fact that this contradicts an earlier statement in the letter (11:5), we cannot take this statement as being representative of the community to which Paul is writing. The fact that Paul felt a need to include such a teaching suggests that things were not as Paul might have wished within the community. It is highly likely that women did play a very active role in the worship of the Corinthian community. A number of women are mentioned in the text as members of the community, some as significant members. Paul may not have approved. He writes trying to curb this activity, but we are not told whether or not the Corinthian community actually took any notice of this teaching or if the position of women in the community changed as a consequence.[16]

When we look more widely at Paul's writings, we can see that the idea of enthusiastic, Spirit-filled worship is reinforced. Familial terms for fellow Christians are common in Paul's writing, and this was not common practice within the Roman and Hellenistic societies of the time. This may indicate a level of intimacy within the community of Christians that is certainly consonant with some form of enthusiastic worship.[17] Edward Phillips also notes the way in which a number of letters end with a request to pass on the holy kiss (e.g. 1 Cor. 16:20).[18] Like familial terms, such displays of intimate affection would probably have been seen as scandalous within the cultural context of the time. Phillips argues that the kiss (which he suggests would probably have been on the lips)[19] was associated, within the earliest Christian communities, with the passing on from individual to individual of

---

[15] I am using the term 'ecstatic' here in the way developed by I. M. Lewis in *Ecstatic Religion, A Study of Shamanism and Spirit Possession*. London: Routledge, 1989.

[16] For further discussion see E. S. Fiorenza, *In Memory of Her, A Feminist Theological Reconstruction of Christian Origins*. London: SCM, 1983, 226–33 and D. F. Sawyer, *Women and Religion in the First Christian Centuries*. London: Routledge, 1996, 103–8.

[17] Meeks, *First Urban Christians*, 129.

[18] L. E. Phillips, *The Ritual Kiss in Early Christian Worship*. Nottingham: Grove Books, 1996.

[19] Ibid., 12.

the power of the Spirit. Such a view once again accords with a community that sees itself, quite literally, as Spirit-filled and within which Spirit possession, particularly within worship, would have been considered as normal.

There is probably very little more that we can say about the gathering described in Chapter 14. Much more, however, has been written about the meal referred to in Chapter 11. When we look at the text more closely, there are, however, few things that we can say for certain about the event that is being discussed. We know that Paul refers to it as the 'Lord's supper' (11:20). This, however, does not really get us very far. This is the only use of this term in the whole of Paul's writing and we have no other clue as to what Paul might have meant by the term.[20] The other point that we can be fairly sure about is that the event that is being described is a communal meal. The sharing of meals was an important part of many different social groups within the ancient world, both Jewish and Hellenic.[21] Such communal meals would normally have been followed by some kind of debate or speech but there is no indication of this in Paul's text.[22]

The evidence that is provided by the letter suggests that the meal was Jewish in form. The earlier references to a 'cup of thanksgiving', or 'cup of blessing', and to the bread that is broken (10:16), both suggest Jewish practices commonly thought to be associated with communal, if not exactly 'ritual' meals.[23] This, however, is not entirely conclusive. There are three other factors that might challenge the idea of a traditional Jewish meal. The first relates to the idea of an 'ideal' Jewish meal. We simply do not have the evidence that we would like for what this might have included at such a date. Gregory Dix and other early commentators have assumed some kind of knowledge based on much later material.[24] However, as Bradshaw makes very clear, referring to the latest Jewish scholarship, we simply do not know.[25] Secondly, the Jews of Corinth would have been Hellenised Jews (as were Paul and other missionaries from Antioch). The Hellenised Jews may also have had different understandings and practices associated with communal meals and could easily have combined elements of, say, Jewish blessings with elements of the Greek symposia.[26] Finally, we must recognise, as Wayne Meeks and others have made clear, that the Christian community in Corinth was most likely a mixture of Hellenised Jews and local Greeks,

[20] Meeks, *First Urban Christians*, 157.
[21] J. Stambaugh and D. Balch, *The Social World of the First Christians*. London: SPCK, 1986, 125 and 140. See also the extended discussion in Smith, *Symposium*.
[22] Smith, *Symposium*, 27–31.   [23] Ibid., 133–72.
[24] G. Dix, *The Shape of the Liturgy*. London: Adam & Charles Black, 1945, 50–70.
[25] Bradshaw, *Search*, 45.   [26] Smith, *Symposium*, 133–4.

probably dominated numerically (if not in influence) by the non-Jews.[27] These Greeks would clearly have found many of the ritual elements of the Jewish meal both novel and alien. What is more, given what Paul tells us of the general sense of disorder during the meal, such non-Jews may not have continued to observe these Jewish elements on a regular basis. This combination of Jews and Gentiles may also have raised other problems. Both groups would have been socialised to avoid eating with the other and this must have caused some element of friction within the meal.[28] This, however, is not the conflict that Paul draws attention to. The conflict Paul is concerned with relates to the obvious status differences within the community, and that, clearly, would have added another layer of confusion. It is difficult, therefore, to say with any kind of certainty what form of meal Paul is discussing.

The other major element of Chapter 11, however, is the statement by Paul of the tradition that he has 'received from the Lord' (11:23), that is, the narrative of the Last Supper.[29] Many scholars have assumed that because this narrative is given such prominence, the meal must have related to it in some way. It is even suggested that the narrative *must* have been read or proclaimed within the context of the meal itself.[30] In my view, this assumption is too easy. We have to ask why Paul chooses to offer this narrative at this stage in this letter, and, just as significant, why he emphasises the fact that this narrative is 'received from the Lord'. The narrative itself has little to say about the main issue of the chapter; the greed of people of high status and the disunity caused by this within the meal being described. The narrative is offered as some kind of justification for the meal. However, the way in which Paul introduces the text suggests that many of the Christians at Corinth would not have been as aware of this tradition as Paul would have liked. The fact that Paul has to stress the narrative in this way suggests that Paul is introducing something relatively new or unusual and is drawing on all the authority he can muster in order to get the Corinthians to accept it. Paul does say that he has passed this narrative on before, but in

[27] Meeks, *First Urban Christians*, 168 and J. K. Chow, *Patronage and Power: A Study of Social Networks in Corinth*. Sheffield: Sheffield Academic Press, 1992, 88–93.

[28] This is the point on which Paul disagreed with Peter during his dispute at Antioch (Gal. 2:11–21). It is clear that the difficulty that Jews and Greeks had in sharing food together has not really been taken seriously enough in any understanding of the early history of Christian meals. Smith argues that the principles determining the sharing of food between Jews and non-Jews would have varied within Jewish communities and so no clear guidance can be offered. Smith, *Symposium*, 159–66.

[29] The account of the Last Supper should not be taken as in any sense a descriptive account of the meal that Paul himself is discussing. It is a narrative account whose reference is the 'tradition'.

[30] Meeks, *First Urban Christians*, 158.

doing this he implies that the Corinthians have probably forgotten it. If this is the case, then why does Paul decide to recount the narrative again at this point in his argument?

In order to provide a possible answer we must note exactly when the letter was written.[31] Towards the end of the letter Paul talks about hoping to stay in Ephesus for Pentecost and implies that this is only a week or so away (16:8). This suggests that Paul is writing sometime in the weeks following Passover. As with communal meals in general, our knowledge and understanding of the practice of Jewish festivals in the first century is more limited than scholars once assumed, especially in areas outside of Palestine and Syria.[32] One thing that is practically certain, however, is that the celebrations for Passover within any Jewish community of the time would have included a festal meal and the reading from Exodus that gives the charter for the feast. What is also clear is that, for Christians, the feast of Passover was intimately linked to the death and resurrection of Jesus. It is not unreasonable, therefore, to assume that at a Jewish-Christian celebration of Passover some reference was made to Jesus' last days; perhaps these were recounted and retold alongside the charter story from Exodus within the context of a festal meal.

In 1983 Etienne Trocmé wrote a short book in which he proposed that the framework for the Passion narrative in the Gospels was originally influenced by the liturgical celebration of Passover among the earliest Christian communities.[33] Much of the liturgical speculation in the second half of the book is a clear case of reading evidence from the end of the second century back to the middle of the first, and must therefore be rejected. In order to make his point, however, Trocmé argues that the Passion narrative probably existed as a distinct unit with a clear shape and content long before it was incorporated into the various Gospels.[34] Some form of coherent narrative, beginning possibly with the anointing at Bethany and concluding with an account of the finding of the empty tomb (Mark 14–16), may well have circulated in the earliest Christian communities in an oral form before anything more formal was written down. It is also plausible, as Trocmé suggests, that this narrative was read, or recounted, at Passover within Jewish-Christian communities, as some

---

[31] In saying this we have to assume that the letter forms a single original text. See Dunn, *Corinthians*, 21–3.

[32] Smith, *Symposium*, 147–50.

[33] E. Trocmé, *The Passion as Liturgy, A Study of the Origins of the Passion Narratives in the Four Gospels*. London: SCM, 1983.

[34] Ibid., 7–46.

kind of justification for the meal, either in place of the Exodus reading or alongside it.[35] Finally, Trocmé argues that we have to see the narrative of the Last Supper as an integral part of this original Passion narrative and not as a distinct or separate unit.[36]

If all this is true, and I agree that it remains speculation, then it is certainly plausible that Paul had recently heard the narrative of the Last Supper within the Christian community at Ephesus as they celebrated their own form of 'Christian' Passover. The narrative would therefore have been fresh in Paul's mind when he came to write the letter to the Corinthians, leading him to associate the narrative of the Last Supper with the event of the 'Lord's supper' that he is discussing. It may also have been the case that the 'Lord's supper' referred to by Paul was itself the Passover meal of the Corinthians, although this would be pure conjecture. While the Corinthians may have read or heard the whole of a Passion narrative as part of their Passover celebrations, and Paul or a colleague would certainly have recounted it when he was with them, the community may not have consciously associated the account of the Last Supper with the meal they were sharing on a regular basis. If this were the case, then Paul is clearly adding something new to their thinking at this point in the letter, as the language he uses suggests.

What is definitely associated with the meal, and more specifically with the bread and wine used at the meal, is the link that Paul makes in Chapter 11, and elsewhere (10:14–22, 11:26), between the bread and wine and the body and blood of Jesus. This emphasis on the body and blood of Christ, and the eschatological nature of Paul's language at this point, could again be related to the links that Paul is making following his own reflection on the themes of Passover and the recalling of the narrative of the Passion.[37] All these passages, therefore, show Paul reflecting on the issues involved in his own distinctive way. They are not presented as traditions 'received from the Lord' and they would not necessarily have been a part of the Corinthians' own reflections on the meal until they came to read Paul's letter.

---

[35] Ibid., 81.

[36] Ibid., 68. It is clear that if Trocmé is right then the account of the Last Supper is part of a wider narrative account and not in any sense a charter for any specific ritual meal. Its shape and structure therefore are probably determined as much by the narrative needs of the text as by any attempt to provide an accurate account of any real or imagined celebration. This would be equally true of the Institution Narrative in 1 Corinthians if Trocmé's overall thesis is correct.

[37] There is considerable evidence within the letter of a wider focus on themes from the Passion. See Barton, 'Christian Community'.

What I am proposing, therefore, is that in his letter to the Corinthians, Paul is aiming to relate the life and worship of the Christian community at Corinth, including a meal that he had previously instituted as a regular event within the community, to a number of Paschal themes. This has laid the foundation for much subsequent Christian reflection on the 'eucharist', but does not in any way allow us to claim that a 'eucharist', or even a 'proto-eucharist', was celebrated within the Corinthian community.[38] Paul himself does not use this term. His letter speaks of the 'Lord's supper', and for Paul this was clearly a meal with some Jewish elements, such as the blessing of the cup and the breaking of bread, that triggered an eschatological connection between the bread and cup and the body and blood of Jesus. Along with the informal Spirit-filled worship described later in the letter, this is probably all that we can safely say about the earliest account of Christian worship available to us.[39]

What I have presented so far is an analysis and discussion of a single text. This analysis has provided some level of insight into the worship and life of a particular Christian community in Corinth some thirty to forty years after the death of Jesus. There are, however, still many questions left open. There are large gaps in our knowledge. We can say nothing in any particular detail about the words that may have been used in worship, the particular relationship of the worship to Jewish or other contemporary models, or even the timing and frequency of such worship. We can say, however, that this worship was focused around a shared meal and a gathering of the community in which each individual brought hymns, words, songs and various forms of ecstatic gifts. The Corinthian community is also only one of many similar Christian communities that were already scattered across the north-east Mediterranean and beyond. The recipients of this letter may not even have been the only 'Christian' community in Corinth at the time. What we have in this letter, therefore, is a mere snapshot of the worshipping life of a particular Christian community at a particular time and place. Can this offer any basis on which to begin a history of Christian worship in any but a very general sense?

[38] If I am right in suggesting that the meal at Corinth that sparked the original concern was itself a Passover meal then it may be the case that this meal was an annual rather than a weekly event. There is no evidence in the letter itself for the frequency of the meal and this reading is certainly plausible.
[39] I have not said anything in this section about baptism. This is primarily because Paul offers no account of the practice of baptism within the Corinthian or any other Christian community. The fact that baptism clearly occurred, however, has to be taken as certain. What form it may have taken is more difficult to guess. See M. E. Johnson, *The Rites of Christian Initiation, Their Evolution and Interpretation*. Collegeville: Liturgical Press, 1999, 22–31.

TEXTS AND CONTEXTS

One way in which we could begin to answer this question, I would suggest, is to take the conclusions that have been drawn from the study of Paul's letter and to test them against other cases where we have less direct and more controversial evidence. In practice this means looking at other texts from the following two hundred years and comparing the data that are available. In doing this, however, we must recognise the nature of the texts that we are dealing with and their specific social and historical contexts. Each of the other texts has a specific history and context of its own. Scholars have come some way in trying to identify the specific origins of each document in the New Testament and the kind of community that might have produced it,[40] but little contextual work has been undertaken beyond this.[41] This work, therefore, is inevitably tentative and controversial and there are very few fixed points around which to make statements with any kind of certainty. This does not mean, however, that we should abandon our task. What it does mean is that we should be very careful of claiming too much for our results.

A full contextual analysis of each text from the perspective of liturgy has still to be undertaken.[42] It is also clear that I cannot mention every single text from the period that may be relevant. I therefore wish to focus on texts from two specific localities for the hundred or so years after Paul's letter to the Corinthians. In doing this I wish to try to contextualise each text and to highlight what the texts themselves may be saying before I go on, in the following section, to try to reconstruct what we know more generally of the histories of worship in this period.

In a jointly authored book Raymond Brown and John Meier recount how, through their independent studies of the Christian literature associated with Antioch and Rome between 50 and 150, they had each come to very similar conclusions.[43] In each case they had seen how the dominant voices in each community had, by the early years of the second century,

---

[40] Barton, 'Communal Dimension'.

[41] See M. Zetterholm, *The Formation of Christianity in Antioch, A Social-Scientific Approach to the Separation Between Judaism and Christianity*. London: Routledge, 2003 for a good recent contribution.

[42] Grove Books has been very good at making the specifically liturgical elements of a number of these texts available for students but these editions rarely provide the contextual material that is necessary. See e.g. D. N. Power, *Irenaeus of Lyons on Baptism and Eucharist: Selected Texts with Introduction, Translation and Annotation*. Nottingham: Grove Books, 1991 and G. J. Cuming, *Hippolytus: A Text for Students with Introduction, Translation, Commentary and Notes*. Nottingham: Grove Books, 1976.

[43] R. E. Brown and J. P. Meier, *Antioch and Rome, New Testament Cradles of Catholic Christianity*. London: Geoffrey Chapman, 1983.

developed a middle line between the 'judaisers' and the 'anti-judaisers' within the Christian communities of each city.[44] In order to demonstrate this, the two authors look in some detail at the literature that was produced by Christians in or around each of these two cities during the first hundred and fifty years of Christianity. Brown and Meier were concerned primarily with the first three generations of Christians. They begin their analysis with New Testament texts (notably Paul's letters to the Galatians and to the Romans, Matthew's Gospel, the first letter of Peter, and Hebrews). This material deals with what Brown and Meier refer to as the first and second generations of Christians. The third generation is represented in Antioch by the writing of Ignatius, who claimed to be a leader of the Christian community in Antioch and was martyred in Rome in about 116, and the Didache, a collection of texts that has proved very controversial, especially for liturgical scholars. In Rome the third generation is represented by Clement, who wrote to the Corinthians a few years before Ignatius' martyrdom, and was something akin to the secretary of the council of Roman churches. This, with the addition of a few less well-attested texts, is as far as Brown and Meier develop their analysis.

In what follows I want to follow Brown and Meier's lead and begin by looking at the literature produced in or around Antioch and Rome, giving particular attention to the literature associated with worship. In Antioch I want, like Meier and Brown, to focus on the writings of Ignatius and the Didache. In relation to Rome, on the other hand, we have far more direct evidence, and I will look briefly at the letter of Clement and then focus on the writings of Justin, who was martyred in Rome in about 160, and a text called the 'Apostolic Tradition' that was, in part at least, produced in Rome at the beginning of the third century. Before going on to look at these texts, however, I need to return to Brown and Meier's main thesis concerning the relationship between the emerging Christian communities and the resident Jewish communities of Antioch and Rome. It is here that we have to begin the process of contextualisation.

The first letter to the Corinthians was written by one man with a very distinctive point of view. The rapid acceptance of Paul's letters across the early Christian communities, and the 'canonisation' of those texts into something approaching sacred scripture, has kept Paul's views at the

---

[44] There is considerable debate in the study of early Christianity about the respective roles of those who wished to retain close links with Jewish practices and traditions and those who wished to reject them. This debate continued until well into the third century but the 'anti-judaisers' quickly gained the upper hand. See Zetterholm, *Antioch*.

forefront of our understanding of the earliest period of Christian development.[45] In many ways, however, Paul was probably something of the exception rather than the rule. The most important of these exceptions is in relation to Paul's attitude to the traditions of his birth. It is not difficult to see that Paul, throughout his writing, is antagonistic to those Christians who maintain Jewish traditions and practices. He understands himself as an apostle to the Gentiles. He questions, if not rejects, aspects of the Jewish law. Even in matters of worship, it is possible that many of the Jewish forms, particularly the celebration of new moons and festivals, are systematically rejected.[46] This is not to say that Paul is not heavily influenced, in all aspects of his writing and theology, by Jewish traditions and ideas. It is simply that Paul goes to some length to set himself up in opposition to the Jewish communities of the cities in which he preached.

What Brown and Meier make abundantly clear, however, is that the earliest Christian communities of Antioch and Rome were far less antagonistic towards the Jews than Paul and his immediate followers. They outline a series of different approaches that could have been held by the Christian communities in Antioch towards the Jews.[47] Paul's position probably sat at one extreme of this series and the exclusively Jewish Christians, who denied the possibility that Gentiles could even become Christians, would sit at the other. This range of positions would also have had an impact on the worship of the different communities.

The text known as the Didache, for example, provides evidence of a more substantially Jewish form of Christian worship than that suggested by Paul's letter to the Corinthians.[48] The text talks of travelling prophets and preachers who clearly used a distinctively Jewish discourse, and the community represented by the Didache modelled many of their prayers on Jewish originals.[49] Liturgical scholars in particular have had difficulty trying to cope with the Didache as a text.[50] It does not fit neatly into a linear history of the eucharist, of ministry or of any other aspect of Christian worship. It is a

---

[45] For more details on this see H. Koester, *Introduction to the New Testament, vol. II, History and Literature of Early Christianity.* New York: Walter de Gruyter, 1987.

[46] See Galatians 4:8–11. Is Paul objecting to the keeping of Jewish festivals and days or pagan ones? Much of the letter argues against judaisers, where a 'slave' is a 'slave under the Law'. V. 8 talks about being formerly slaves to 'those who by nature are not gods', which implies paganism. Then in v. 17 Paul goes on to talk about 'those people' who are 'zealous to win you over', i.e. those who want the Galatians to be circumcised, i.e. judaisers. It is all rather confusing.

[47] Brown and Meier, *Antioch and Rome*, 2–8. See also Zetterholm, *Antioch*.

[48] Niederwimmer, *The Didache.* [49] Ibid., 156–64.

[50] See W. Rordorf, 'The *Didache*', in R. Johanny (ed.), *The Eucharist of the Early Christians.* New York: Pueblo, 1978 as an example of a Roman Catholic approach to the document that clearly fails to engage with the text as it stands.

document that was written for or by a Christian community in the process of change. It recognises the authority of travelling preachers and teachers but also suggests that authorities from within the community itself, such as 'bishops', are superseding these.[51] It has been traditionally associated with a rural community, either in Palestine or, more likely, in the region around Antioch, and was compiled towards the end of the first century.

The Didache begins with a section laying out, in a Christianised version of a traditional Jewish text, the ways of life and the ways of death. This is followed by a series of instructions on worship and the ordering of the community. There is a short passage on baptism, which suggests that baptism should occur in running water (7:1–4).[52] There are also two passages that deal with meals (9:1–10:7 and 14). Most scholars have assumed that one or other of the references is 'eucharistic' while the other relates to a formal communal meal. This assumption is made primarily because of the need that scholars have felt to fit this text into their linear historical tradition.[53] If we look at the text itself, however, what we see are two references that could very easily be to the same event. Chapters 9 and 10 deal with a full meal (10:1), although the text itself focuses on prayers of thanksgiving over the wine and the bread at the beginning of the meal and a longer, more general prayer of thanksgiving at the end. These prayers follow what most scholars agree is a form of the Jewish blessings later used at all formal Jewish meals. Chapter 14 refers only to thanksgiving and the breaking of bread, and is given a sacrificial gloss. There is no reason why these two passages should not be referring to the same event. If this were so, then, within the community that produced the Didache, a shared meal with a distinctly Jewish series of blessings or thanksgivings[54] was celebrated on a weekly basis (14:1).

This brings us back to the question of the influence of Jewish worship on that of the earliest Christian communities. Many liturgists have tried at various times to suggest that the forms of Christian worship that emerged in the second century in different parts of the Roman world are all derived

---

[51] The text talks of *episcopoi* and *diakonoi* in the plural (15:1). Niederwimmer comments that this represents a very early understanding of elected officials with responsibility only to the local congregation (*The Didache*, 200–1).

[52] Where running water is not available other possibilities are offered. See Johnson, *Christian Initiation*, 35–7.

[53] Rordorf, 'The Didache'.

[54] Roger Beckwith, while stressing the close relationship between Jewish and Christian language for worship, notes the different emphasis of blessing (Jewish) and thanksgiving (Christian) although this may be a later distinction as we do not have Jewish texts that are contemporary with the Didache to confirm the position. R. T. Beckwith, *Daily and Weekly Worship: From Jewish to Christian*. Nottingham: Grove Books, 1987, 38–9.

from at least a family of Jewish models.[55] Unfortunately, when we come to look at the evidence we find that there is as little known about Jewish worship in the first century after Jesus as there is about Christian worship. While the links between Christian and Jewish forms are clear in many cases, as with the Didache, the exact nature of the Jewish model that has been followed is almost impossible to reconstruct.[56] The question we must ask, therefore, is not so much whether Paul and the compilers of the Didache were exceptional in their respective attitudes to Jewish traditions of the time. Clearly they were. Rather we need to ask whether either author had any lasting effect on the emerging liturgical life of the wider Christian communities. In order to explore this further, however, we need to move on and look at a contemporary of the compilers of the Didache who also emerged from the Christian communities of Antioch.

Ignatius wrote a series of seven letters to Christian communities in Asia Minor while on his way from Antioch to Rome, where he was due to be martyred.[57] In these letters he proclaims himself to be 'the Bishop of Syria' (Romans 2:2)[58] and provides a considerable amount of detail about his current situation. He also offers advice to the range of Christian communities that he is writing to. He says very little, however, about the situation in Antioch as he left it.[59] Ignatius is centrally concerned in all his letters to encourage the local Christian communities to a greater sense of unity under the leadership of a single 'bishop', a group of elders and the deacons. Whether Ignatius reflects the situation in Antioch at the turn of the first century or is promulgating an ideal position for his own purposes is difficult to determine.[60] Whether his message was accepted widely within Asia Minor is also uncertain. Polycarp, Bishop of Smyrna and one of the people to whom Ignatius wrote, does not appear to have taken this message on board in his own letter to the Philadelphians after Ignatius' death.[61] He makes no reference to 'bishops' at all.

---

[55] See R. T. Beckwith, 'The Jewish Background to Christian Worship', in C. Jones et al. (eds.), *The Study of Liturgy*. London: SPCK, 1992, 68–80.

[56] Bradshaw, *Search*, 36–46.

[57] W. R. Schoedel, *A Commentary on the Letters of Ignatius of Antioch*. Philadelphia: Fortress Press, 1985.

[58] This is the only time Ignatius refers to himself as a 'bishop' although all the later commentators describe him as Bishop of Antioch. It is interesting that Ignatius refers to himself as 'the bishop' rather than 'a bishop', so claiming an authority and role of the bishop that is significantly different from that in the Didache. See Schoedel, *Commentary*, 171.

[59] C. Trevett, *A Study of Ignatius of Antioch in Syria and Asia*. Lewiston: Edward Mellen Press, 1992, 1.

[60] For further details about Ignatius' possible relationship with the church in Antioch see Trevett, *Ignatius*, 37–66 and Zetterholm, *Antioch*, 203–10.

[61] A. Roberts and J. Donaldson (eds.), *The Apostolic Fathers*. Edinburgh: T. & T. Clark, 1867, 65–78.

In a number of his letters Ignatius makes references to the 'eucharist'. This is the first time that the word itself appears to be used in a technical sense in Christian literature.[62] These references relate the eucharist directly to Ignatius' ideas about the unity of the church as focused on the bishop (Phil. 4, Smyrn. 8:1–2). What is not clear from these references, however, is exactly what kind of event the 'eucharist' actually is or how frequently it was celebrated. In his letter to the Ephesians Ignatius encourages the community to assemble more frequently for prayer and thanksgiving (Eph. 13:1) but offers no suggestion for an appropriate frequency. The eucharist could easily be a meal, much like the one mentioned by Paul and the Didache. In the letter to the Smyrnaeans the words 'eucharist' and 'agape' (love-feast) appear to be used interchangeably (Smyrn. 8:1–2), but the word 'agape' is not defined any more clearly than 'eucharist'.[63] The content of the worship is not Ignatius' concern. What we do know is that bread and wine were involved. Ignatius refers to this as 'medicine for the soul' (Eph. 20:2). The eucharist is also related, albeit very loosely, to discussion of the flesh and blood of Christ (Phil. 4, Smyrn. 7:1). It is the unity of the event, however, as the central defining feature of the Christian community gathered around its bishop, that Ignatius is most keen to stress and this he does with great emphasis.

Interestingly, in his letter to the Smyrnaeans Ignatius refers to a Christian community that does not celebrate the eucharist 'because they do not confess that the eucharist is the flesh of the saviour Jesus Christ' (Smyrn. 7:1). Whether this is an accurate portrayal of that community or a slur on Ignatius' part is also difficult to determine. Other references to worship include the constant reference to prayer, usually of an intercessory nature, and to communal prayer meetings. Baptism is also referred to in passing, again as a sign of unity under the bishop (Smyrn. 8:1–2). Finally, while there is no direct reference in any of the letters to speaking in tongues or to any other form of ecstatic experience, certain members of the church at Philadelphia are referred to as 'prophets' and Ignatius suggests that he is also adept at prophetic utterances.[64]

This brings me back to the central question of Ignatius' writings. Is Ignatius simply stating what he takes for granted at Antioch, or is he trying to impose some kind of model that he feels should reflect the life of the

---

[62] 'Eucharist' is a form of the Greek word for 'thanksgiving' and it is used widely in a generic sense, as for giving thanks in the Didache and other texts. Ignatius is the first to use it in a technical sense for a specific rite involving bread and wine. R. Johanny, 'Ignatius of Antioch', in Johanny, *The Eucharist*, 48–70, 52.

[63] Schoedel, *Commentary*, 224.   [64] Trevett, *Ignatius*, 131–8.

ideal Christian community? It is very difficult to answer this. The first three letters, written from Smyrna, are written to those churches that have representatives in the city. In each case one of these representatives is referred to as the 'bishop' and the letter encourages the whole community to abide by his authority. In the letter to the Philadelphians, which is written from Troas, Ignatius makes it clear that he has passed through Philadelphia earlier in the voyage and is responding to a situation of disunity among the Christians there, related primarily to the on-going question of the Jewish law. It is in the Philadelphian letter that the strongest statements of the need for unity are made. Personally, I feel that Ignatius is actually over-stressing his point. What he has found in Asia Minor is clearly a much more informal arrangement of churches and communities than he would really like. Given the continuing worries over those who disagree, from the position both of the 'judaisers'[65] and of others, he feels that a stronger more centralised organisation is preferred and uses all his authority as a potential martyr to try to impose one. In doing this he draws on the eucharist and baptism as central images and sets them up as the defining rites of the church. This tells us little or nothing, therefore, about the actual practice of the Christian communities either in Antioch or in those other cities that Ignatius passed through on his way to Rome.

At this point, therefore, we need to follow in Ignatius' footsteps and move on to Rome itself. More specifically we need to look at the writing of Justin Martyr and the Apostolic Tradition. Before doing this, however, I need to make a few comments about Clement and the letter he sent on behalf of the Roman church to Corinth at the very end of the first century.[66] Clement is addressing a disturbance in the church at Corinth, which has led to the expulsion of a number of elders. While he offers a great deal of sound practical and theological advice he does not make any significant reference to worship. Towards the end of the letter, in a discussion of order that draws heavily on Old Testament imagery, Clement uses terms such as offerings (*prosphorai*) and services (*leitourgiai*) which he says should not be celebrated 'randomly and without order but at determined hours and times' (40:2).[67] Clement, however, never uses the term 'eucharist' in any technical sense, or makes any direct reference to a

---

[65] Ibid., 169–73.
[66] Clement never identifies himself by name in the letter but is referred to in the Shepherd of Hermas as the one who writes to other churches on behalf of the churches in Rome and is mentioned by Dionysius, Bishop of Corinth, as the one who wrote a letter to the Corinthians. Brown and Meier, *Antioch and Rome*, 160–1.
[67] G. Blond, 'Clement of Rome', in Johanny, *The Eucharist*, 24–47.

communal meal or to bread and wine. It is unclear, therefore, whether the 'offerings' referred to in the text relate to prayers or to some kind of offering of bread and wine. Without further evidence, the offering of prayer and praise on a regular basis is probably more likely.[68] Despite his insistence on order, Clement also fails to develop the idea of *episkopos*, bishop or overseer, in the way that Ignatius was to do ten or so years later. It is clear that the Corinthian community at the turn of the first century, and we must assume the Roman community of which Clement was a member, was run by a council of elders rather than by a single bishop.[69]

Justin, writing fifty years after Clement, is a very different kind of Christian from those who wrote most of the literature that we have looked at so far.[70] He was born in Samaria and clearly travelled extensively. He was a Roman citizen and spent much of his life exploring different forms of philosophy, most notably the works of Plato, before finally coming to Christianity. His writings are primarily apologetic and are written for non-Christians, whether Roman authorities, Jews or Greeks.[71] In the course of this writing Justin provides us with the first account of what actually happened at worship within a Christian community in the city of Rome. The account comes towards the end of an apology that is addressed to Antonius Pius, the Emperor.[72] For most of the first sixty chapters Justin addresses the main charges that were commonly put against the Christians: that they were atheists, that they were lax in morals and so on. In the final few chapters he presents two accounts of what the Christians did when they came together for worship. The first describes a baptism followed by the sharing of bread and wine and the second recounts an act of worship with readings, teaching, prayers and the sharing of bread and wine standing alone without baptism.

The feel of both of these accounts is very informal. In relation to the second rite the community meets on Sundays, presumably in the evening, and readings go on for as long as time allows. Then the president presents his teaching. Prayers are offered standing and, in the first, baptismal, rite,

---

[68] The regular nature of these 'offerings', presumably more than one a day, reinforces this reading. The language is simply taken from Old Testament sources but the reality appears to have been a series of prayers throughout the day; whether individual or communal is not clear.

[69] Brown and Meier, *Antioch and Rome*, 164.

[70] For further discussions on Justin see L. W. Barnard, *Justin Martyr: His Life and Thought*. Cambridge: Cambridge University Press, 1967.

[71] For editions see M. Dods, G. Reith and B. P. Pratten, *The Writings of Justin Martyr and Athenagoras*. Edinburgh: T. & T. Clark, 1867.

[72] Dods et al., *Writings*, 7–69; for the passages relevant to worship see R. C. D. Jasper and G. J. Cuming (eds.), *Prayers of the Eucharist, Early and Reformed Texts*. Oxford: Oxford University Press, 1980, 14–16.

members of the community greet one another with a kiss. Bread and wine are brought in and the president offers a thanksgiving to the best of his ability. The gifts are shared very informally and some of the bread is kept back to take out to the sick and infirm. The food is referred to as 'eucharist' and only believers can participate. Like Paul, the Didache and Ignatius, Justin also relates the bread and wine to the body and blood of Jesus. He also offers the Institution Narrative from the Last Supper as an explanation for the event. However, no examples of specific prayers are given. Justin also chooses the term 'president' rather than 'elder' or 'bishop' for the principal celebrant, making it very difficult for us to draw any conclusions about the structure of his community or to answer further questions about the place of bishops in the Christian communities of Rome. He does however use the term 'deacon' for those who take the bread and wine to the sick (65:5) and the term 'lector' for those who read (67:4), distinguishing both of these from the president.

It has been argued that the nature of the text itself, an apology written for non-Christians, led Justin to be less specific about what was happening than he might otherwise have been.[73] Justin, in this view, is simply saying all that needs to be said to indicate how inoffensive the activity was. This is perfectly plausible, but we have no reason to assume that there was anything more to the rite than Justin is telling us.[74] Those who want to read more formality and structure into the event are generally looking back at it from later accounts. What Justin describes is just as plausible as a development of the rite from the context of all that we have looked at so far.

One further point relates not to the Apology itself, but rather to the earliest account we have of Justin's martyrdom.[75] It is very difficult to date these popular texts but it is clear that this account is very early, and probably reliable. In this text Justin is recorded as saying that Christians do not all meet in one place in Rome for worship, but rather worship where they choose and where they can.[76] He claims that he has never joined any of the other congregations in Rome but has always worshipped with his own followers in his own house above the home of Martinus near the baths of Timotinius.[77] The picture given here is of a distinct group, meeting around

---

[73] See for example Bradshaw, *Origins*, 98–9.
[74] No mention is made of a meal, although 67:2 does say that thanks is given for 'all that we eat'. It is unclear whether this stands alone or is more directly related to the account of the rite that follows.
[75] Dods et al., *Writings*, 367–70.
[76] Martyrdom account, Chapter 2. In the First Apology, by contrast, Justin says that 'all who live in the city or the countryside meet' (67:3). This suggests a single congregation but is not necessarily at odds with the idea of a specific congregation meeting at Justin's house.
[77] Martyrdom account, Chapter 2.

Justin whenever he is in town (which is not all that often from this account), and celebrating the rite described in the Apology within the context of the philosopher and his disciples.[78] The sense of informality would clearly be reinforced by this context, as would be the lack of any formal Jewish meal, which would probably have been alien to Justin's experience. However, if this is anything like an accurate account of Justin's own situation in Rome, somewhat detached from the main congregations, then what can we say for this rite being representative of the worship of the wider Christian community in Rome? Justin, in his writings, was defending Christians against the threats posed by Jews and the wider pagan culture. While he was active in Rome, however, there were many different kinds of Christian within the city, including followers of Marcion, Valentinus and others who were later considered heretics.[79] These different communities were no more favourable to each other than the 'catholics'[80] were to these other communities. A later generation, the fourth if we follow Brown and Meier, was to take the threat of these so called 'heresies' very seriously and adapt their worship accordingly, but it is not at all clear whether Justin was part of the same community as Clement, or of that to which Ignatius wrote asking them to support him in his martyrdom.

One of the authors who wrote extensively against the 'heretics' from within the Roman context was Hippolytus.[81] Hippolytus was writing at the beginning of the third century, almost fifty years after Justin. As well as writing against the heretics he is also thought to be the author of a work entitled the 'Apostolic Tradition'. The text that we have of this work has had to be put together from later translations and adaptations. The major problem, therefore, is that we really do not know whether the liturgical events described in this text ever occurred in the form in which they are presented, or, more specifically, whether the prayers that are reproduced were ever used. This has been a matter of constant debate for over a hundred years. First, it is not at all clear that Hippolytus actually wrote the text as we have it.[82] Secondly, Hippolytus himself was clearly a conservative and, in some accounts, the leader of a community that was opposed to the dominant 'catholic' group. It could therefore be argued that

---

[78] For more information on the context of the philosopher's meal see Smith, *Symposium,* 47–65.
[79] G. Lüdemann, *Heretics, The Other Side of Early Christianity.* London: SCM, 1996.
[80] Ignatius was also the first to use this term of his own community. Trevett, *Ignatius,* 152.
[81] P. F. Bradshaw, M. E. Johnson and L. E. Phillips, *The Apostolic Tradition.* Minneapolis: Fortress Press, 2002, 5.
[82] Because of the complexity of the textual traditions of this text each editor appears to present a different version of the supposed work. For the most recent edition and commentary see ibid., 1–6.

the Apostolic Tradition represents what Hippolytus might have liked to see, rather than what was actually happening at the time of its composition. This does not necessarily discredit the text completely, as, at the very least, it would still represent an example of what one particular author thought could happen at a fairly specific date and place. However, it is clear that we have to treat the text with a great deal of care in terms of general liturgical history.

The text can be divided into four parts: the first deals with ordinations and includes an account of the eucharist (1–14);[83] the second covers information on baptism and preparation for baptism (15–22); the third deals with fasting, eating, meals and food (23–34); and the fourth covers a range of miscellaneous issues to do with times and places for prayer and other rites (35–43). What becomes very clear from this text is that the community it refers to appears to be far more organised and formal than anything we have seen before. Baptism is severely restricted to people of good character and only permitted to those who have been within the community for at least three years. Ordination, or the commissioning of ministers, is provided for bishops, presbyters, deacons, confessors, widows, readers, virgins, subdeacons and those with a gift of healing. The eucharistic rites,[84] while slightly more formal than those mentioned by Justin, are in their structure almost identical. The Apostolic Tradition, however, does offer a suggested prayer of thanksgiving over the bread and wine while continuing to stress that the bishop could still pray in his own words if he wished. It is very clear that the community had come a long way by the time this text was written in terms of organisation and formality. The core of what was happening in terms of worship, however, is little different from much that we have already seen.[85]

What we have seen throughout this brief survey of texts from Antioch and Rome are two things. First, we have seen a gradual formalisation of worship, both in terms of those who can lead it and in terms of the shape or structure of the rites themselves. It is possible to argue that this increasing formalisation is, in fact, something of an illusion, as each text chooses to say a little more about the nature of the rites being described, ending with Hippolytus' apparently prescriptive order. What is very clear, however, is that Paul's ecstatic and disordered gathering in which each person brought

---

[83] I am following Bradshaw et al. (*Apostolic Tradition*) in my chapter numbering.

[84] As with Justin, two rites are described, one with a baptism and one following the ordination of the bishop. See G. J. Cuming, *Essays on Hippolytus*. Nottingham: Grove Books, 1978.

[85] Perhaps the most interesting element refers to the use of food and meals, but I will come back to this below.

a hymn or a psalm or a spiritual experience had no part to play in Hippolytus' own understanding of Christian worship. The second trend we have seen is a gradual move away from whatever Jewish forms may have influenced the worship of Christian communities during the first century. Again this may be illusory, as it appears to be within the Roman context in particular that this move has taken place. Beyond Ignatius, and perhaps even with him, we have little knowledge of similar developments in Antioch. Such a progression is, however, understandable and while it is clear that the Christian communities at the beginning of the third century were even more diverse than they were at the end of the first, Christians had clearly established themselves with a distinctive identity very different from that of contemporary Jewish communities. Finally, we must note the diverse and disjointed nature of the texts that we have been looking at. None of them, it could be argued, is a witness to the dominant tradition in either Rome or Antioch. Each is contested in its own way, and the whole, when seen together, should begin to raise serious questions about our ability to construct anything like a coherent history of worship at this time.

THE SPIRIT AND THE MEAL

Despite my closing remarks above, all the texts that we have looked at so far in this chapter are generally accepted as being within the mainstream development of Christian worship. When we looked at Paul's letter to the Corinthians, however, we identified two distinct ritual acts within the text: an ecstatic gathering for worship and a shared meal. We have seen that both of these events continued to have some kind of presence in the mainstream. The meal has inevitably received most attention because this, in the form of the eucharist, has become the principal ritual event of the Christian church. However, by focusing on the eucharistic aspects of the meal at the expense of other ritual activity, the impression can be given that there is far more continuity and consistency within the early history of Christian worship than is perhaps the case. In this final section of the chapter, therefore, I want to begin by tracing the development of the ecstatic gathering through the first three centuries. Only after having drawn a number of conclusions in relation to this do I then want to come back and focus again briefly on the meal before moving on to my conclusion.

Given that there are no further detailed accounts of worship in the New Testament apart from that given in the letter to the Corinthians, we have no direct evidence for the wider use of informal Spirit-filled times of worship at this period. However, the evidence that we do have of praying together, worship times, preaching, prophecy, visions and healing are all compatible with the kind of scenario we are presented with in Paul's letter. Many scholars have seen visionary Spirit-filled communities behind the writings of Luke, John and others in the New Testament. J. D. G. Dunn argues that charismatic experience was the bedrock of early Christian communities.[86] Gerd Theissen argues, from the basis of his reconstruction of Matthew's community, that the 'first followers of Jesus' were wandering prophets and teachers moving from community to community leading ecstatic and 'Spirit-filled' worship.[87] Finally, whatever we may want to say about Luke's presentation of the Christian community in Acts Chapter 2, his stress on Spirit possession and its consequences at Pentecost must contain some kind of continuing Christian memory.[88] It is clear, therefore, that this form of informal, Spirit-filled, worship was common to most, if not all, of those communities that produced the texts that now make up the New Testament.

It is possible, therefore, as we have seen, to characterise the history of Christian worship in the first two centuries as little more than a process of formalisation, from the charismatic excesses of Corinth to the formal liturgies of Hippolytus and others. This, however, would not be the whole story. If we trace what history we have, from Corinth forward through the texts of the New Testament and beyond, we see a number of references to prophets and prophecy. We hear of Paul staying with 'Philip the evangelist, one of the Seven' (Acts 21:8). He had four unmarried daughters who prophesied. Eusebius offers later accounts referring to the death and burial of Philip and his daughters in Hierapolis in Asia Minor (3:31).[89] John, the author of the Apocalypse, was also aware of, and may have practised, prophetic ecstasy. He was clearly a visionary and accepted ecstatic gifts as entirely normal. John was writing on the Island of Patmos off the coast of Asia Minor. What is most significant, therefore, is where all these events took place. This is the same region that Ignatius wrote to

[86] J. D. G. Dunn, *Baptism in the Holy Spirit: A Re-Examination of the New Testament Teaching on the Gift of the Spirit in Relation to Pentecostalism Today*. London: SCM, 1970, *Jesus and the Spirit: A Study of the Religious and Charismatic Experience of Jesus and the First Christians as Reflected in the New Testament*. London: SCM 1975 and 'Models of Christian Community in the New Testament', in D. Martin and P. Mullen (eds.), *Strange Gifts?* Oxford: Blackwell, 1984, 1–18.

[87] G. Theissen, *The First Followers of Jesus, A Sociological Analysis of the Earliest Christianity*. London: SCM, 1978.

[88] See the discussion of the relevant literature in E. Haenchen, *The Acts of the Apostles, A Commentary*. Oxford: Basil Blackwell, 1982, 166–75.

[89] Eusebius, *The History of the Church from Christ to Constantine*. Harmondsworth: Penguin, 1965.

concerning the damaging effect that prophecy was having on the unity of the Christian community in Philadelphia.[90] It was also in the same region, some fifty years after Ignatius' letter, that Montanus, Priscilla and Maximilla began to prophesy.[91]

One of the problems that Montanus and his companions faced was that which all prophetic movements face at some stage within their life. The wider 'catholic' church was already becoming more formal in its administration and teaching. Part of this formalisation involved the routinisation of authority and particularly the routinisation of the authority of revelation. Christians had already begun to distance themselves from the eschatological thinking of the very earliest communities and therefore looked to the revelation of scripture, and the growing definition of what Christian scripture would consist of, in order to define truth within the community. Prophecy that defines itself as direct revelation from God undermines this certainty in authority by claiming for itself an alternative source for authority with a direct link to God. This is exactly what Montanus and Maximilla claimed: that God spoke to the church through their prophetic ministry.[92] Many in the church simply could not accept this challenge to their institutional authority, and hence conflict was bound to arise.

It has also been suggested that the association between prophecy and women was another reason for condemnation in an increasingly male-dominated church. Paul suggests in 1 Corinthians that the women were engaged in ecstatic prophecy (11:5). It is Philip's daughters who were the prophets, although there was a later dispute as to whether their prophecy was truly ecstatic or not.[93] The 'New Prophecy' that Montanus inaugurated is best known for the role of women in prophecy and leadership, even in formal ministerial leadership.[94] Some of the most vitriolic attacks on the movement were aimed at the role of women within it, rather than the action of prophecy in itself, and it appears that once again the ecstatic nature of women's prophecy is what caused most offence. How widespread women's leadership was outside of the New Prophecy is difficult to determine but it is clear that within the 'catholic' churches it was dying out, even if it had not gone completely.

What is most significant, however, is the widespread impact that Montanus and his prophetic version of Christianity had. It was not easy

---

[90]   Trevett, *Ignatius*, 93.
[91]   C. Trevett, *Montanism: Gender, Authority and the New Prophecy*. Cambridge: Cambridge University Press, 1996, 16.
[92]   Ibid., 82.   [93]   Ibid., 174–5.   [94]   Ibid., 151–97.

for local church leaders to silence the prophets and to claim a legitimate authority in tradition. One question that this raises concerns the possible widespread nature of prophecy, or at least the memory of charismatic gifts within the Christian communities of the early third century. Was the New Prophecy's experience really that unusual? Certainly there were many within the Christian community at the time who were willing to recognise what was happening as legitimate, and willing to follow the new revelation of the prophets. Unfortunately we will never really know how far the expression of charismatic gifts of any kind, particularly prophecy, had begun to die. Other early evidence give us glimpses of a woman prophet in Cappadocia who performed wonders in a state of ecstasy, of Nanas in Phrygia who spoke in tongues and had visions of angels, and of various martyrdoms of women in which visions play a very important role, all of which suggests that charismatic gifts were still continuing, especially among Christian women.[95] However, it is very difficult from the evidence to say anything more. The 'Montanists' themselves were surprisingly popular in the second and third centuries but had largely died out by the end of the fourth.[96] An interesting final glimpse of spiritual gifts being acknowledged, and of female liturgical roles, is found in the Testamentum Domini, a Church Order from the late fourth century which is thought to originate among an extreme anti-Arian group in central Asia Minor, the same region in which Montanus and the New Prophecy had developed.[97]

If I now move on to the meal, the first point to note is that there is no further reference to a shared meal in any of Paul's other letters.[98] This, however, is not true for all the texts in the New Testament. Most scholars agree that, along with Paul's first letter to the Corinthians, the writings attributed to Luke are among the most valuable in trying to gain a glimpse of what might have occurred during worship in the earliest Christian communities.[99] Luke does not give us detailed accounts of worship.[100] However, there are descriptions and references to shared meals that could be described as 'worship' scattered throughout both the Gospel and, more particularly, the Acts of the Apostles.

---

[95] Ibid., 171–2.   [96] See ibid., 198–232.

[97] G. Sperry-White, *The Testamentum Domini: A Text for Students with Introduction, Translation and Notes*. Nottingham: Grove Books, 1991.

[98] Smith sees references in Galatians and Romans as indicating the context of a shared meal but this is not made explicit in the text. See Smith, *Symposium*, 180–4.

[99] Bradshaw: *Search*, 53–6.

[100] The nearest Luke comes to actual descriptions of worship are the various accounts of baptism in the Acts of the Apostles and the account of the meeting at Troas in Chapter 20.

Within the Gospel, for example, there are a number of different meal stories (e.g. 7:36–50, 14:5–14, 24:30–5). Meals clearly played an important role within Luke's Christian experience.[101] Unfortunately, the evidence of what actually happened at these meals and the kind of meals that we are dealing with is severely limited.[102] When we move on to Acts, however, we have very different kinds of evidence. Luke is not at this stage attempting to recreate the life and culture of Jewish Palestine, something of which he may have known very little. Rather he is attempting to present a very specific view of the founding of the church. The accounts of worship are incidental to this view and that makes them even more valuable. Apart from the account of the immediately post-Pentecost life of the early Christian community, Luke is clearly not trying to make any polemic points about worship.[103]

Within Acts we have just three accounts of the Christian community meeting for the 'breaking of bread'. The principal reference comes in the description of the post-Pentecost context, where Luke is probably presenting an idealised or nostalgic view of the earliest Christian community (2:46). The second comes in the middle of the all-night worship in Troas, shortly after the boy who fell out of the window is healed (20:11). This could be seen as a simple meal break or it could have more ritual significance.[104] The third reference is to Paul on board ship caught in the middle of a storm on the way to Rome (27:35). In this context it is highly unlikely that a full ritual meal is being referred to.[105] The informality of all three references should be noted, along with the lack of any other reference to specific gatherings for sharing bread *and* wine. Is the action too common to be worth mentioning, or does it play only a very small part in Luke's own

---

[101] Studies of the kind of community that might have produced Luke's Gospel are less common than those that have discussed Paul's letters or even the Gospels of Matthew and John. Philip Esler's book (*Community and Gospel in Luke-Acts: The Social and Political Motivations of Lucan Theology.* Cambridge: Cambridge University Press, 1987) is an exception. See also H. Moxnes, *The Economy of the Kingdom, Social Conflict and Economic Relations in Luke's Gospel.* Philadelphia: Fortress Press, 1988.

[102] As with the situation in Paul's letter to Corinth references to giving thanks and the breaking of bread at the feeding of the five thousand (9:16) and at Emmaus (24:30) suggest a Jewish model for the meal. However, this does not really tell us very much about how the meals might have been understood. See also Smith, *Symposium*, 253–72.

[103] Many scholars see the brief description of the Christian community following Pentecost in Chapter 2 as an ideal image of the church rather than a clear description of reality. See discussion in Haenchen, *Acts*, 190–6.

[104] The text simply reads 'then he went upstairs again and broke bread and ate. After talking until daylight he left.' The reference to eating suggests a full meal, but it is ambiguous.

[105] In this text the giving of thanks is also mentioned; it continues 'then he broke it and began to eat', after which everybody else also eats. The simple act of giving thanks does not make this a ritual meal.

consciousness? The breaking of bread was common to all Jewish meals.[106] A ritual form of this meal, including both bread and wine, does not appear to be a central part of the traditions that Luke was drawing on.[107] We must doubt, therefore, whether such meals had any particularly eucharistic overtones for Luke or his community.

Beyond the writings of Paul and Luke it is very difficult to find any specific reference to a ritual meal within Christian writings until we reach the Didache and the writings of Ignatius at the beginning of the second century. Within the non-Pauline Epistles, for example, there is no reference at all to shared meals, with the exception of an oblique reference to the 'love feast' in Jude (v. 12).[108] The other references that may be interpreted as 'eucharistic' are found in the Gospel of John.[109] John's Gospel is very different from that of any other Gospel writer and scholars have argued that it was written for a small, separatist community of Christians who developed their own ideas independently of wider Christian thinking.[110] John 6 contains an extended meditation on the eating and drinking of the flesh and blood of Jesus and, according to some commentators, acts as a substitute for an account of the actions of the Last Supper. This text appears to extrapolate from the words assigned to Jesus in the supper narrative to produce general statements about the eating of Jesus' body and blood. John's line of thought, however, appears to be entirely independent of Paul's at this stage and is not related to any specific meal, ritual or otherwise.[111] As with all the other texts we have looked at, therefore, there is no direct evidence that a ritual meal akin to the later eucharist was actually happening in the Christian communities of the first century.

[106] Smith, *Symposium*, 145–7. Joachim Jeremias states that 'the constantly repeated assertion that "breaking of bread" is an expression used in Jewish sources meaning "to have a meal" is an error that seems impossible to eradicate' (*The Eucharistic Words of Jesus*. London: SCM, 1966, 120). I am not asserting this; I am simply stating that it is more likely to refer to the meal, of which breaking bread is an initial act, than to anything that may be 'ritual' in nature, although it is, of course, impossible to distinguish with any certainty what is 'ritual' from what is not in this case.

[107] I am not including Luke's account of the Last Supper in this discussion because, if what I have said in relation to 1 Corinthians and Trocmé's analysis of the Passion narratives is correct, Luke took this over from an earlier Passion narrative and it does not provide clear evidence of Luke's own thinking.

[108] This is particularly surprising given the emphasis on ministry in a number of these letters. Ministry appears to be closely associated with prayer and preaching, even baptism, but not meals.

[109] As with Luke, the Gospels of Matthew and Mark have references to shared meals and to the Last Supper, but the same comments can be made about these as I have already made for Luke.

[110] S. C. Barton, 'Christian Community in the Light of the Gospel of John', in Barton, *Life Together*, 165–86.

[111] See B. Chilton, *A Feast of Meanings, Eucharistic Theologies from Jesus through Johannine Circles*. Leiden: Brill, 1994.

We have already looked at the principal evidence of the first and second centuries. We have seen that some kind of meal continued through the Didache and Ignatius. This meal was associated with bread and wine and enabled the relevant authors to make a link to the body and blood of Jesus. With Justin in Rome we saw that the bread and wine element appears to have been separated from the meal, for whatever reason, and Hippolytus reinforces this. Over a third of the Apostolic Tradition, however, does concern itself with questions of eating and it is clear that some kind of communal meal is still continued within Hippolytus' community.[112] By the beginning of the third century this separation appears to be almost universal. This does not mean, however, that ritual meals had died out in Christian circles, any more than ecstatic spiritual experiences had died out. The evidence we have from Egypt, in particular, provides clear evidence of the continuation of the meal, usually referred to as an 'agape'. Clement of Alexandria devotes two chapters of his *Paedagogus* to ritual meals and Origen, his successor, continues to refer to the importance of the meal.[113] This may have something to do with the continuing Jewish influence on the Christian community in Alexandria but once again only really serves to highlight the importance of contextualisation and the need to focus on exactly where and when the evidence we are discussing comes from.

TEXT, LOCALITY AND HISTORY

In order to try to draw some of these ideas together it is worth moving our focus slightly and looking at the work of an author from the beginning of the third century and from an entirely different part of the Christian world. Tertullian was a member of the church in North Africa in the early years of the third century, although it appears that he never held a formal position within that church.[114] At some point in his career he took on the teachings and practice of the Montanists, and he maintained a consistently critical attitude to the leaders of the 'catholic' church in his region. One of the questions that has been raised, therefore, is whether Tertullian had to leave the 'catholic' church in order to enter a 'Montanist' church or whether the Montanist group maintained itself within the structures and authority of the wider catholic church.[115] Either way it is clear that in liturgical terms

[112] Bradshaw et al., *Apostolic Tradition*, 136–75.
[113] A. Méhat, 'Clement of Alexandria', in Johanny, *The Eucharist*, 99–131.
[114] See D. Rankin, *Tertullian and the Church*. Cambridge: Cambridge University Press, 1995.
[115] Trevett, *Montanism*.

Tertullian's conversion had two distinct effects. First was his acceptance of prophecy and free prayer as part of everyday worship, including eucharistic worship. Second was his rejection of the agape or meal, which Tertullian describes as being exclusively 'catholic'. This places Tertullian in an interesting position in relation to the discussions of the previous section.

More interesting from our point of view in this conclusion is the long debate that Tertullian engaged in with church leaders in Rome concerning the nature of baptism. Tertullian wrote a full treatise on the subject and referred to the issue in a number of his other writings.[116] The main debating point within these writings is whether it is possible to readmit to the church somebody who had been baptised and had subsequently, under pressure of torture or the threat of death, denied their Christianity. Here, Tertullian took a much harder line than the leaders of the church in Rome and this, in itself, threatened to lead to a split within the church. Tertullian's own position focuses on the need for perfection within the individual Christian and the purity of the Christian community.[117] It is the emphasis on purity and perfection in turn that leads Tertullian to make such a clear statement on the importance of baptism.

Baptism, as the boundary rite for all forms of Christianity within the first three centuries, was inevitably an area of dispute and contention.[118] It is interesting to note that during the period when many of the texts of the New Testament were written baptism was a serious issue. It was important for Paul and other New Testament writers to be clear about what it is that makes a person a Christian. The emphasis, however, is not institutional. Baptism is not seen primarily as the rite of entrance into a bureaucratic structure. Baptism for New Testament writers is the sign of a change of life, the distinguishing feature of those who have received the Spirit. It is the internal changes in the individual that dominate the discussion of baptism in these writings and it is as a marker of one who has chosen, or been called, to a higher, more perfect life, that baptism is presented. For the hundred years from the end of the first century to the end of the second baptism is noted as an important rite. The Didache, Ignatius and Justin all refer to it in passing, as we have seen. Baptism is not, however, a significant point of dispute within the growing Christian communities. The Apostolic Tradition presents a list of people for whom baptism was not permitted

---

[116] Evans, *Tertullian's Homily on Baptism*.
[117] This undoubtedly comes from his interest in Montanism, or may have been the reason for that interest. See Trevett, *Montanism*.
[118] Johnson, *Christian Initiation*, 33–88.

and this list, although in a far more formal and institutional way, only reinforces the emphasis from the New Testament writers on baptism as a marker for a way of life, a way of perfection in moral and spiritual terms.

By the time we move to the writings of Tertullian, however, and of writers from Rome and North Africa in particular for the next hundred years, we see baptism as once again a significant source of concern. At this point it is not so much the moral nature of the individual coming for baptism that is of primary concern (although the dispute is still couched in terms of individual apostates and heretics). The concern is to monitor and define the boundaries of the Christian church. This is an institutional concern that has arisen because of the disputes and debates within that church. It is directly related to the writings on heresy and is part of a developing institutionalisation of the Christian community. Baptism as debated at the beginning of the third century is clearly a rite of entry into the 'church'.

This emphasis on baptism at times of crisis or dispute about the nature of Christian identity is only to be expected from a sociological perspective. As any community is attempting to define its own distinct identity, to establish the symbols around which it is to coalesce, then the task of defining and defending the boundaries becomes central.[119] Likewise when the nature of that identity is called into question, boundary maintenance once again becomes significant. It is not surprising therefore that these are the times of significant discussion of baptism within the early Christian communities, nor should we be surprised by the nature of debate in each case. This brings us directly back to the question of context and social structures. Unfortunately, however, this is almost as far as we can go with this discussion, as scholars have not, as yet, undertaken the detailed contextual analysis of baptism that would be necessary to take the argument further. The same could also be said about the meal and the Spirit-filled worship we looked at earlier. Far more work still remains to be done.

Within this chapter we have looked at a very limited number of authors and the texts that they produced. However, this small group of 'authors' cannot be said to be representative of the whole of the Christian community of this time. The people who put pen to paper are exceptional in many ways. They have a point to make. They may be particularly devout, charismatic leaders, visionaries of one kind or another. They are not, in any sense, the 'ordinary' Christians. Whatever these writers may offer us in terms of hints and allusions as to the practice of worship during the first

---

[119] A. P. Cohen, *The Symbolic Construction of Community*. Chichester: Ellis Horwood, 1985.

three centuries they cannot begin to show how ordinary members of this new and still slightly suspect community actually felt about worship either within a specific context or in relation to worship as a whole. What is more, all these texts derive from a small corner of what was, even at the time, a much larger world. They almost certainly do not reflect the totality of Christian experiences of worship, as we shall see in the following chapters. It is unwise, therefore, to suggest any kind of continuous link between the ideas and practices represented in these texts and the ideas and practices of other early Christian communities. The 'origin' of Christian worship must forever escape us. It is with this thought in mind, therefore, that we must move on to a time of greater coherence and uniformity.

CHAPTER 2

Worship and the Christianisation of public space, 300–600

INTRODUCTION: CHRISTIANISATION

The so-called 'conversion of Constantine' in 311 did not mark a sudden shift of a whole society from paganism to Christianity. Many ordinary members of society, both Christian and pagan, would not have noticed any immediate difference. As part of a wider process, however, the relaxation of persecution by the state, and the official encouragement that Constantine gave to certain factions within the emerging church, did mark a significant step in a process that some scholars have come to call the 'Christianisation' of the late Roman Empire. This process clearly had its impact on worship as well as on many other areas of social life. At the most basic level, worship in the major centres of the Empire became much more formal, more elaborate and, perhaps most significantly, more public as the fourth century progressed. What is not so clear, however, is whether the increasingly public nature of worship was a consequence of, or one of the many causes of, the wider process of Christianisation. This is what I wish to look at in this chapter.

'Christianisation' is the term that some scholars have given to the process that is believed to have taken place across Europe, North Africa and much of the Middle East between the fourth and the seventh century.[1] The use of the term 'Christianisation' recognises that while during this period the formal structures of the church grew and by the end of the period the vast majority of the population were at least nominally Christian, the 'conversion' of the Empire did not happen in one simple movement.[2] The process is recognised to be complex, involving many different facets of society. It

---

[1] See R. McMullen, *Christianizing the Roman Empire*. New Haven: Yale University Press, 1984 and the discussion of the process in J. C. Russell, *The Germanization of Early Medieval Christianity: A Sociohistorical Approach to Religious Transformation*. Oxford: Oxford University Press, 1994, 26–39.
[2] Russell distinguishes between 'conversion' of individuals and the 'christianization' of societies. Russell, *Germanization*, 26–7.

also moved at different rates in different parts of the Empire, in different social strata, and between women and men, with many social groups or geographical locations probably never being fully Christianised. The majority of the theorists who have written about Christianisation have been interested in the shifts in ideas and attitudes over this period,[3] in the Christianisation of the way people thought or of their identity, or in the gradual change of public discourses.[4] This is despite the fact that many of those writing in this field come with a strong sociological or even anthropological interest.

There is no doubt that between 315 and, say, 550 there was a dramatic change in many different aspects of life within the Empire. It has even been argued that the very fundamental ways in which men and women thought about their own identity underwent a radical change over this period.[5] In terms of discourses we can argue that during these few centuries the power balance within society began to change. A new dominant discourse was slowly introduced and this gradually filtered throughout the whole of society. However, it must be clear that the Christian discourses of the political elite, those of the clerical and theological elite within the churches and those of individually influential figures in specific cities or regions were probably very different. One of the principles of a process of 'Christianisation', which as James Russell suggests implies some kind of 'end point',[6] is that for the majority of the period there is no real consensus concerning the discourses of society. No one discourse was dominant enough for us to say of any society in the Early Middle Ages that it was 'Christian'. It took another series of changes in the eighth and ninth centuries to make Christian discourses unquestionably dominant, at least in the Eastern and Western Empires. The period surveyed in this chapter is one of struggle between discourses and it is in this context that we need to look at Christianisation and worship.

Despite the recognition that these fundamental changes took place, and despite the fact that historians are able to track these changes in documentary and archaeological evidence, there is still considerable dispute about the underlying causes of these changes. It is not adequate to say that the

---

[3] An excellent example of this is C. W. Bynum, *The Resurrection of the Body in Western Christianity, 200–1336*. New York: Columbia University Press, 1995.
[4] Significant exceptions to this are P. Brown, *The Cult of the Saints: Its Rise and Function in Latin Christianity*. Chicago: University of Chicago Press, 1981 and F. S. Paxton, *Christianizing Death, The Creation of a Ritual Process in Early Medieval Europe*. Ithaca: Cornell University Press, 1990.
[5] M. Kuefler, *The Manly Eunuch: Masculinity, Gender Ambiguity and Christian Ideology in Late Antiquity*. Chicago: University of Chicago Press, 2001.
[6] Russell, *Germanization*, 30–1.

changes in attitudes and behaviour were simply a result of the growth and development of Christianity. There were other dramatic changes in society going on at the same time, totally unconnected with the growth of the Christian religion. There were invasions from the North and the East from tribal groups that were not Christian.[7] There was an increasing use of foreign mercenaries in the armed forces and a demilitarisation of the aristocracy.[8] There were famines and droughts and regular epidemics that took many lives in both urban and rural areas.[9] The centre of power was moving from West to East and the population of Rome, for example, probably declined by almost two thirds in the period from 300 to 500.[10] The very infrastructure of the Empire was, in many places, simply collapsing. None of this had anything directly to do with Christianity or the increasing popularity of Christian discourses.

It has been argued, therefore, that the growth of Christian discourses came at an opportune time. Given all the dramatic social change, the old religious discourses were beginning to lose their credibility and people, especially people of influence, were beginning to look for something new. Christianity simply happened to be in the right place at the right time.[11] However, such an interpretation of Christianisation does not go far enough. Christian discourses had to have something to offer. Their thought processes, their grammar, their basic assumptions and their underlying values had in some way to be matched to the needs of the time. Christians were also becoming far more visible and their own ideas and practices were clearly changing in responses to the changing situations around them.[12] Worship, I would argue, had a significant role to play within this process. Worship provided a focus for the Christian discourse, a context for teaching, but also a series of rituals and activities that could form the habitus of the people involved.[13] Worship also made Christianity visible. As the worship of the church moved from private to public spaces, and from semi-public, specifically Christian spaces, out into the genuinely

---

[7] J. M. Wallace-Hadrill, *The Barbarian West 400–1000*. Oxford: Blackwell, 1985.

[8] Kuefler, *Manly Eunuch*, 37–69.   [9] Wallace-Hadrill, *Barbarian West*, 41.

[10] Estimating populations for ancient cities is always very difficult. See N. Purcell, 'The Populace of Rome in Late Antiquity: Problems of Classification and Historical Description', in W. V. Harris (ed.), *The Transformations of Urbs Roma in Late Antiquity*. Portsmouth: Journal of Roman Archaeology, Supplement Series 1999, 135–62.

[11] Kuefler, *Manly Eunuch*.

[12] Robert Markus calls his book *The End of Ancient Christianity* (Cambridge: Cambridge University Press, 1990) in order to emphasise that the process of Christianisation did as much to change fundamental Christian discourses as it did to change the balance of discourses within society.

[13] See the discussion of habitus on pp. 16–17 above.

public spaces of the city and countryside, it became increasingly more difficult to ignore the Christian discourses associated with them. Worship provided the public face of Christianity for the vast majority of the ordinary populations of the Empire.[14] It is this gradual colonisation of public spaces that I wish to focus on in this chapter.

Over the fourth century Christian worship began to move into, and take over, the public spaces of practically all the major urban centres of the Empire. This was not entirely unplanned or gradual. In those cities that were being constructed or reconstructed from scratch, a public role for the Christian ritual, and the spaces needed to perform it, was built into the fabric of the city itself. We can see this particularly in the designs of Constantinople and Jerusalem.[15] Even in these cities, however, we still have to acknowledge the entrepreneurial role of significant bishops and a level of response and development from the political leaders or the people. There was also a clear desire on the part of the church to Christianise the spaces being created, what John Baldovin calls 'an intense desire to "show Christianity off"', that to some extent predated the official support from the state.[16] The colonisation of public space by the liturgy, however, was not entirely 'planned' in a strict sense. It was in part the continuation of a long-standing use of public space by various pagan cults.[17] As Christianity came to be the dominant religious discourse, however, it naturally began to usurp some of the roles of previous discourses and their associated practices. We see this particularly in the use of processions and the claiming of important sites and streets within a city. The way in which Christian discourses defined space, however, was significantly different from that of the pagan traditions and this inevitably had a long-term impact on the shape, the visual impact, the soundscape and the uses made of the cities that were involved.[18]

---

[14] It has to be remembered that, despite the importance of the Councils and the activities of bishops and theologians for the formation of the Christian discourses over time, these were not public events in the sense that ordinary people in cities and villages across the Empire could follow every nuance of the arguments. On the other hand, riots and persecutions in previous centuries had been 'public' events, visible to a wide cross-section of the population, and these had their own impact on the spread of Christian discourses. The move of worship, however, from the privacy of Christian buildings out onto the streets and other public spaces was a very different kind of public event and it is this that I will be looking at in detail.

[15] See pp. 64–6 and 72–3 below.

[16] J. F. Baldovin, 'The Urban Character of Christian Worship in Jerusalem, Rome and Constantinople from the Fourth to the Tenth Centuries: The Origins, Development and Meaning of Stational Liturgy'. Ph.D. dissertation, Yale University, 1982, 112.

[17] K. Dowden, *European Paganism, The Realities of Cult from Antiquity to the Middle Ages*. London: Routledge, 2000, 188–91.

[18] The ideological uses made of the city also changed within Christian discourse; see Augustine, *Concerning the City of God, Against the Pagans*. Harmondsworth, Penguin, 1984.

It was not only urban areas, however, that were colonised and transformed by the Christian rite. I want to argue that we can see an analogous
transformation in many of the rural areas of the Empire, particularly in the
rise of monasticism, and even a 'Christianisation' of space in the 'wild
spaces' beyond the Empire. Even by 311 Christianity was no longer confined by the boundaries of the Empire. It had already spread through trade
routes, army manoeuvres and the wider movements of peoples and populations to areas well beyond the boundaries of the Empire itself. It is too
easy to link the history of Christianity to the history of the regions covered
by the Roman Empire. From a very early date ordinary Christians and
Christian missionaries had moved beyond the Empire and set up churches
in areas as far apart as Ireland, South India, Ethiopia and Siberia. These
Christians often developed their own patterns of worship and theology and
it is important to see them, not as marginal to the mainstream traditions of
Rome and Byzantium, but as central to their own understandings, from
which Rome and Byzantium were themselves seen to be marginal.

In this chapter, therefore, I want to look at the process of
Christianisation in relation to worship with a specific reference to the use
of public space. I will begin with the urban centres of the Empire and
slowly move out to rural spaces, villages and wild spaces within the Empire.
I will then look beyond the Empire to the furthest reaches of the Christian
world, before drawing the argument together again at the end of the
chapter to look once again at the theoretical questions of space and
Christianisation.

THE COLONISATION OF URBAN SPACE

Jonathan Z. Smith, in a book exploring the relationship between ritual and
'place', provides a fascinating account of the liturgical development in
Jerusalem in the fourth century.[19] Throughout the book Smith is aiming
to show how different kinds of ritual transcend the specifics of place
through different mechanisms that allow them to be universalised. So,
for example, the ritual of the Temple at Jerusalem, as outlined in Ezekiel, is
shown to be so dependent on idealised dualities between pure and impure
that the system could be universalised within Judaism even when the
Temple itself was destroyed.[20] In the case of the Christian use of
Jerusalem, however, things are not quite so simple.

---

[19] J. Z. Smith, *To Take Place, Towards Theory in Ritual*. Chicago: University of Chicago Press, 1987.
[20] Ibid., 47–73.

Smith begins by discussing the way in which Constantine 'rediscovered' the sacred sites of Jerusalem and how Macarius (the Bishop of Jerusalem at the time) was able to adapt these for the development of a very specific liturgical experience within and around the city.[21] Smith is not the first author to suggest that the development of the liturgy at Jerusalem in the fourth century marked a turning point in the way in which Christians understood their worship. Others have shown that the presence of the real places, the holy sites of Jerusalem, allowed the church there to fit the liturgy to the place in a unique fashion, so historicising what had, up until this time, been primarily theological commemorations.[22] It was, of course, the cycle of events surrounding the death and resurrection of Jesus at Easter that held out the best opportunity for this historicisation, as these were known to have happened in and around Jerusalem itself. Constantine's workers claimed to have found the site of Golgotha, the wood of the cross and the tomb in which Jesus was buried. Other principal sites, such as the upper room, Gethsemane and the Mount of Olives, were already known and churches were soon built on these sites.[23] The worshippers in Jerusalem therefore were able to celebrate each point in the story at the place in which it actually happened. What is more, Smith argues, they chose to celebrate these rites not just at the right place, but also at the right time, relative to each other and the Gospel narratives, so creating the sense of sharing in the Passion and death of Christ through real time and space.

It was the association of time and space, Smith argues, that was the most significant liturgical development in Jerusalem. Clearly this was possible in Jerusalem and led to the dramatic sense of pilgrimage that is seen so clearly in the contemporary accounts, such as that of the Spanish nun Egeria.[24] However, outside of Jerusalem, this association of time and space was not possible. Nowhere else was the specific geography of the ritual so closely associated with the narrative of the rite. The Jerusalem liturgy could only be celebrated in the 'place' of Jerusalem. However, as Smith argues, even if the spatial aspects of the rite could not be transferred to other places, the temporal elements clearly could. So, Smith concludes, the origins of a historicised liturgical year can be found in the worship of the church in

---

[21] Ibid., 74–95.
[22] In liturgical scholarship the association of historicisation with Jerusalem can be traced back to Gregory Dix (*The Shape of the Liturgy*. London: Adam & Charles Black, 1945, 331). See also T. J. Talley, *The Origins of the Liturgical Year*. Collegeville: Liturgical Press, 1991.
[23] See P. W. L. Walker, *Holy City, Holy Places? Christian Attitudes to Jerusalem and the Holy Land in the Fourth Century*. Oxford: Oxford University Press, 1990.
[24] See John Wilkinson's *Egeria's Travels*. Warminster: Aris & Phillips, 1999 for a more detailed discussion of the text and context of Egeria.

Jerusalem and it is this temporal transcendence of the specifics of place that allowed the church at large to reproduce the worship of Jerusalem in different specific contexts.

Clearly there is a great deal about Smith's argument that is attractive. The theoretical neatness of the analysis is appealing, even if it might not be entirely convincing when we come to look at some of the other facts. Jerusalem was a very important site within the Constantinian church. We know a surprising amount about the liturgies that were celebrated there in the fourth century and it is clear that these do take full advantage of their unique location.[25] However, to see in this the sole origin of the Christian year, or to see this as the only way in which Christian communities interacted with their geographical context, is to narrow our vision considerably. Smith himself argues that Constantinople was itself 'deliberately crafted, over time, as a stage for the distinctive drama of the early Byzantine liturgy'.[26] This, however, had very little to do with the historicised liturgies being developed in Jerusalem. Also, Rome was developing, at much the same time, the fundamentals of its own 'stational' liturgy in which the Pope celebrated the principal liturgy in a different church depending on the day or the season.[27] This use of the particular geography of the city was again very different from that in Jerusalem. In each case it is important to emphasise Smith's central point, the importance of 'place' for the celebration of ritual. The way in which this 'place' was expressed, however, was very different in each of these three cities. It is this that I wish to explore in more detail within this section.

When Constantine came to construct his new imperial city he chose a site between Europe and Asia, on the Bosphorus peninsula. At the time there was already a substantial town on the site and Constantine did not have a completely blank canvas on which to work. There were geographical restrictions to the site, as significant buildings such as the hippodrome were already in place. There were also restrictions of convention, of what an imperial city could and should look like. Finally there were the inevitable restrictions on cost and the limitations of the builders. The city that was eventually built, therefore, was not something entirely new and revolutionary. It had royal palaces, a hippodrome, public fora and religious temples. The only major difference from all the cities that preceded it was that the temples built at the core of the city were Christian (although

---

[25] For fuller details see Baldovin, 'Urban Character'.   [26] Smith, *Place*, 75.
[27] Baldovin, 'Urban Character'.

Constantine also included a significant number of traditional pagan temples in other parts of the city).[28]

Christian architecture differed in a number of significant ways from the religious architecture of the pagan religions. Most pagan temples contained a small inner sacred space that was restricted to the priests, and were surrounded by more public arcades, walkways and squares. For the Christians the inner space had to contain the whole Christian congregation and the basic shape of the building came to follow that of the basilica, or public hall, rather than that of the temple.[29] Constantine built two basilicas within the central, royal space of his new city, Hagia Sophia and Hagia Eirene. He also began the Church of the Holy Apostles towards the north of the city, which he hoped would contain the bodies of all the apostles as well as being his own mausoleum. Subsequent emperors added further buildings, both in the central complex and on more distant sites, although by the mid-fifth century the city still only had fourteen churches, far fewer than any other city of a comparable size.

The principal basilica, or church, in Constantinople was the Great Church, or Hagia Sophia. Constantine's original church was destroyed during riots in 404 and again in 532. The Emperor Justinian (527–65) rebuilt the church on a grand scale as part of a major building programme in the mid-sixth century. Internally the new church was divided into separate spaces: for the clergy, including a low screen separating off the area around the altar (so creating once again the inner sacred space of the old pagan temple); for the men on the main floor of the building; for reading and singers; for the Emperor; and for women and children (both of the latter being in the galleries).[30] The building was, of course, designed for the worship of the Christian community, but equally clearly it reflected the social structures and norms of the time, and the worship of the community came to adapt itself to the space within which it had to function.

Hagia Sophia provided one place of worship for the Christian community in Constantinople, but, as already mentioned, there were other churches built by Constantine, his successors and other influential figures in the city. The Christians in Constantinople, however, understood themselves to be one congregation. These separate churches, therefore, did not function to serve distinct congregations; they functioned more as the

---

[28] Ibid., 300–9.
[29] See R. Giles, *Re-Pitching the Tent, Re-Ordering the Church Building for Worship and Mission in the New Millennium*. Norwich: Canterbury Press, 1996, 29–44.
[30] R. F. Taft, 'Women at Church in Byzantium: Where, When – and Why?' in R. F. Taft, *Divine Liturgies – Human Problems in Byzantium, Armenia, Syria and Palestine*. Aldershot: Ashgate, 2001.

smaller pagan temples had in previous cities. They celebrated particular saints or mysteries. They contained the relics of martyrs or of finds from Jerusalem and the Holy Land. They were spaces to visit at specific times of the year, not for the regular worship of local congregations. This demanded a particular relationship between the worship of the Christian community, the bishop, the Emperor and the city.

In order to worship at an appropriate church on a particular day, usually one that celebrated some aspect of the dedication of the church or some relic that it contained, the clergy, the Emperor and the people had to process, in public, through the streets of the city from Hagia Sophia or some other point within the imperial complex, to the church designated for the celebration. This public, processional worship came to be the defining form of worship for the church of Constantinople.[31] Processions became particularly important in two contexts: as public statements of support for specific factions within the church and as elements in imperial ritual. Arian processions, for example, competed in splendour with those of the Orthodox. They also competed for the attentions of the Emperor and led to riots throughout the city. Processions were also called whenever the city came under threat, whether from earthquakes, plague or invasions, and in that way became the most significant form of worship of the city, especially for the ordinary person in the streets.[32]

The worship of the church in Constantinople, therefore, was not historicised in the way that Smith argues for Jerusalem. The geographic and temporal movement of the liturgy grew around the layout of the city and the yearly cycle of the Emperor's activities. Yet this does not explain all the different movements from Hagia Sophia to some of the smaller 'stational' churches. The whole process was one that had its own rhythms and reasons. Over time this in some ways entirely arbitrary movement became ossified and caught up in the increasingly detailed regulation of the Byzantine state, and the various movements in time and space took on a life of their own. This, however, is a matter for the next chapter.

If we move our attention to Rome, we need to look back beyond the time of Constantine in order to understand the growth of the Christian geography of the city.[33] One of the principal issues is the relationship between the original houses in which the many diverse communities of Christians met for worship and the 'titular' churches that were subsequently built on the same sites. The process of building churches on the

---

[31] R. F. Taft, *The Byzantine Rite, A Short History.* Collegeville: The Liturgical Press, 1992, 29.
[32] Baldovin, 'Urban Character', 418.   [33] See ibid., 156–82.

site of residential houses where Christians had met is not unique to Rome.[34] Aquileia and Poreč around the top of the Adriatic offer clear examples where later archaeology has uncovered the original domestic buildings under the churches.[35] In the case of most of the Roman titular churches, however, we do not have this kind of archaeological evidence of previous use.[36]

The titular churches of Rome still have names that in many cases refer to the families whose house or land was donated for the building of the churches. These churches are spread widely around the city, and are not generally in the more fashionable residential areas. Alongside the titular churches built within the city, we must also note the churches built in the cemeteries and catacombs beyond the city walls. These became the sites for the burial of the martyrs of the Roman church and therefore for the memorials of these martyrs in worship. The two groups of buildings were the most significant Christian places within Rome before the conversion of Constantine.[37] A limited form of stational liturgy also appears to have begun within these churches before 315 as the bishop tried to draw together the diverse communities throughout the city by worshipping with each one in turn.[38] The bishop was also involved in the celebrations for the martyrs and would announce at each act of worship where he would be celebrating the next. The more formal pattern of stational worship, however, began some time after the reign of Constantine, who initiated the building of four new basilicas, dedicated to St John, St Peter, St Paul and St Lawrence. Over time other places of worship developed, and a Christian geography of the city, representing the memorials of the original Christian communities, began to grow. Within all this growth, however, one specific

---

[34] For North Italian examples see M. Humphries, *Communities of the Blessed, Social Environment and Religious Change in Northern Italy, AD 200–400*. Oxford: Oxford University Press, 1999.

[35] The church at Aquileia also shows up another characteristic of at least the larger North Italian churches at this time, that is the double church. The original church at Aquileia had two halls, plus a baptistery between them. The smaller of the two halls/churches appears to have been used specifically for baptismal-related eucharists rather than on a regular basis (Humphries, *Communities*, 74–8). Milan had two distinct churches, very close to each other, that were used in a stational liturgy probably based on that of Jerusalem (C. Alzati, *Ambrosianum Mysterium: The Church of Milan and its Liturgical Tradition, Vol. I*. Cambridge: Grove Books, 2000).

[36] At St Anastasia, St Clement and SS. John and Paul, house walls have been found which date to the second or third century. G. G. Willis, *Further Essays in Early Roman Liturgy*. London: SPCK, 1968, 58.

[37] Deaconries, or spaces where doles were handed out to the poor, were also set up in the poorer districts of the city but churches were not built on these sites until the sixth century. Willis, *Further Essays*, 73.

[38] Baldovin, 'Urban Character', 252–8.

area, the old ceremonial centre around the forum, remained clear of Christian buildings until the end of the sixth century.[39]

It was within the context of this wide range of churches that the 'stational' liturgy of Rome took on its principal form, although a complete 'system' was not in place until the mid to late fifth century. As with Constantinople, there was a clear sense that the congregation of the church in Rome was a single community that met to worship in many different churches, rather than each church having its own distinct congregation.[40] Through Lent, in particular, the liturgy of the bishop was celebrated in a different church on each fast day (Wednesdays and Fridays), covering practically all the titular and other churches over the season.[41] On each of the major feasts there were also liturgies in the different basilicas around the city. Added to this was the growing practice of sending a piece of the consecrated bread out from the Pope's liturgy to those eucharists being held in all other churches and so the development of a series of secondary processions of the sacred elements began.[42] This must have had a major impact on the people of the city. Processions were not something new, but in Rome they were relatively understated until the sixth century, when Byzantine influence led to an increase in their splendour and popularity.[43] As the population of the city declined, therefore, the size and splendour of the Christian basilicas along with the regularity of the processions must have gone a long way to developing the identity of Rome as a 'Christian' city.

Having looked at the ritual context of Constantinople and Rome, therefore, and having seen different associations between worship and space, which are not related to the ideas developed by Smith, we have to come back to Jerusalem and to ask how space is being used within worship here and whether Smith actually helps to make sense even of this situation. One of the first things to note about the liturgical context in Jerusalem is that space is not simply working on one level. We need to look at the use of

---

[39] Ibid., 160. See also M. Salzman, 'Christianization of Sacred Time and Sacred Space', in W. V. Harris (ed.), *The Transformations of Urbs Roma in Late Antiquity.* Portsmouth: Journal of Roman Archaeology, Supplement Series, 1999, 123–34.

[40] Baldovin notes that Rome had the largest Christian population at this time, and it would, in fact, have been impossible for the whole congregation to meet in one church, however large. See J. F. Baldovin, 'The City as Church, the Church as City', in J. F. Baldovin, *City, Church and Renewal.* Washington: Pastoral Press, 1991, 3–11.

[41] Baldovin, 'Urban Character', 271–6.

[42] The earliest example we have of this is an account in Eusebius of Pope Victor sending holy communion to an Asiatic community in Rome. Most scholars, however, date the origins to the early fourth century. Ibid., 252.

[43] Ibid., 298.

space within each building (and in Jerusalem that means primarily within the complex built around the Holy Sepulchre). We need to look at the use of space across the city (which is Smith's primary focus). And, finally, we need to look at the wider use of space that situates the city within its landscape (and here the pilgrim's itinerary becomes central).

A great deal has been written about the complex that Constantine created around the tomb of Christ and the site of Golgotha. Much of this, however, has been archaeological in nature.[44] Much of the specifically liturgical writing has tended to overlook this micro-spatial context. It is the city of Jerusalem and the surrounding churches, as they have been used within the context of Lent and Holy Week, which have provided the principal focus for liturgical writers and which have led to the assumption that the development of the Jerusalem liturgy is a process of historicisation. In a similar way it is only historians who have tended to be interested in the wider context of the pilgrimage to the Holy Land while liturgists have ignored this to a greater or lesser extent.[45] In trying to rectify this balance we need to begin by looking at the various levels of space independently before we begin to see if there are any connections between them. I will begin with the Holy Sepulchre complex itself.

The origins of the Holy Sepulchre complex are surrounded by mystery and legend and it is still somewhat difficult to determine exactly what might have happened. In 325 Bishop Macarius attended the Council of Nicaea and used the opportunity to raise the status of the Jerusalem Church (which until that time had been subject to the control of Caesarea, the centre of government administration). Macarius also appears to have gained permission, or even a commission, from the Emperor Constantine, to undertake major building work in the city. This led to the demolition of the Temple of Venus, just off the Roman Forum, which local Christians claimed was the site of the crucifixion and the burial of Jesus.[46] In the process of the excavation that followed, both the tomb of Jesus, hence the site of the resurrection, and the 'wood of the cross' were found. What is difficult to determine is which of these was seen at the time to be the more significant. Different authors clearly focus on different

---

[44] See S. Gibson and J. E. Taylor, *Beneath the Church of the Holy Sepulchre, Jerusalem, The Archaeology and Early History of Traditional Golgotha*. London: Palestine Exploration Fund, 1994. For a discussion of the complex beyond the medieval period see the essays in A. O'Mahony (ed.), *The Christian Heritage in the Holy Land*. London: Scorpion Cavendish, 1995.

[45] E. D. Hunt, *Holy Land Pilgrimage in the Later Roman Empire AD 312–460*. Oxford: Oxford University Press, 1982.

[46] P. Walker, 'Jerusalem and the Holy Land in the Fourth Century', in A. O'Mahony (ed.), *The Christian Heritage in the Holy Land*. London: Scorpion Cavendish, 1995, 22–34.

aspects, with Eusebius (who was bishop of Caesarea and wrote on church history and the life of Constantine) emphasising the tomb and the resurrection while other authors, including Cyril (Bishop of Jerusalem c. 350–86) and, it appears, Constantine himself, preferred to stress the wood of the cross.[47] Either way, these 'finds' confirmed the site as that of the death and resurrection of Jesus, and the building of a major church on the site was begun. The actual building took most of the subsequent century with the main body of the church, the Martyrium, being completed first and the building covering the site of the tomb, the Anastasia, only being completed in 347.

In liturgical terms there are a number of sites within the complex that are important. The Anastasia is clearly the most sacred site; however, it is not the space within which any of what we might usually take to be the most important liturgical actions were performed. There is some dispute about Egeria's account of the normal Sunday eucharist, with some scholars assuming that the eucharist was divided into two with the second half taking place within the Anastasia, or even that there were two eucharists.[48] This, however, is unlikely and is not really warranted by the text. What Egeria says is 'when the dismissal has taken place in the church in the way which is usual everywhere the monks lead the bishop with singing to the Anastasia'.[49] Egeria does then talk about a 'thanksgiving' within the Anastasia but this is more likely to refer to a prayer of thanksgiving than to another celebration.[50] In other words, after the eucharist itself, which is celebrated in the Martyrium, the whole congregation processes to the Anastasia for an elaborate dismissal rite in which the bishop, standing in the mouth of the tomb, blesses each member of the congregation individually.[51] In the case of baptism there is also very little of the rite itself that actually takes place at the Anastasia. Most of the rite takes place within the baptistery, as would be expected. However, once again following the main rite with the washing and anointings, the candidates process to the Anastasia before entering the Martyrium for the eucharist.[52]

---

[47] Walker, *Holy City*, 235–41.
[48] G. Dix, *Shape*, 436–8. See also J. F. Baldovin, *Liturgy in Ancient Jerusalem*. Nottingham: Grove Books, 1989, 21.
[49] Baldovin, *Liturgy*, 21.   [50] Wilkinson, *Egeria*, 145.
[51] Ibid. The only possible time that the eucharist may be celebrated in the Anastasia is on Easter morning after the vigil and a eucharist in the Martyrium, where Egeria says, 'Once more the bishop makes the offering' (Wilkinson, *Egeria*, 157). It is not entirely clear, however, what exactly this passage means.
[52] Baldovin, *Liturgy*, 19.

What does take place within the Anastasia, however, are elements of the daily round of services of prayer and praise. The first takes the form of a vigil office before the main liturgical action of the day gets under way (or rather before the bishop is called to take part). This consists of the singing of psalms and is associated by John Baldovin with the development of the monastic office.[53] The principal morning office follows, which consists primarily of intercessory prayer by the bishop within the tomb itself and closes with the elaborate form of blessing already mentioned for the eucharist. There may also be other acts of worship during the day, especially in Lent, but it is the afternoon or evening office that brings everybody back to the Anastasia for the lighting of lamps, more prayer and singing of psalms, and a procession around the sacred sites of the complex before the usual dismissal.[54]

Through all the daily services that take place at the Anastasia one element that is clearly missing, and which we would take entirely for granted today, is any form of reading.[55] It is only at the Sunday morning office that any reading from scripture is heard on a regular basis. This is the reading of the resurrection from John's Gospel, proclaimed from within the lighted tomb.[56] This site, therefore, which is undoubtedly the most sacred within the Holy Sepulchre complex, is associated almost exclusively with intercessory prayer, praise and blessing. It is a space of power within which it is possible to have direct and uninterrupted communication with the divine.[57] It is this heightened sacredness, I would argue, that makes the space unsuitable for the eucharist or for any of the baptismal rites (both of which need to create the same kind of bridge to the sacred as part of their ritual development and cannot begin in such a sacred space). It is also this direct source of sacred power that helps to develop the sense of awe and fear in worship that a number of commentators comment on as a major part of the development of worship in Jerusalem and Syria during the fourth century.[58]

---

[53] Ibid., 31.   [54] Wilkinson, *Egeria*, 143–4.

[55] Psalms were clearly included but it is questionable whether these should be considered as 'readings' in the sense that I am using the term here.

[56] Wilkinson, *Egeria*, 144–5; other readings are proclaimed within the Anastasia during the Easter services. I will come back to this reading when I consider the wider role of worship in the context of pilgrimage below.

[57] It is interesting to note at this point that the source of power situated in the Anastasia is greater, or perhaps of an entirely different order, than that of the wood of the cross. The wood is venerated during the rites for the Friday of the Great Week (Wilkinson, *Egeria*, 155), but it has nothing of the same spiritual power as we can see associated with the Anastasia and the tomb.

[58] E. Yarnold, *The Awe-Inspiring Rites of Initiation, The Origins of the RCIA*. Edinburgh: T. & T. Clark, 1994.

If we now turn our attention away from the Holy Sepulchre complex itself to the way in which liturgy is used to define the sacred geography of the city of Jerusalem, we see both an increasing trend towards historicisation and some of the themes that we have already seen from Constantinople and Rome. The first point to note, however, is that the move towards historicisation is not necessarily the primary feature in the use of space. It is only as the fourth century moves into the fifth century, and as new sites are added to the list of stations for the liturgy, that a truly historicised use of space begins to develop. Towards the end of the fourth century, as evidenced from the writings of Egeria, we can see a kind of half-way stage.[59] The second point is that when scholars discuss the development of historicisation they tend to focus almost entirely on the liturgy surrounding Holy Week and Easter. While this was clearly significant, and an obvious highpoint in the liturgical life of the city, it was, in fact, only one of three major festivals. The cycle surrounding the festival of the Epiphany is the time of year about which we know least, and which was clearly still developing in the second half of the fourth century. Matching the great cycle of worship surrounding Easter, however, was the feast of *Encaenia* in October. This feast celebrated the finding of the true cross and the dedication of the Martyrium.[60] It is in no sense a historicised festival, and is unique to Jerusalem. However, at this feast there are similar developments in the use of space as at Easter and this may change the way we have to look at the Easter festivities themselves. Finally, we have to recognise that there was a stational element to the non-festive worship of Jerusalem, with a liturgy celebrated in the church of Sion on all fast days throughout the year. Baldovin claims that this is the earliest form of stational worship in Jerusalem, as Sion probably marked the site of the pre-Constantinian Christian community in the city.[61]

Let me begin, however, with the Great Week (Holy Week) as recounted by Egeria. Apart from the daily and weekly round of worship at the Holy Sepulchre, which we have already explored, the Great Week adds a further development that leads the worshipping community out of the Sepulchre into the city, and beyond. One way of looking at the liturgical use of space through the week is in terms of a series of movements from the Sepulchre, the most sacred site in the city as we have seen, out to the margins of the

[59] Interestingly Eusebius, Bishop of Caesarea (313–39), appears to have understood the sacred geography of Jerusalem and its surroundings in a very different way. Walker presents Eusebius as presenting a tripartite structure with Golgotha, the Mount of Olives and Bethlehem forming three parts of a single complex. See Walker, *Holy City*.
[60] Wilkinson, *Egeria*, 80.   [61] Baldovin, 'Urban Character', 116.

city, and back into the centre again. On the Saturday before the Week begins there is a procession out to Bethany and the church called the Lazarium, which commemorates the raising of Lazarus.[62] On Palm Sunday this movement takes the crowds out to the Mount of Olives and the procession comes back via the site of the Ascension to the Anastasia.[63] On Maundy Thursday the procession goes out later but follows the same route, staying on the Mount of Olives overnight, and stops at Gethsemane on Good Friday morning before going back into the city and to the site of the cross, behind the Martyrium.[64] Similar processions took place to various sites on the days following Easter. The morning worship would begin in different places, either within the Sepulchre complex or on the Mount of Olives or at the Church of Sion. Each afternoon the newly baptised along with any others who wished to join them would go out to the Mount of Olives and the church marking the site of the Ascension before coming back to the Anastasia for the evening worship.[65] Not all the sites visited in these processions are closely linked with the stories they are assumed to celebrate (although this is clearly one of the determining features of each procession).[66] There seems to be a need, just as we have seen in Constantinople and Rome, to claim the city itself as a site for Christian worship, to claim the city for Christ.[67]

We can see this more clearly, perhaps, if we look at the feast of the *Encaenia* in the autumn. Here, as we have seen, there are no historical stories to commemorate, but once again we see the use of processions out of the city and back to the centre, to the Sepulchre, on significant dates during the feast.[68] If this happens as part of this non-historicised rite, then why should we assume that the same pattern at Easter is necessarily historicisation? Obviously with time, as the bishops and other liturgical leaders of the city begin to see the advantages of visiting historical sites during the Paschal Feast, then the historicisation of the rite does become much clearer. This is seen particularly in the Armenian and Georgian Lectionaries for the early fifth and sixth centuries.[69] Not only are a number of new churches added to the processions, but these have clearly been built with a sense of historicisation in mind.

---

[62] Wilkinson, *Egeria*, 150–1.   [63] Ibid., 151–2.   [64] Ibid., 153–5.   [65] Ibid., 158.
[66] Egeria refers to the reading of John 13–15 as taking place in a cave under the church of the Eleona on the Mount of Olives and claims that this is 'what the Lord said to his disciples when he sat in the very cave which is in the church', but later this was transferred, more reasonably, to Sion, the supposed site of the upper room. Ibid., 153.
[67] Baldovin, 'City as Church'.   [68] Wilkinson, *Egeria*, 164.   [69] Ibid., 175–94.

When it comes to the wider context of pilgrimage within the Holy Land, we see yet another use of space associated with specific liturgical practices. Pilgrimage to Jerusalem and the region around it predates the Constantinian developments. Melito of Sardis visited Jerusalem sometime before he wrote his Paschal Homily, which is usually dated between 160 and 170, and Alexander, Bishop of Jerusalem from 212 to c. 251, encouraged many pilgrims, including Origen, who visited a number of sites in the area.[70] John Wilkinson notes that pilgrimage and the visiting of hilltop and other shrines had been a part of the religious life of the Holy Land area for as long as records exist.[71] The fact that many of the sites related to caves (even that of the ascension) suggests some earlier sacred associations of these sites before they were Christianised in the fourth century.[72] Even by the fourth century, however, a significant number of the sites visited by pilgrims were linked with the Old Testament rather than with the life of Christ.

From a strictly liturgical point of view these shrines offer very little of interest. The rites that were performed were simple and unimpressive. In most cases they consisted of prayers, perhaps a hymn or a psalm, and a reading of the relevant passage of the Old or New Testament.[73] Baldovin suggests that the Sunday morning office at the Holy Sepulchre (the only office to include a reading) was of a similar kind, hence the reading of the resurrection Gospel at this time.[74] Whether this is true or not the principle of reading a passage from scripture to fix a site within a sacred context is significant. It is not as liturgy that the pilgrimage is primarily to be understood, however. Rather, it is as part of an extended time of worship that pilgrimage comes into its own. It is time out from the ordinary run of life. It is time within a sacred landscape, time spent moving between sacred sites. It is a sacralising of a period of time that becomes special and distinct because of the action taken.[75] Spending the Great Week at Jerusalem is a deeper and more significant part of this wider time, but equally only a part, not the whole. Within the context of the pilgrimage, Jerusalem, the Great Week and even visits to the Holy Sepulchre must be seen only as moments in something much larger.

What we have seen, therefore, in this brief exploration of the colonisation of urban space by Christian worship is a conscious attempt by the

---

[70] J. Murphy-O'Connor, 'Pre-Constantinian Christian Jerusalem', in A. O'Mahony (ed.), *The Christian Heritage in the Holy Land.* London: Scorpion Cavendish, 1995, 13–21.
[71] Wilkinson, *Egeria*, 5.   [72] Walker, *Holy City*, 26.   [73] Wilkinson, *Egeria*.
[74] Baldovin, *Liturgy*, 33.
[75] See J. G. Davies, *Pilgrimage Yesterday and Today, Why? Where? How?* London: SCM, 1988.

churches of these three cities to claim their city for Christ. In many ways this desire and the methods used to achieve it, the stational liturgies and processional worship, are common to all three cities. Each of these cycles, for example, is dependent on the bishop of the local city for its liturgical focus,[76] and each aims to bring the whole Christian community together in a single coherent system. Underlying this apparent unity, however, are three very different spatial discourses that drive the specific details of worship in each city. For Constantinople the underlying discourse is imperial; it is the Emperor who is the primary focus and motivation for the worship.[77] In Rome the discourse focuses on the memorial of the martyrs and the history of the city,[78] and in Jerusalem, the underlying discourse is rooted in the Gospel narratives and the ability to reproduce these in time and space within the city. In each of these cities Smith's emphasis on 'place' is essential. Each is fundamentally different, however, in its development, its structure and its relation to geography. This is important to remember as we go on to look beyond the cities at the Christianisation of the countryside.

DEFINING RURAL SPACE

In all of the three examples that we have just been looking at, with the possible exception of Rome, we could perhaps ask whether what we have explored is actually a process of Christianisation. Christianisation is usually understood by scholars to be a process whereby the older pagan culture was slowly transformed into a new Christian world. In at least two of the cases, Constantinople and Jerusalem, it is arguable that there was no older pagan context to be transformed; the building work and the construction of the city were beginning with what was effectively a blank canvas. As I hope that I have explained, this is not the whole story even in these two cities; the older pagan cultures, and to a very small extent the remnants of the Jewish culture in Jerusalem, had a considerable impact on the way the Christians chose to use their space and the kind of rituals that they developed to colonise that space. It is also clear that in both Constantinople and Jerusalem, there was a very large pagan population (perhaps even constituting the majority until well into the fifth century). Jerome was able to complain at the end of the fourth century that Jerusalem was far from being a Christian city, with immorality, violence and prostitution rife among the

---

[76] Baldovin, 'Urban Character', 145.   [77] Taft, *Byzantine Rite*, 28.
[78] Salzman, 'Christianization', 124.

ordinary members of the population despite, or perhaps even because of, the importance of the city as a Christian pilgrimage site.[79]

When we move out from the cities, however, we begin to see a very different pattern developing for the Christianisation of space. From the fourth century on, the balance between urban and rural space, like that between the centres of the Empire and its periphery, was in a process of flux. As the coherence of the Empire began to decline, the people who lived outside of the cities began to look more to their own resources and less towards the principal urban centres. This process was exacerbated, especially in the North, by the invasions of tribes from the East. The rural dwellers, even those most influenced by the Empire and by Roman ways, began to look increasingly to their own resources in order to define their life and their world. In part this led to a reinforcement of Roman values as the conservative elements of the rural population aimed to maintain a way of life in isolation from a centre that was already dying rapidly. Part of this process also became intimately linked to the spread of Christianity within these areas. Within both of these processes, the physical nature of place and the meanings given to space were beginning to change.[80]

It is clear therefore that the decline of Empire, or at least of the influence of Empire, had an effect on the rural church and its worship. It is also possible that the effects were very similar in different parts of the Empire. In both Gaul and Egypt, for example, the starting point was much the same. Both provinces had been thoroughly Romanised and each had been divided into large estates run by noble families with historic ties to the Empire.[81] As the links to the centre began to decline, it was this local aristocracy that began to take more control of the local situation and to influence the development of the social, economic and political nature of each province. As these noble families turned to Christianity, they also had considerable influence over the religious life of their region.[82] In order to understand this process more fully, however, we have to look in more detail

---

[79] A. O'Mahony (ed.), *The Christian Heritage in the Holy Land.* London: Scorpion Cavendish, 1995, 29.

[80] Seeing this as a simple process of Christianity replacing an older pagan tradition is probably too simplistic. The evidence we have for Egypt, for example, makes it clear that the older pagan traditions were already dying through a lack of resources in the mid-third century and it is not until the end of the fourth century that we begin to see archaeological and textual evidence of the rise of Christianity. It is impossible to know what existed for the hundred years or so between these two processes but it is clear that Christianity did not simply replace paganism in any direct sense. See R. S. Bagnall, *Egypt in Late Antiquity.* Princeton: Princeton University Press, 1993, 260–72.

[81] Ibid.

[82] The reasons why Christianity was particularly attractive to members of the aristocracy is not really part of this study. For more details on this process see Kuefler, *Manly Eunuch.*

at the kind of evidence that we actually have. I want to focus primarily on Egypt, as we have more specifically liturgical evidence from here than from Gaul at this time. However, I will compare my findings with the situation in Gaul at each stage to provide a wider comparative perspective.

Colin H. Roberts argues, from manuscript evidence, that the church in Egypt was present in the rural areas (i.e. outside of Alexandria) from a very early date.[83] George Every picks this up and draws specific attention to the particular problems in governing Egypt.[84] These have to do with the way in which the irrigation system had to be managed and the need for centralised authorities within Egypt with considerable local knowledge in order to achieve stability. After the decline in interest from the Empire, however, the management of the irrigation system was left largely in the hands of the local aristocracy. This put considerable pressure on the economic and social structure of the country. Anthony, for example, often considered as the founder of Egyptian monasticism, was heir to one of the larger Egyptian estates after the death of his father in 314.[85] Being a very shy youth, however, Anthony never wanted anything to do with the running of the estate and appeared to abandon it to its fate. Anthony is presented in the monastic literature as retreating further and further into the desert as the authorities, and in later years his disciples, tried to catch up with him. Whatever the initial motivation, however, what becomes clear is that the move into the desert and the building of monasteries, with their small central churches surrounded by sometimes hundreds of cells for individual monks, came to be seen as the distinctive form of Christian life in rural Egypt. This produced two significant changes in the understanding of rural space as a consequence of Christianisation. First, we see a change in the meaning of the desert as opposed to the village, with the former moving from a space of chaos to one of holiness and perhaps even divine order. Secondly, we see a personalisation of the desert, and of space generally, as specific sites become associated with real people and the myths and legends of the ascetics who inhabited the desert. We will see this again when we come to look at Gaul towards the end of this section.

The desert communities of monks and nuns began to produce a considerable body of literature from a very early date and it is from this literature that we can see that the primary reason for their existence was

---

[83] C. H. Roberts, *Manuscript, Society and Belief in Early Christian Egypt.* Oxford: Oxford University Press, 1979.
[84] G. Every, *Understanding Eastern Christianity.* London: SCM Press, 1980, 31–42.
[85] Ibid., 36–7.

to become focused in worship. It was not only in the desert, however, that this life of perpetual prayer could be lived. Other monastic communities were established in abandoned villages in the Nile Valley and even within urban centres.[86] All of these establishments put the perpetual life of prayer and work at their heart and tried to interpret their lives through the biblical injunction to pray without ceasing,[87] thus bringing the desert, as it were, into the heart of the community, or the praying heart of the community into the desert.

Another justification that was given for the movement into the desert was the need to engage with the spiritual forces of evil. The life of the ascetic was understood, in many ways, as spiritual warfare and one of the most important weapons in the armoury of the monk or nun, alongside asceticism and discipline, was prayer and reflection upon the scriptures. The pattern of life for these ascetics revolved around worship, both corporate and individual. The earliest prayer life of the monks or nuns, encouraged by Anthony and others, was rooted in the recitation of psalms and meditation on scripture. There is even some evidence that the eucharist or other forms of communal worship played no part in the life of the earliest, priestless, communities.[88] Psalms and the scriptures would have been learnt by heart and the whole Psalter would have been recited each night within the individual cells. Over time this recitation was expanded to form the beginnings of the monastic office.[89] In the desert monasteries it was only once or twice a week that the community as a whole would meet in the communal church for a eucharist and an agape, or shared meal. For the monasteries in the valley this would have been very different. Monks and nuns would have met twice a day for readings and psalms[90] and again for the eucharist on Sundays.

What comes through very clearly from the literature of these early monasteries is the very physical nature of their worship. Within the valley monasteries psalms and readings were read by one of the community while the rest sat, worked on their basket making, and meditated on the words. At the end of each block of readings the monks would rise, raise their arms in prayer, kneel, prostrate themselves and then return to their seats for the

---

[86] Bagnall, *Egypt*, 295.
[87] R. Taft, *The Liturgy of the Hours in East and West, the Origins of the Divine Office and its Meaning for Today*. Collegeville: The Liturgical Press, 1986, 68–72.
[88] Ibid., 66.   [89] Ibid., 60.
[90] While it is clear that the valley monasteries did not read psalms in order like those of the desert, there is no lasting evidence of the order or structure of reading that they did use. Psalms at this stage were treated as readings, speaking to the monks, rather than being presented as prayers in themselves directed at God. Over time, however, this was to change. Ibid., 63.

next series of readings.[91] Within the desert monasteries, where the ascetics would pray alone, perhaps for the whole night, the sense of physical struggle and bodily discipline became central. This was often expressed in stories of physical temptation in which the devil and other demonic tempters are presented in a very realistic form, challenging the resolve of the monks and nuns.[92]

Clearly many of the desert communities were dependent on those living in towns and rural estates for their livelihood, and in some cases for their priestly ministry. It was also important for the local church to maintain order and authority over these distant and potentially dangerous groups of men and women. The desert monasteries, therefore, were never entirely isolated.[93] It is also clear that over time pilgrims and other visitors began to visit the monasteries with increasing regularity, making their purpose as isolated spaces for prayer even more difficult to maintain. Although similar forms of monasticism were growing up in many other places, Egypt was seen as the originator and source of all monasticism. This attracted yet more pilgrims and visitors and enabled Egypt to export its monasticism, along with its distinctive form of worship, to Palestine and Syria and beyond.[94] It was, however, the worship of the desert monasticism that was exported to the East, not that of the valley. This meant that the reading of psalms in sequence became a distinctive feature of all monastic worship across the Christian world.

The Egyptian form of monasticism was also 'exported' into Gaul in the late fourth century by Cassian and others. Obviously there were no deserts as such in Gaul at this time, but the social structure of the province was very similar to that of Egypt. What becomes particularly clear from looking at the evidence from Gaul is the link between the growth of monastic communities and the changing role and attitudes of the aristocracy: the noble families of Gaul were turning to Christianity in relatively larger numbers than was the case in Egypt. For some this meant taking on a full ascetical lifestyle and themselves becoming monks or nuns. For others it meant sponsoring communities of monks or nuns to come and live on their estates. The monks themselves often sought wilder, more remote locations,

---

[91] Ibid., 60.

[92] There are many stories of demons physically tempting or struggling with the monks during prayer. See ibid., 67–8.

[93] Bagnall also comments that these so-called 'desert' monasteries were never all that far from residential communities, maybe a day's walk or so, although this did not stop them feeling more isolated. Bagnall, *Egypt*, 295.

[94] S. Rubenson, 'The Egyptian Relations of Early Palestinian Monasticism', in A. O'Mahony (ed.), *The Christian Heritage in the Holy Land*. London: Scorpion Cavendish, 1995, 35–46.

but the pressure from the owners of the estates meant that many, often smaller monasteries were founded across the country. Many of the heads of the noble families also maintained their own links between the urban centres and the country estates by becoming bishops in their own right and living both in the cities near their main episcopal churches and out in the countryside alongside the growing monastic communities.[95]

The ascetics and the monasteries, however, for all their numbers and their increasing symbolic importance, were not the only expression of rural Christianity in Egypt or Gaul.[96] The first point to note as we look at the wider worshipping life of each province is that we cannot assume that there was one unified liturgical tradition for the whole of Egypt, or of Gaul. The evidence that we have from the fragment of Sarapion's prayer book and from the Canons of Hippolytus (both of which were produced in Northern Egypt in the early fourth century) is that even in the fourth century there is considerable variety in forms of prayer outside of Alexandria.[97] The structure of rites, however, seems to be fixed around what was to become the standard Egyptian shape. There were also considerable disputes between different factions of the church, and we have no way of knowing whether the liturgical traditions of the various groupings were identical.[98] A number of the texts that we do have offer evidence of having been constructed in order to clarify or challenge particular points within the doctrinal disputes of the time and it can be argued that the increasing concern for 'orthodoxy' led to the increasing uniformity of the rites.

The textual evidence we have from Gaul at this time is even less clear. The texts that scholars have defined as 'Gallican', that is, originating from Gaul before imposition of a more Roman form of worship in the eighth century, indicate a considerable level of variety. Many of the earliest written liturgies indicate a wide range of acceptable variation according to the day or season in which the liturgy is being performed. The eucharistic liturgy from Gaul, however, appears to have by far the widest range of

[95] For a discussion of the conflict between desert and city in the religious discourses of Gaul see Markus, *Ancient Christianity*, 157–211.

[96] F. E. Brightman argued that the development of the episcopacy in Egypt was slow and that the development of the parochial system was far more rapid, making many of the priests in the local communities relatively independent from an early date. F. E. Brightman, 'The Sacramentary of Serapion', *Journal of Theological Studies*, 1 (1900), 88–113, 247–77, 256.

[97] P. F. Bradshaw, *The Canons of Hippolytus*. Nottingham: Grove Books, 1987 and R. J. S. Barrett-Lennard, *The Sacramentary of Serapion of Thmuis: A Text for Students, with Introduction, Translation and Commentary*. Nottingham: Grove Books, 1993. For a wider discussion see M. E. Johnson, *Liturgy in Early Christian Egypt*. Nottingham: Grove Books, 1995, 17.

[98] Bagnall, *Egypt*, 303–9.

such variation, with a different eucharistic prayer for each celebration and considerable variety in other parts of the rite.[99] Whether this reflects a previous local or spatial variation that has been slowly brought together to inform a temporal variation is impossible to say from the evidence that we have.

A second point about the wider rural church concerns the evidence we have for the layout of churches and their surroundings. The Canons of Hippolytus provide an interesting insight into various spatial aspects of the church in rural areas within Northern Egypt. The text refers, for example, to the feeding and the housing of the poor within the church, or more probably within a church compound.[100] If we link this to details about the times of prayers, particularly those in the middle of the night, and what appears to be a public act of worship at cock-crow, as well as the regular prayers throughout the day, and the emphasis on fasting etc., then the impression given is of a semi-monastic community existing in and around the rural or estate church, regardless of what was happening in the deserts. Regular and persistent prayer is a central part of many writings of this period.[101] What this suggests is that the church compound itself played a very significant and central role within the life of the people of the village, small town or country estate. It was becoming the beating heart of that community, with constant activity, a small population of people living and working in and around the compound, and a regular meeting point for the whole community – if not daily then at least on one or more occasion each week.

Something very similar is seen in Tours in the later fourth century. As bishop of Tours, Martin opened his church during the week as a kind of hospital for the mentally ill and other outcasts from society.[102] This is noted in his life as something particularly significant, more for the scale of this activity rather than as something unusual in itself. However, on Sundays the sick were relegated to the porch, and if the congregation had to pass through what was in effect a hospital ward before they came to the liturgy each week, this must have had a very significant impact on their

---

[99] R. C. D. Jasper and G. J. Cuming (eds.), *Prayers of the Eucharist, Early and Reformed Texts.* Oxford: Oxford University Press, 1980, 105–8.

[100] Bradshaw, *Canons.*   [101] Taft, *Hours,* 35.

[102] C. Donaldson, *Martin of Tours, Parish-Priest, Mystic and Exorcist.* London: Routledge and Kegan Paul, 1980, 100–2. This can also be seen in the Testamentum Domini from central Asia Minor, where a detailed description of the church compound includes houses for the various orders, including virgins and widows, as well as accommodation for travellers and the poor and/or sick. See G. Sperry-White, *The Testamentum Domini: A Text for Students with Introduction, Translation and Notes.* Nottingham: Grove Books, 1991.

experience of worship and their understanding of Christianity.[103] The church compound at Tours, however, is clearly a pinnacle of Christian presence within the province of Gaul. It also illustrates very clearly, in its intimate association with St Martin, the increasing personalisation of the Christian landscape that went hand in hand with the rise of the cult of the saints in the West.[104] It is, in many ways, the end point of the process of Christianisation in terms of space. On the arch above the sanctuary at Tours an inscription proclaimed 'How awesome is this place! It is none other than the house of God, and this is the gate of Heaven.' It does, however, show how, by the end of the fifth century, a single church, and the symbolic associations that it held, had come to dominate the lives of the people not only of the town or city concerned but also of the region as a whole, and, through the development of pilgrimage, of a far wider international community of believers. We will come to look at this process in far more detail in the following three chapters.

MOVING TO THE MARGINS

The rural areas of Egypt and Gaul, even those areas defined as wilderness within these regions, were still loosely within the ambit of the late Roman Empire. Christianity, however, had long broken free of these boundaries and had begun to take a hold within societies beyond the cultural influence of the Empire. There was still, however, a process analogous to the Christianisation of the Empire happening within these cultures. In liturgical terms, many of these regions were beyond the direct control and influence of the councils and hierarchies of the imperial church that attempted to impose some form of uniformity on the theologies of the Empire. In these regions is was also easier for local cultures to have a far greater impact on the development of worship. This led to an even greater diversity of worship beyond the boundaries of the Empire than within it. In order to explore this further I will begin by looking at the church under the Persian Empire and the societies scattered along the Silk Road towards China. I will then look briefly at Ireland and Ethiopia before drawing the chapter to a close and gathering some of the themes together.

[103] It has been claimed that St Sulpitius' *Life of St Martin*, written before his death, is the only account of the life of a parish community in the Late Roman church. Donaldson, *Martin*, 102.
[104] For more on this see S. Farmer, *Communities of St Martin, Legend and Ritual in Medieval Tours*. Ithaca: Cornell University Press, 1991.

The situation in Persia was clearly different from the Roman Empire, as Christianity was a minority (often a persecuted minority) within a Zoroastrian state. This clearly had a significant impact on the life of the churches in this Eastern Empire. However, the impact on the practice of worship appears, from all the evidence, to have been minimal. The liturgical development of the Syrian-speaking church, from which the Persian church grew, had much closer links with Judaism than many in the West. The earliest eucharistic prayer that we have from the region, that of Addai and Mari, has been shown by liturgists to have had a strong Jewish influence.[105] The development of imagery in the early East Syrian church also took a very different turn from that of those further west.[106] The 'hymns' of Ephrem (c. 306–73) in particular are full of exciting and provocative imagery.[107] 'Hymn' in this context, however, refers to a poetical form of theology rather than texts that were used in the context of worship. The impact of Zoroastrianism on the continuing development of this liturgy seems, therefore, to have been very limited. This might strike us as odd, given that Zoroastrianism was the state religion of the Persian Empire and had to be acknowledged by all those who lived within the limits of that Empire. Was Christianity so obviously an imported religion? Did Christians continue to maintain significant links with Roman-dominated Syria? Is it only in Manichaeism that Christianity truly engaged with its Zoroastrian context?[108]

It is clear that by the time of the conversion of Constantine and the development of the Christian Empire focused on Constantinople, many Persians had converted to Christianity and the hierarchy of the Persian church was Persian in origin.[109] This made these bishops particularly skilled in anti-Zoroastrian polemic. The Zoroastrians in turn, backed by a relatively weak empire, engaged in a series of persecutions of the Christians including an attempt at the forced conversion of Armenia in about 450. In the light of this hostility, and the ever-present converts from

---

[105] B. D. Spinks, *Addai and Mari – The Anaphora of the Apostles: A Text for Students with Introduction, Translation and Commentary.* Nottingham: Grove Books, 1980.

[106] See R. Murray, *Symbols of Church and Kingdom, A Study in Early Syriac Tradition.* Cambridge: Cambridge University Press, 1975.

[107] S. P. Brock (ed.), *The Harp of the Spirit: Eighteen Poems of Saint Ephrem.* London: Fellowship of St Alban and St Sergius, 1983. See also S. P. Brock, *The Luminous Eye, the Spiritual World Vision of St Ephrem.* Kalamazoo: Cistercian Publications, 1992.

[108] For more information on Manichaeism, a partially Christian dualist tradition, see S. N. C. Lieu, *Manichaeism in Mesopotamia and the Roman East.* Leiden: Brill, 1994.

[109] A. V. Williams, 'Zoroastrians and Christians in Sasanian Iran', *Bulletin of the John Rylands University Library of Manchester*, 78:3 (1996), 37–54.

Zorastrianism within the Persian church, it is not surprising that the church failed to inculturate as much as it might have done, especially in the area of worship. One area where there was some Zoroastrian influence, however, appears to have been in the role and understanding of priesthood.[110] Zoroastrian priests, with their emphasis on ritual purity, had always kept a distance between themselves and the laity, not even sharing in meals. Some of this respect and distance can also be seen in the developing Christian context. The antagonistic relationship between the church and the Zoroastrian state continued on and off up until the Islamic invasion of Persia in the mid seventh century.

One of the problems with looking further east towards Central Asia and China is that we simply do not have the evidence for what was going on in terms of worship in the various churches along the Silk Road. George Every points to the central role of merchants in the spread of Christianity throughout Asia, which gives a very particular social context to the churches of this part of the world.[111] Christianity, it appears, remained the religion of the foreigner. There is some evidence for a thriving Christian community in Xian in the seventh century and for Christian communities among some of the nomadic tribes in Siberia in the following century.[112] The language of these Christians, however, was clearly Syriac and there is no reason to believe that their worship was anything other than that being developed in Syria and Persia at the time. It is interesting to speculate on the impact of Buddhism and other religions of the East on Christian worship, but again we simply do not have the evidence to be able to pursue this very far.

In the South, Christianity had spread as far as Ethiopia and India. The church in India was, like that of the Silk Road, clearly under the orbit of the Syrian-speaking churches. That of Ethiopia was linked more closely with the churches of Egypt and Nubia. When Ethiopia began to take on a particular feel of its own within its worship is very difficult to determine. By the time of the expansion of the Aksumite Empire, however, from the fifth century onwards, the worship of the Ethiopian church had a very distinct style. I will be looking at India in more detail in Chapter 5, and Ethiopia in Chapter 4.

---

[110] Ibid. [111] Every, *Eastern Christianity*, 18–30.
[112] In 1625 Jesuit missionaries found a bilingual stone erected in 781 giving information about the early mission to China. K. Parry, 'Images in the Church of the East: The Evidence from Central Asia and China', *Bulletin of the John Rylands University Library of Manchester*, 78:3 (1996), 143–62.

When we come to look north we have to focus on the church in Ireland. This was always, in a technical sense, beyond the political control of the Roman Empire.[113] However, it is clear that the Irish church shared a great deal of common ground with that in Gaul. Irish or Celtic Christianity is often portrayed as being very different from that of the Catholic mainstream. This, however, is probably an overstatement of the facts. The Irish church was closely related to that in Northern Gaul and much of the textual descriptions we have of Gallican liturgy comes from Irish texts. We must not, therefore, get too caught up with the idea that Irish worship was all that different in practice from the worship of churches in many other parts of Northern and Western Europe.[114] However, there were clearly some significant differences. These are seen primarily in the disputes that emerged in the Council of Whitby in 763. Here the main point of disagreement concerned the timing of Easter, as the British (and Irish) church was still working to an older tradition. The form of the tonsure among Irish monks was also distinct, and the social structure of the Irish monasteries was closer to that of Egypt than the more Benedictine forms that had subsequently developed in the rest of Latin Europe.[115]

Another area where the Irish church clearly differed from that of Rome in particular was in the elaboration of its imagery. In this the liturgy of the Celtic traditions was subject to a similar set of circumstances to that of the church in Persia. In both cases the freedom to develop a more elaborate and symbolic imagery had been released by the lessening of hierarchical and dogmatic controls. In both cases the use of poetry rather than formal theological discourse was the norm for all forms of Christian writing, not just the liturgy, and in both cases the boundaries of the imagery was stretched to its very limits. As with the Christian poetry of Syria, the use of feminine imagery and the role of women were emphasised in the Irish tradition.[116] This emphasis produced some really beautiful texts that were only in a few cases part of the official liturgy of the church.

In all these situations we need to be conscious of the way in which Christianisation was functioning. Unfortunately we simply do not have the textual evidence necessary to trace this process in the kind of detail that has

[113] H. Mytum, *The Origins of Early Christian Ireland*. London: Routledge, 1992.

[114] F. E. Warren's book, *The Liturgy and Ritual of the Celtic Church* (Oxford: Oxford University Press, 1881), still remains the best account of Irish liturgy despite the recent rise in interest in Celtic Christianity. Warren argues strongly for the commonality of Irish liturgy with that of the rest of Western Europe at the time.

[115] M. and L. De Paor, *Early Christian Ireland*. London: Thames and Hudson, 1958, 49–72.

[116] C. Harrington, *Women in a Celtic Church, Ireland 450–1150*. Oxford: Oxford University Press, 2002.

been possible for the heart of the Empire. However, to ignore these marginal sites of Christianity would be to miss some very important elements in a potential theory of Christianisation. It is clear that it is not only the social structures of these areas that are different from the Empire; it is also the thought processes and the religious traditions into which Christianity was being introduced. This must make a difference to the very process of Christianisation. It is also possible that the form of Christianity being introduced to some of these outlying regions was very different. It was certainly beginning to move in very different directions shortly after contact with these areas. Unfortunately the work needed to explore this further has not been done as yet, but I am sure that when it does, worship will be found to have played a very significant role.

SPACE AND THE CHRISTIANISATION OF THE IMAGINATION

In his book *The End of Ancient Christianity*, Robert Markus presents an argument concerning the transformation of social ideas, or discourses, about space over the three centuries covered by this chapter.[117] He suggests that at the beginning of the third century a pagan discourse on space, which identified specific sacred 'places' (as defined by Smith) and which saw the city itself as one of these places, was still dominant. Christian discourses at this time, however, tended to reject the idea of sacred 'places' and to situate the sacred in people, whether these were the Christian congregation gathered for worship or, more specifically, the holy person or martyr. Over the following three centuries, Markus claims, the Christian understanding gradually gained the ascendancy and was then slowly transformed, through the cult of the martyrs, back towards the older pagan discourses of sacred 'places'. We have seen something of this move in the present chapter. However, it should also be clear that the development is not quite as straightforward as Markus appears to be suggesting.

In Jerusalem we have seen that the idea of Smith's sacred 'place' was established very quickly in Christian discourse following the discovery of the tomb of Christ. Peter Walker shows very clearly that this did not go uncontested.[118] Eusebius, who had been Bishop of Caesarea before Constantine's conversion, and who as principal bishop in the region continued to have considerable influence, appeared to reject this particular kind of discourse on space. According to Walker, he did not want Jerusalem and the sacred sites to be the focus of intensive pilgrimage and

---

[117] Markus, *Ancient Christianity*, 139–55.   [118] Walker, *Holy City*.

devotion that they inevitably became. Eusebius wished to maintain Markus's earlier Christian discourse that placed the sacred in people rather than places. Of course, Eusebius lost this particular battle, but that was not the end of the story.

One aspect of the discourse about the sacredness of people, according to Markus, focused on the worshipping congregation. This, as we have seen in relation to Hagia Sophia in Constantinople, led to a Christian architecture that provided considerable space for the congregation within its church buildings. Here again, however, the discourse of the sacred people was only half the story. As Edward Yarnold shows so clearly in relation to baptismal teaching, it was not long before the sense of the sacred, and the awe associated with that sacredness, was transferred away from the congregation onto the eucharistic elements, the body and blood of Christ made real within the congregation.[119] This in turn led to the need to curtain these elements off from the congregation and to restrict access to these uniquely sacred objects from all those who were considered unworthy. The great preachers of the Syrian tradition in particular developed this theology during the fourth and fifth centuries. These preachers also brought these ideas to the capital, to Constantinople, where the veneration of the Emperor had already laid the foundations for the increasing splendour and detachment of the worship from the ordinary members of the congregation. Curtains quickly became walls, with gates, and the sacred was once again forced to reside in a specific place.

The development of monasticism and the legends surrounding the ascetics form another element of this wider process. Monks in Egypt left the cities for the desert. The desert of the time was a place of emptiness and chaos; it was very far from the pagan idea of a sacred 'place'. The very presence of the monks and nuns, however, with their prayer, their asceticism and their struggle with the forces of evil, turned the deserts of Egypt into a whole series of sacred places of the first order. These became sites of pilgrimage and healing, spaces to be sought out and visited for the sacred power that was directly associated with them. In Gaul, however, the process did not work out in quite the same way. The older pagan discourses had endowed many sites within the landscape beyond the cities as sacred, and the link between the wilderness and the sacred practitioner was already present in the activity of druids and other pagan traditions. The ascetics were able to draw on this tradition in order to enhance their own discourses of power and sacredness among the people and were, through their own

---

[119] Yarnold, *Awe-Inspiring Rites.*

healing miracles, able to associate the same or similar spaces with a new Christian power of 'place'. With the death of the greatest monks and nuns a further level of sacredness was made available.

Finally, therefore, we must note the rise of the cult of the saints, as outlined so clearly by Peter Brown, and see the importance of relics for the increasingly Christian discourses of 'place'.[120] Ambrose of Milan famously brought the relics of two martyrs discovered near Milan into the city, so challenging pagan discourses that associated the city with the sacred and death with pollution.[121] Death and the bodies of the dead were to be kept out of the cities in the ancient Roman world. The bodies of the martyrs, however, were not polluting; they were the site of sacred power and the focus for worship. If the churches of the cities were to become the sacred places of the new discourses, then the sacred dead needed to be brought in to sanctify these spaces. It was no longer enough simply to have a worshipping congregation; something more concrete, a specific sacred 'place', was needed, and this was provided by the relics of the martyrs and saints.

Worship, therefore, by the end of the sixth century was something very different from that at the beginning of the fourth. What is more important to note, however, is that the discourses surrounding that worship were even more different than the specific details in ritual and liturgical activity. The very idea of what it meant to worship and the nature of the spaces within which that worship took place had changed beyond recognition in the three hundred years since Constantine first saw the sign of the cross over the battlefield at the Milvian Bridge. What is more, it was going to change yet again in the following three hundred years, as we shall see in the next chapter.

---

[120] Brown, *Cult.*
[121] J. Moorhead, *Ambrose: Church and Society in the Late Roman World.* London: Longman, 1999, 129–56.

CHAPTER 3

Hegemonic discourses in the worship of empires,
600–900

INTRODUCTION: HEGEMONY

In the previous chapter I suggested that the process of Christianisation was a slow and gradual movement developed through the individual actions of many different people, and that it represented a gradual change in the direction of discourses within the society as a whole. As we will see in Chapter 5, however, there are many conflicting worldviews vying for a place within the discourses of all complex societies. Over against this complete and widespread view of Christianisation there were clearly other forces at work that had an equally important impact on the development of Christian worship. While much of the process discussed in the previous chapter could be described as bottom-up (at least in principle) there were also top-down movements that involved the imposition of Christian ideas and practices as part of state policy. In the period between about 600 and 900 this involved attempts by ruling authorities to manipulate and control liturgy for political ends. It is these attempts, and their consequences for the development of Christian worship, that I wish to explore in this chapter.

It is difficult to define exactly how a particular state establishes and maintains its authority. There are many theories within the political sciences from Machiavelli to Gramsci and beyond. No one theory could ever be used in isolation to explain every single instance. Here again, as with the specific situations we have already looked at in the previous two chapters, a detailed analysis of the complexity of the local situation at a particular time and place is the only real way of exploring these issues. However, once again, we do not have the space within a book such as this to undertake that kind of study. For the purposes of my own argument within this text, and with the perspective firmly on the role of liturgy in the imposition of order, identity and authority, I would like to draw on the work of Antonio Gramsci and the concept of 'hegemony' to try to understand how worship has been used as a tool of political authority in the empires of the Early Middle Ages.

Hegemony is a process that was described and theorised by Gramsci in his *Prison Notebooks* in the 1930s, although most scholars agree that Gramsci was notoriously vague about what exactly he meant by the term.[1] Hegemony was developed as part of a wider Marxist project to try to understand the process of domination within modern Western societies. As Gramsci presents the theory, hegemony refers to a process whereby the state aims to maintain its control over the subaltern majority of the society by controlling the discourses of consent.[2] Within any one society there is a wide range of different, and often conflicting, discourses that are available to ordinary members of the society to use in order to explain and under- stand different aspects of their lives. At some times in history two or more of these discourses may be in open conflict and the political manoeuvring of the ruling elite will be as much for control of these discourses as for military or economic power. We can see this in the processes of Christianisation that we explored in the previous chapter, where Christian and pagan discourses competed for supremacy as the discourse that could explain the world. Christianity, in most parts of the late Roman Empire, won out and came to be the dominant hegemonic discourse.

However, according to Gramsci the process of hegemony is not simply one of a power struggle between two or more distinct discourses that one side or the other may eventually win. It is a process by which the winning side maintains its own discourse as the dominant one to the exclusion of all others, and the process by which the ruling elite uses its dominant discourse to maintain its own position of power. This works primarily by establish- ing a legitimacy for the discourse to an extent that no other, alternative, discourse can be conceived or allowed to challenge the dominant form, and by establishing a consensus within society. Any form of speculation or political manoeuvring has to be undertaken through the medium of the dominant discourse and that discourse is systematically weighted in favour of the political elite. It is also worth noting that Gramsci does not equate hegemony with ideology; it is not simply a question of ideas. As with Foucault's discussion of 'discourse' there is a clear sense that hegemony 'involves "practical activity", and the social relations that produce

---

[1] A. Gramsci, *Selections from the Prison Notebooks*. London: Lawrence and Wishart, 1971.

[2] At some points in his writing Gramsci appears to suggest that the state uses coercive power while civil society uses hegemony. As Kate Crehan demonstrates, however, this distinction is purely methodo- logical, and underlying the distinction is the principle that the state uses both coercive and hegemonic power. K. Crehan, *Gramsci, Culture and Anthropology*. London: Pluto Press, 2002, 99–105.

inequality, as well as the ideas by which inequality is justified, explained, normalised and so on'.[3] We can see this with the discourse of capitalism and market forces in the contemporary world, but we can also see it with Christianity in the empires of the seventh to the ninth centuries, particularly in the classic period in Byzantium and in the political manoeuvring of the Merovingians and Carolingians in France.

It is of course possible to look at the great Christological debates of the fourth century onwards, and the suppression of so-called 'heretical' theologians through exile or death, as a crude means of enforcing a dominant discourse. This, however, is not really a process of hegemony, although one of the consequences of these debates for the Emperor was to establish the hegemonic control of 'orthodox' Christianity. The process of hegemony relies for its success on more subtle means of control, and here the role of the liturgy, and the increasing textualisation of worship, becomes particularly important. It is clear that the arena within which the ordinary member of any society learns its consensual Christian discourse, and the habitus and power relations that are associated with that discourse, is that of the liturgy and other forms of popular devotion. Societies of the seventh to ninth centuries were not universally literate, and popular literature or other forms of written media were not available to the majority of the population. Many forms of popular entertainment were also banned. It was worship, therefore (and arguably the space of worship as this was planned and decorated as well as the practice of the rite itself), that provided the source of the hegemonic discourse for the vast majority of the population. Control of the liturgy, therefore, equalled control of the discourse.

In her book on liturgy and technology, Susan White dates the first revolution in information processing to the sixth or seventh century.[4] This was the time when the increasing complexity of the rites, the need for doctrinal orthodoxy and missionary expansion, and the improved copying facilities of the growing Benedictine scriptoria in the West and their equivalents in the East facilitated the distribution of significant numbers of near identical texts. The rulers of the day took advantage of this process to regulate and codify liturgical texts and to impose as much uniformity of rite on their churches as they could manage. This, I would argue, is a classic example of the processes of hegemonic control of discourse in action and it is this, alongside similar processes, which I wish to explore further within this chapter.

---

[3] Ibid., 174.
[4] S. J. White, *Christian Worship and Technological Change*. Nashville: Abingdon Press, 1994, 42–5.

In looking at the impact of hegemony in practice I want to focus on two specific contexts. The first is the development of the liturgy within the city of Constantinople during the classic era of the Byzantine state and at the time of the Iconoclast Debate. Secondly, I wish to examine the Carolingian Empire in Northern Europe towards the end of the eighth century. Here again the deliberate manipulation of the church and its liturgy was a significant part of the political activity of Charlemagne and his advisers. In order to highlight the issues raised in the analysis of these two contexts, and to provide a useful contrast in a number of signifcant ways, I wish to preface the main analyses by a brief look at the conversion of Armenia and the development of the highly distinctive Armenian rite.

THE CONVERSION OF ARMENIA

Armenia is generally considered to be the first Christian nation, the first state in which the conversion of the ruler led to the subsequent, often forced, conversion of the rest of the population. This was clearly a political act, although there is no evidence that the conversion itself was undertaken for any specifically political motives. According to the writings of the historian Agathangelos, Trdat, the King of Armenia, was converted by his childhood friend Gregory the Illuminator.[5] In 289 King Trdat came to the throne through the intervention of the Roman Emperor. Gregory meanwhile had been educated as a Christian at Caesarea in Cappadocia before coming back to Armenia; there, he was tortured for his faith and thrown into a pit. Following a fit of madness and bad dreams the king was advised to turn to Gregory for healing. Miraculously Gregory had survived in the pit for fifteen years and the successful outcome of the healing led to the king's conversion to Christianity in 301. The king insisted that the people should follow his example, and Gregory organised a major evange-listic campaign, was consecrated bishop in Caesarea and became the first Catholicos of Armenia.

Clearly there is no way of verifying a legend such as this, or of knowing how many within the population of Armenia might already have been Christian. The assumption within the story was that the king, as king, had the unquestioned right to determine the religious allegiance of his subjects.

---

[5] R. W. Thomson, 'Armenian Christianity', in K. Parry et al. (eds.), *The Blackwell Dictionary of Eastern Christianity*. Oxford: Blackwell, 2001, 54–9.

This right is not disputed, particularly in a story written from a Christian perspective, yet it would have been considered very strange, if not offensive, from an earlier Christian point of view. The assumption within the earliest Christian writers was that conversion to Christianity was entirely a personal choice, something that individuals needed to make for themselves in order to gain salvation. The idea of a 'forced' conversion would have been anathema to writers such as Paul, Justin, Irenaeus and Tertullian. This does not appear to have worried King Trdat. Gregory the Illuminator, however, was aware of the enormity of the task that was given him and the considerable opposition from both the nobles and large sections of the population. He is recorded as setting about his task of conversion with considerable organisational skill.

It is here that one further element of the legends becomes significant and is particularly apposite for our current theme. It is said that on conversion King Trdat asked that the priests who had served in the old national cult should become Christian priests in order to serve the nation in its new religion. The priests, however, were reluctant to do this because it would mean giving up one particular ritual act that provided their sustenance and, interestingly, their link with the people. This act was a form of votive sacrifice in which a lamb or chicken was killed at the fire shrine within the temples on behalf of a particular individual and then shared and eaten by that individual, their family and their friends. It was agreed, therefore, according to legend, that the priests, while converting to Christianity and being ordained to perform Christian rites, could continue to receive votive offerings and continue to sacrifice sheep and chickens as part of their priestly duties. This right is maintained to the present day within the Armenian Church and each church is provided with a space where, on Saturdays and Sundays, animals can be bought and killed in a sacrificial manner.[6]

This particular story can be seen from two directions. At one level there is a very clever bit of political manoeuvring going on here on the part of the king. He wins the support of the priests by allowing them to continue the one rite that provides their income and their link with the people. This must also have had a bearing on the level of support for the action of the king from the people themselves. However, from another angle we can see here the importance of ritual in the maintenance of order. We can see how the continuity of action maintains a sense of stability while the meanings

---

[6] I have not found a written reference to this legend but was informed of it during a visit to Armenia in 2002 during which we were able to see the sacrificial sites and were informed of contemporary practice.

associated with that action change.[7] We can also see the way in which the
apparent continuity of ritual activity allows for the imposition of a very
radical change in worldview and meaning systems on the part of the
political authorities. How far the people understood that the actions they
continued to perform had changed in meaning is impossible to know. As in
most other nations it would have taken many decades, even centuries, for a
full process of Christianisation to have been completed. That process,
however, was helped, if we believe the legends, by a shrewd piece of
political intervention in the liturgical life of the people on the part of the
king. It was also an important basis for the subsequent hegemony of the
Christian discourse among the Armenian people.

Armenia, of course, was rarely independent for long during its troubled
history, and larger powers to the West and the South continued to
influence or invade it. This history is reflected in the subsequent development of its liturgy, which despite the constant cycle of invasion and
oppression has managed to remain unique. Textual analysis of the rite
has shown a series of four principal influences.[8] The most significant came
from Cappadocia, as might be expected given the recorded origins of the
conversion process. Gabriele Winkler shows, however, that even in the
account by Agathangelos, the rite used by Gregory for the baptism of King
Trdat in the Euphrates has a distinctively Syrian shape.[9] This Syrian
influence on the baptismal rites was to continue despite many changes in
other areas of worship. From the fifth to the ninth century the primary
influence on Armenian worship came from Jerusalem and the liturgy of the
Holy City. This is not as surprising as it may sound, as both Armenia and
Georgia within the Caucusus maintained very close links with Jerusalem
throughout this period and many of the monks of this region had close
relations with monastic communities in Palestine. It is the office, therefore,
that shows most influence from Jerusalem, with Armenia maintaining it in
a form far older than that of many of the other Eastern churches.[10] From
the tenth century there was considerable influence from Byzantium and

---

[7] Behind this analysis lies the theory of Robertson Smith who argued, in relation to the sacrifices of the
Semitic peoples, that ritual action remains constant while the justification for that action changes.
Here we can see Robertson Smith's argument in action. See W. Robertson Smith, *Lectures on the
Religion of the Semites*. London: A. & C. Black, 1907.

[8] See R. F. Taft, 'The Armenian "Holy Sacrifice (*Surb Patarg*)" as a Mirror of Armenian Liturgical
History', reprinted in R. F. Taft, *Divine Liturgies – Human Problems in Byzantium, Armenia, Syria
and Palestine*, Aldershot: Ashgate, 2001.

[9] G. Winkler, 'Armenian Liturgy', in Parry, *Dictionary*, 60–2.

[10] R. F. Taft, *The Liturgy of the Hours in East and West, the Origins of the Divine Office and its Meaning
for Today*. Collegeville: The Liturgical Press, 1986, 219–24.

then, into the twelfth and thirteenth centuries, the crusading armies from the West left a distinctly Latin influence on the rite. The overall effect, matched with a distinctively Armenian approach to language and architecture, has led to a unique liturgical tradition that continues to the present day.

ICONOCLASM, POLITICS AND RITE

Having looked briefly at Armenia, we must now turn our attention westward to Byzantium. Here again we have to see the development of hegemony not simply as a process by which the Emperor and the Patriarch imposed a particular discourse on the people. There is actually very little evidence of this, and given the continuing Christological debates it is very uncertain as to exactly which Christian discourse was being 'imposed' at any one time.[11] The process of hegemony has much more to do with the relationship between the ruling elite and the people such that the people begin to accept the discourses of the ruling elite as their own and as the only discourse within which power, authority and legitimacy can be discussed. Christianity is clearly the hegemonic discourse in question, whether it be Arian, Monophysite, Chalcedonian or whatever. What is interesting, therefore, is the way in which worship enables and encourages the popularity of the Christian discourse and the way in which this popular discourse is associated with the discourses of the elite. It is the popular aspects of Byzantine worship, therefore, that will be my main concern in this section.

J. M. Hussey, in his history of the Byzantine Orthodox Church, dates the origins of a truly Byzantine state, as opposed to the vestiges of the late Roman Empire, to the beginning of the seventh century.[12] In 613 the Persian army had conquered most of Syria and Asia Minor and was camped on the Asian side of the Bosphorus just outside the city of Constantinople. At the same time the Slavs and Avars from the North had conquered most of the Balkans, and the Persian Emperor was calling on the Avar leaders to join him in the final push against Byzantium. As it happens this push never came and over the next fifty years or so the Byzantine emperors were able to push the Persians back and to bring the Slavs into their own sphere of influence. However, with the rise of Islam from the South, taking advantage as it did of the conflict between Persia

---

[11] See the extended discussion in J. M. Hussey, *The Orthodox Church in the Byzantine Empire.* Oxford: Clarendon Press, 1986, 9–110.

[12] Ibid., 10–11; see also J. F. Haldon, *Byzantium in the Seventh Century, The Transformation of a Culture.* Cambridge: Cambridge University Press, 1990.

and Byzantium and the subsequent weaknesses of both, the Eastern Roman Empire was never going to be the same again.

The following three hundred years were to be the most significant in the consolidation and definition of the Byzantine Church since the reign of Emperor Justinian in the sixth century.[13] These were three hundred years of controversy and political manoeuvring in which Christological and Iconoclastic debates dominated the political discourses of the time. They were also to be defining times for the identity of the Orthodox community. It is at this time that the Byzantine liturgy came to take its classical form,[14] and it is at the end of this period that this liturgy begins to be exported to other states under Byzantine influence. It is therefore important to look at the issues that were prevalent at this time and see how they impacted on the development of worship in order to see the processes of hegemony at work.

In this section I want to look at three aspects of the worship of Constantinople and to see what impact these had on the development of the popular understanding of worship within the Byzantine tradition. The first concerns the development and use of processions within the city. The second focuses on the Iconoclast Controversy and the consequences that this had for the development of the rite and popular devotion. The third examines the development of official commentaries on the liturgy from the beginning of the Iconoclast Controversy to the end of the millennium. In loose terms these three aspects develop in chronological order, but this should not be seen as a history of the Byzantine rite as such. There were many other influences and factors involved in the development of the minutiae of the rite that I am going to have to pass over within this text.[15] What interests me here are those aspects of the worship of the city, the Emperor and the church that impact on the relationship between church and state and relate directly to the ideas of discourse and hegemony.[16] Underlying all three aspects, however, is a process that we can see

---

[13] Hussey, *Orthodox Church*, provides a detailed summary of this period and its impact on the Byzantine Church.

[14] Although the fall of Constantinople to the Latin armies in 1204 and the subsequent rebuilding of church and state saw the establishment of many elements of the rite that we know today. R. F. Taft, *The Byzantine Rite, A Short History.* Collegeville, Liturgical Press, 1992 .

[15] See Taft, ibid., and H. Wybrew, *The Orthodox Liturgy, The Development of the Eucharistic Liturgy in the Byzantine Rite.* Crestwood: St Vladimir's Seminary Press, 1996, for good short introductions to the history of the rite.

[16] We have to recognise the importance of theological and political conflicts between the church and the state as part of the wider hegemonic process, but in this section I wish to concentrate primarily on the question of worship. For a useful discussion of the wider context see Haldon, *Byzantium*, 281–323.

developing throughout the history of Byzantine worship: the development of codification and textualisation.

The very word 'Byzantine' has become synonymous with the idea of highly elaborate, even convoluted and excessive, bureaucracy in which every little element is coded and every action and response outlined in meticulous detail. This is clearly something of a caricature. However, it is evident that as the Byzantine state began to rebuild from the seventh century it took excessive pains to control and codify vast areas of its life.[17] The Roman emperors, from before Constantine's move to his new capital, had always been involved in a complex round of ritual and political activity. This was not dropped with the conversion of the Emperor to Christianity, as we have already seen in the previous chapter.[18] In the first half of the tenth century the Emperor Constantine VII Porphyrogenitus commissioned a text outlining and codifying in minute detail exactly what the Emperor was to do on each day and in relation to every conceivable form of ceremony.[19] *De Cerimoniis Aulae Byzantinae* was compiled for the Emperor's son and, in his preface, Constantine openly admits that his aim in producing the document is to restore a set of traditions that had already begun to decay. The emperors by the tenth century were already beginning to retreat from public life, and Constantine set out, very deliberately, to try and halt that process.[20] *De Cerimoniis* gives a clear picture of the kind of complex ritual activity that the court was expected to be involved in at this time, with rites and ceremonies for practically every day of the year and detailed prescriptions for the full range of officials associated with the imperial household. However, this is very much the end of a process.

In order to understand where *De Cerimoniis* came from, therefore, we need to go back a number of centuries and trace through some of the developments that led to this text. I will begin with what is undoubtedly the core of Constantine's document, the processional nature of Byzantine worship. As we have already seen, processions formed a significant part of the liturgy of Constantinople from the very beginnings of the city as an imperial capital.[21] They were in some ways a continuation of a pagan past, as with the sacrifices of the Armenian clergy. They were also part of the process of Christianisation. They enabled the new religious authorities to

---

[17] See ibid.
[18] See pp. 64–6 above and J. F. Baldovin, 'The Urban Character of Christian Worship in Jerusalem, Rome and Constantinople from the Fourth to the Tenth Centuries: The Origins, Development and Meaning of Stational Liturgy'. Ph.D. dissertation, Yale University, 1982, 397.
[19] Baldovin, 'Urban Character', 377–89.　　[20] Hussey, *Orthodox Church*, 300.
[21] See p. 66 above.

assert their own religious discourses over and against those of the pagans. It is not surprising, therefore, to find the procession at the heart of conflict within the city over rival religious discourses. This is seen principally in the conflict between Nicaean and Arian discourses at the end of the fourth century. John Chrysostom, we are told, deliberately engaged in nocturnal processional activity as part of his attempts to oust the Arian patriarchs.[22] Certainly the popular support for ecclesial processions within the city can, in part, be traced to this kind of early conflictual activity.

The Emperor Justinian rebuilt Constantinople following riots in 532, and as part of that rebuilding programme consolidated many of the current processional activities. The dedication and rededication of the new Great Church in 537 both began with processions in which the Patriarch travelled by chariot and the Emperor on foot.[23] Established routes, set stations, and to some extent the words and music used within the processions began to be fixed from this time. The processions themselves were always accompanied by music. It would have been unthinkable to conduct a procession in silence. It was the psalms sung antiphonally that formed the texts for the processions, and the chants were developed with open-air processional activity and popular participation in mind.[24] Another factor that was consolidated at this time was the association between the processions and the secular or ecclesial hierarchies. Processions were public events that involved the participation of some of the leading figures of the society. Processions brought the Emperor and the patriarchs, as well as nobles, bishops and others, out on to the streets and into the public gaze. It was essential, therefore, that the necessary distance and power were maintained and that the order of the procession, as well as other ritual accompaniments, was of a kind that maintained the sense of due order and awe. Justinian, for example, made it a punishable offence to hold a procession without ecclesiastical sanction and a crime to disturb those processions that had such authority.[25]

In Constantinople, however, the processions did not remain an entirely ecclesial affair, used solely to celebrate the feasts of the church. They clearly took on a much more central role in the life of the city that came to have a significant impact on the liturgical calendar by default. The procession

---

[22] Baldovin, 'Urban Character', 337; Taft, *Byzantine Rite*, 31–2.
[23] Baldovin, 'Urban Character', 346.
[24] Baldovin, ibid., argues that the antiphonal nature of the psalmody, with the refrain repeated by the population after each verse, or collection of verses, added to the popularity of the processions themselves.
[25] Ibid., 419.

with its popular, public expression became the principal ritual act with which the city came to approach any kind of disaster. A seventh-century chronicle claims that processions were held in response to a series of earthquakes, plagues, invasions and other disasters from 447 onwards.[26] As John Baldovin says, 'by the early seventh century commemorating the salvation of the city and liturgical processions went hand in hand'.[27] This, in itself, shows the importance and impact of the procession within the life of the city. Whether the city was under threat of invasion, of earthquake, of plague or of any other kind of disaster, the natural and obvious response was to hold a procession, either to a church dedicated to a saint who could help, or to the gates or walls of the city itself, or even beyond into the fields surrounding the city. These processions in the face of disaster often took on a penitential form, and we are told that the Emperor would often process barefoot.[28] The words and music used would also have reflected this mood. What is more, should the procession prove successful, the event was almost inevitably commemorated through further penitential processions held on an annual basis. This began to fill the calendar with commemorative processions, many of a penitential nature, which came to characterise the worship of the city.

It was not just the Emperor, however, who was visible within the procession; the whole of his household clearly took an active part in the public liturgical life of the city, and this included the Empress and other female members of the household.[29] There is evidence, for example, of a far greater liturgical role for virgins and widows in the liturgies of Byzantium than in many other equivalent cities of the time. J. A. McGuckin demonstrates how, in the first half of the fifth century, the Empress, as well as other noblewomen, virgins, widows and ascetics, played a considerable part in the regular liturgical life of the capital.[30] Robert Taft also provides extensive evidence of the active, if more detached, role of women, including imperial women, within the liturgy of the Great Church over the whole sweep of the Byzantine Empire.[31] For the most part these women were confined to a particular space in the nave of the church (the *gynaecium*) or in a gallery above the nave, but this was as much a public space as any other,

---

[26] Ibid., 343; see also Taft, *Byzantine Rite*, 30.   [27] Baldovin, 'Urban Character', 343–4.
[28] Ibid., 343.
[29] S. J. White, *A History of Women in Christian Worship*. London: SPCK, 2003, 69.
[30] J. A. McGuckin, 'Nestorius and the Political Factions of Fifth-Century Byzantium: Factors in His Personal Downfall', *Bulletin of the John Rylands University Library of Manchester*, 78:3 (1996), 7–21.
[31] R. F. Taft, 'Women at Church in Byzantium: Where, When – and Why?' in R. F. Taft, *Divine Liturgies – Human Problems in Byzantium, Armenia, Syria and Palestine*. Aldershot: Ashgate, 2001, 154.

from which, according to Patriarch Athanasius I (c. 309), they could not only partake in worship but also parade their latest fashions for the gossip of the populace.[32] It was Nestorius who, as Patriarch in the fifth century, tried to suppress the role of women, as it did not equate with what he knew from his hometown in Syria.[33] The role of women, including imperial women, in processions, therefore, appears to have declined considerably after Nestorius. However, women continued to play an important role in the religious life of the city, not least in their support for private religious foundations.[34]

Almost all of the processions within the city would have ended in a celebration of the eucharist, and every principal celebration of the eucharist would also have begun with a procession through the streets. The procession and the eucharist, therefore, became closely linked in the minds of the clergy and people. It is this that led to the situation, as the number of processions began to decline in the seventh and eighth centuries, in which elements from the processions began to be added to the opening of the liturgy itself.[35] As well as the rites associated with the entrance into the church, the psalms, or more usually their antiphons, and the stational prayers were added to the opening rites to combine the remnants of the procession with the celebration of the eucharist. The Trisagion, for example, was originally an antiphon to a penitential psalm that, according to legend, had been revealed to a young boy during a procession to pray for delivery from a violent earthquake during the time of Patriarch Proclus (434–46). On the singing of the antiphon the quake ceased and over time the prayer became an important statement of orthodoxy in its own right, a regular part of many processions which was eventually sung as part of the introductory rites of the liturgy itself.[36]

What we see here is a clear example of the expansion or elaboration of what Taft refers to as the 'soft points' of the liturgy, those points at which actions originally occurred without words.[37] This merging of processional elements with the entrance rites was only the beginning of the development of these soft points. Up until the beginning of the eighth century, as Hugh Wybrew suggests, the liturgy itself 'still preserved its early simplicity of

[32] Taft, 'Women at Church', 154.   [33] McGuckin, 'Nestorius'.
[34] J. P. Thomas, *Private Religious Foundations in the Byzantine Empire*. Washington: Dumbarton Oaks Research Library and Collection, 1987 .
[35] Wybrew, *Orthodox Liturgy*, 76–80.   [36] Ibid., 78–9.
[37] R. F. Taft, 'How Liturgies Grow: The Evolution of the Byzantine Divine Liturgy', in R. F. Taft, *Beyond East and West, Problems in Liturgical Understanding*. Washington: The Pastoral Press, 1984, 167–92.

structure'.[38] It was during the Iconoclast Controversies, however, of the eighth and ninth centuries that the emperors began to retreat from the public ritual of the city and the procession became less significant in the life of the population. Increasingly, therefore, as worship retreated within the churches, the growth in the splendour and ritual of that worship, especially of its internal processions at the soft points of the rite, was reflected in the decline of the public expression of ritual in external processions. It is the consequences for worship of the Iconoclast Controversy that we need to look at next.

Icons, or images of one kind or another, had been produced within the Christian church since the end of the third century. They developed alongside the rising fashion for relics that followed Constantine's 'discovery' of the true cross at Jerusalem in 318.[39] At what point images or relics actually became the focus for devotion is difficult to determine, but the increasing troubles of the sixth and seventh centuries led many ordinary people in Byzantium to turn to icons, relics and other images as a focus for their prayers and petitions. In some cases specific icons were seen to have the power to save the city or to protect the community and were treated with a new kind of reverence, even adoration. They were, for example, carried in a number of the processions that I have already mentioned. As the icons grew in popularity there was a constant undercurrent of opposition to their use in devotion and even to their very existence, based on a reading of the second commandment against any representation of God. This undercurrent, however, never surfaced into a popular movement until the Iconoclast Controversy, and even then it is still very unclear how popular the iconoclast activity actually was.

The roots and motivation for the Iconoclast Controversy are also difficult to determine.[40] It appears as though the driving force and impetus for the whole event was the action of the Emperor. Leo III came to the throne at a difficult time in the history of Byzantium. He was a soldier, born in North Syria. Whether he brought iconoclastic ideas from his hometown, or whether Islam had in some way influenced him is impossible to determine, but in 726 he ordered the destruction of a mosaic of Christ over the entrance to the palace.[41] This was followed by a wholesale destruction of images led by the Emperor himself. Many people went along with this action and many church leaders fell in behind the Emperor.

---

[38] Wybrew, *Orthodox Liturgy*, 103.   [39] See pp. 69–70 above.
[40] The whole period of the Iconoclast Controversy is currently undergoing considerable reinterpretation and the academic debates will no doubt continue for some years. For a detailed account of this period from the perspective of the older 'orthodoxy' see Hussey, *Orthodox Church*, 30–68.
[41] Ibid., 37.

Whether this was for entirely political or for other religious reasons is also difficult to assess. The fact that Leo and his son Constantine V, who succeeded him, were successful generals who brought the army under control and began to rebuild the empire through campaigns in Asia Minor and the Balkans clearly has something to do with the popularity of iconoclasm, especially among the military.

This act of destruction, however, was just the first of what was to become a recurring theme of Christian worship, in different places and at different times. We will meet it again when we come to consider the Reformation in Western Europe in the fifteenth and sixteenth centuries.[42] Many of the same activities were involved in the different forms of iconoclasm. It consisted of the destruction of all images, especially those within the space of worship. At its crudest the justification was the accusation that ordinary people were being induced into worshipping the images them-selves rather than that which they represented. At its most subtle it was claimed that the images were a distraction from the worship of the true God. The result, therefore, was seldom the substitution of abstract pattern for figurative frescos as might have been found in Islamic architecture, but rather the whitewashing of the inside walls of the church to leave the worship space blank, devoid of all forms of distraction.

The iconoclast phase did not last long in Byzantium. It was caught up in the disputes about the nature of Christ and was proclaimed a heresy in 787, a matter of doctrine not just of practice.[43] After the death of Constantine V, the iconophiles eventually came back to power and, apart from the brief return to iconoclasm at the beginning of the ninth century, the Byzantine church was never again to fall into this 'heretical' state. Icons were to become ever more central to the life and worship of the people of the Byzantine church and of all those other churches that were heavily influ-enced by Byzantium. In fact the final victory of the iconophile party in 843 was celebrated annually within the liturgical calendar on the first Sunday of Lent, as the Victory of Orthodoxy.[44] The understanding of icons had also changed through the controversy, from the idea of images being seen as lessons leading people to greater faith, to the understanding of icons as sacramentals in their own right, making present for the worshipper that which they represented.[45]

---

[42] See p. 184 below.   [43] Hussey, *Orthodox Church*, 49.   [44] Ibid., 63.
[45] To claim that these two positions were the only ones held before and after the controversy and that there was not a continuing debate about the nature of icons is, of course, very simplistic. The two positions, however, do sum up the majority view on either side of the debate.

What the Iconoclast Controversy also allowed, however, was the possibility for the reconstruction of the liturgy, not so much in its words, but in the actions of the Emperor, the clergy and most importantly the people. Icons and relics came to play an even larger part in the ritual of the various liturgies of the church following the Controversy. In particular ordinary people began to develop devotional practices in relation to icons. The immediate response to the crisis was to replace practically all the decorative aspects of the churches with iconographic imagery.[46] The first change was to replace the image of the cross that had been in the roof of the apse of Hagia Sophia by a representation of the *Theotokos*, or Mary, and child.[47] Individual icons and images also began to take on specific importance as the population came to associate the images with miraculous healing and other events. Finally, it became increasingly common for members of the congregations to light candles and pray before icons during the liturgy itself, so enabling the people to participate in the rite in a very specific way. The place of the icon, therefore, developed over the centuries to be one of the most significant features of Orthodox devotion.

De Cerimoniis itself was in part a response to iconoclasm in that it laid out what the Emperor and his court ought to be doing and highlighted the importance of the material elements of the worship.[48] The production of liturgical books also followed the reconstruction of the rite as a sense of the necessity for order prevailed. However, the vast majority of the manuscripts that we actually have for the Byzantine rite date from the tenth century or later, even though the scribes who produced them were often copying texts that can be dated much earlier than this. The earliest specifically liturgical manuscript, the *Codex Barberini*, dates from about 800 and contains prayers said by the celebrant primarily from the Liturgy of St Basil, but also from what was to become the Liturgy of St John Chrysostom.[49] What is noticeable, therefore, is that the number of manuscripts that have survived from the fourth to the tenth century is remarkably few. Obviously a manuscript that is being used day after day in the context of worship, with constant handling and in an atmosphere of incense and candles etc., is unlikely to survive. That said, however, the number of texts that we have from copies of such manuscripts is still significantly lower than we might expect if the use of liturgical books was

---

[46] Taft, *Byzantine Rite*, 61.   [47] Hussey, *Orthodox Church*, 67.
[48] It has been suggested that the 'what it used to be' of the *De Cerimoniis* relates to the period immediately after the restoration of Orthodoxy in the mid ninth century. Hussey, *Orthodox Church*, 64.
[49] Wybrew, *Orthodox Liturgy*, 108.

the normal practice of most churches. It is simply impossible to get behind this lack of manuscript evidence to say whether there were books used within worship, from which the priests and others officiating at the rite might have read, or whether we are dealing with an essentially oral process of transmission. Either way, the consistency of the record and the ability of monks and others to memorise large tracts of scripture and prayer has to be recognised.

The real question, however, is why, in the eighth and ninth centuries, the Byzantine church suddenly felt the need to codify and, more specifically, to begin to textualise their worship. Susan White suggests that this reflects a change in technology: paper was becoming cheaper, and copyists were becoming more available.[50] I will look at these arguments in more detail when I come to look at the work of the Western church below. In the case of Byzantium I think that there was probably another factor involved, the need to codify and the need to preserve a tradition that the people concerned clearly felt was in danger of dying. This is the action of a church and people who felt threatened by the world in which they lived. Preservation was a prime motivator and one that is difficult to ignore. There was also the need to control, which would be clearly related to the need to preserve. The result, I would suggest, was a mindset, and a tradition, that began to close in on itself and to ossify.

This is not, however, the only process involved. With the disruption to worship that was caused by the Iconoclast Controversy there was also a need to reconstruct the tradition. In doing this, however, the church of Byzantium drew not on its own past but on the worship of others.[51] This is, in part, a process of consolidation from across the Empire. It can also be seen as a consequence of a new ecclesial order following Iconoclasm in which the monks became the dominant figures in the life of the church for the first time.[52] We can see these movements, for example, in the changes to the daily prayer of the Great Church, where the Palestinian monastic office was introduced into Byzantium. This happened following the first phase of the Iconoclast Controversy through a series of reforms led by the iconophile St Theodore of Stoudios (d. 826) who brought monks from the Palestinian monastery of St Sabas to Constantinople.[53] St Theodore's reforms included an expansion of the hymnody in the office and a complete

[50] White, *Technological Change.*   [51] Taft, *Byzantine Rite*, 52–61.
[52] Hussey, *Orthodox Church*, 66. The revisions to the office suggested by the monks can also be seen as part of an attempt on their behalf to gain hegemonic control of the Christian discourse at this time.
[53] Taft, *Liturgy of the Hours*, 276.

revision of the Easter Triduum, based on the Palestinian models.[54] However, there still remains the question of why, specifically, it was the Palestinian monastic office that proved so influential.

One answer to this question relates to a situation that we have already touched on very briefly for Armenia. There we saw that between the sixth and the tenth century the primary influence on the worship of Armenia was the practice in Jerusalem. The same principle could easily be applied to Constantinople. It was the Jerusalem liturgy that was being introduced into the city, and in this Byzantium was simply following a wider fashion. With the invasion of the Persians in 614, Jerusalem was sacked, but this made the city and all that it stood for, in terms of the sites of the death and resurrection of Jesus, even more appealing. There was also a need to preserve what was special about Jerusalem outside of the city itself, as there was the ever-present potential for the entire destruction of the city. The monks of St Sabas in the Palestinian wilderness reformed the monastic structures of Jerusalem and preserved the tradition during a period of unequalled creativity and reform.[55] It was this tradition, therefore, that was adapted to the urban context of Byzantium and from there spread to Mount Athos, Georgia, Rus and Southern Italy.

It was not just the writing down of the words and actions of the liturgy that developed over the eighth and ninth centuries. Alongside this came the development of theological commentaries on the rites. In many ways these commentaries are even more important than the writing of the texts themselves; in one case at least they came to be contained within the official form of the rite. The commentaries become most important, however, as with processions and the response to the Iconoclast Controversy, because of their impact on the popular imagination and the people's own responses to the liturgy. These commentaries, therefore, can be seen as a central part of the growing hegemony of specific quasi-monastic or mystical Christian discourses within Byzantium.

The earliest of the popular commentaries on the liturgy is that of Maximus the Confessor, who wrote his *Mystagogia* while travelling to North Africa between 628 and 630.[56] Maximus writes primarily for a monastic audience and presents both the building of the church and the practice of the liturgy as an opportunity for a long and detailed meditation on both the life of Christ and the journey of the individual soul. This

---

[54] R. F. Taft, 'In the Bridegroom's Absence: The Paschal Triduum in the Byzantine Church', in R. F. Taft, *Liturgy in Byzantium and Beyond*. Aldershot: Ashgate, 1995, 72.
[55] Taft, *Liturgy of the Hours*, 276.   [56] Wybrew, *Orthodox Liturgy*, 94–101.

meditative approach, along with the interpretation of each aspect of the building or the rite in terms of symbolism and figures, was to set the tone for all subsequent commentaries. Maximus' *Mystagogia* was followed in the early eighth century by the *Ecclesiastical History and Mystical Contemplation* of Germanus.[57] Germanus was Patriarch at the height of the Iconoclast Controversy, from 715 to 730, and was deposed by the iconoclast Emperor Leo III. In many ways the *Ecclesiastical History* followed the pattern of the *Mystagogia*, providing contemplative and symbolic interpretations of all aspects of the rite, although it also included commentaries on posture and vesture as well as the building and the ritual of the liturgy. Germanus, however, aims his text at a lay audience rather than the monastic audience of Maximus, and roots his commentary far more in the historical life of Christ,[58] so reflecting a major theme of the iconophiles, rather than in mystical theology. These commentaries were followed in the eleventh and the fourteenth centuries by other similar texts, including the famous commentary by Nicholas Cabasilas.[59] The earlier commentaries, however, continued to be read and to influence the way in which the liturgy was understood, and Germanus' *Ecclesiastical History*, in later edited versions, eventually became part of the official text of the rite.[60]

What is interesting in relation to the commentaries is the importance that has been placed, within Byzantine worship, on the interpretation given to the liturgy as well as to the words that are actually used.[61] In many ways, especially for the ordinary worshippers, the interpretation, or commentary, was perhaps more important than the texts of the prayers, as the words themselves could not have been followed.[62] It was the commentary that was widely known and came to influence the way in which ordinary worshippers understood both the action of the rite and, more importantly, their own part in it as mystical participants in a grand heavenly drama. Over time the commentaries also came to influence the development of the liturgy itself as the private personal prayers of the clergy, in Taft's soft points or the rite, came to reflect the commentaries and were then codified and textualised in later editions of the liturgy.[63]

---

[57] R. F. Taft, 'The Liturgy of the Great Church: An Initial Synthesis of Structure and Interpretation on the Eve of Iconoclasm', in Taft, *Liturgy in Byzantium and Beyond*.

[58] Taft argues that this reflects an Antiochene theology focusing on the incarnation rather than the more mystical, monophysite, Alexandrian tradition. Taft, 'Liturgy of the Great Church'.

[59] Wybrew, *Orthodox Liturgy*, 158–64.   [60] Taft, 'Liturgy of the Great Church', 74.

[61] Taft, *Byzantine Rite*, 67–75.

[62] Much of the liturgy took place behind a screen and was either recited in a soft voice or said silently.

[63] Taft, *Byzantine Rite*, 74–5.

While the Emperor was as much a participant in this drama as any ordinary worshipper it is not immediately clear how these commentaries could be seen as a significant part of the hegemonic discourses of the state. The fact that the Emperor took part must have affected the way in which his role was understood, but this is not enough. As we have seen, hegemonic discourses need to be popular discourses that reflect significant elements of the elite worldview in order to make that worldview the only possible way in which ideas and arguments can be expressed.[64] This is exactly what the commentaries do. Taft, for example, argues that the commentaries, especially that of Germanus, were inspired primarily by the space created within the Great Church of Hagia Sophia.[65] Without the sense of heaven on earth created by the sheer vastness of the building and the play of light within it the commentaries would have developed in an entirely different direction. This church, however, was constructed by Justinian to be the spiritual centre of the Empire, as much a part of the self-expression of the state as any imperial ceremonial. The expression of this space within the commentaries, therefore, simply developed and popularised an implicit discourse of power that put Byzantium, the Great Church and the Emperor at its heart.

The Byzantine Empire was rooted in liturgy and that liturgy linked heaven and earth; it provided a space for heaven on earth, in the physical form of the Great Church, which could also be claimed by the Emperor as well as the Patriarch in the many disputes that ensued between church and state. The various parties may have used the space as part of their disputes but its increasingly hegemonic meaning, reinforced by the commentaries, was eventually set as being beyond dispute. Underlying this was an attempt to use the liturgy and its commentaries in the process of establishing a hegemonic discourse about the space of worship throughout the Empire and beyond. This, however, is a story that we will pick up in the following chapter. At this point we must continue to move even further west, to France and to the very different way in which the new emperors of the West were using their liturgies for similar hegemonic purposes.

CHARLEMAGNE AND THE INVENTION OF THE WESTERN RITE

On Christmas Day in the year 800, Charlemagne was crowned Emperor in Rome. He had persuaded the Pope that this was an appropriate and politically astute thing to do despite the bitter opposition of the Eastern

---

[64] Crehan, *Gramsci*, 102–4.   [65] Taft, 'Liturgy of the Great Church', 47.

Emperor in Constantinople.[66] The coronation, however, was only the latest stage in a series of dramatic events that had led to the re-formation of a 'Roman' Empire in the West. The details of all the tribal movements across France and Spain and the particular intrigues of the Franks and other Germanic tribes are probably not relevant to a history of Christian worship such as this. However, it is clear that the story of the rise of the Carolingian kings among the Franks, and the Merovingians before them, cannot be separated from an understanding of the church in this period.[67] It was not insignificant that Charlemagne sought to be crowned Emperor in Rome, by the Pope. He needed the full authority both of the discourses rooted in the old pre-Christian Roman Empire and of those of the Catholic Church, that had in many ways inherited the mantle of the Western Empire, in order to reinforce his own discourses of authority.

When the early Franks first came to prominence in what is now Belgium, most of the tribal groups in Western Europe would still have been using liturgical texts that were, to a greater or lesser extent, related to the old Gallican liturgies.[68] Many of the northern tribes that had overrun the Latin Empire had been Arian rather than Catholic and this divide was significant for the political manoeuvring of the various tribal leaders.[69] The conversion of the first Merovingian king, Clovis, in 493 or 503[70] has been hotly disputed, but one of the significant factors was an alignment with Rome and the Catholic Church against the Arian Goths and Visigoths.[71] Alongside the tribal groups, all primarily nomadic but all integrated to a greater or lesser extent into the local social setting, were the old Gaulish aristocracy who in a number of significant cases maintained positions of

[66] The coronation and its motivation are, like so much else associated with the life of Charlemagne and his predecessors, open to debate and controversy. The sources can usually allow us to determine what happened, and this can be disputed because of the political slant of the authors, but only very rarely can we assess the motives behind these actions or their immediate consequences. See e.g. J. M. Wallace-Hadrill, *The Barbarian West 400–1000*. Oxford: Blackwell, 1985.

[67] It is in relation to this rise of the Franks in particular that Russell refers to the Germanization of Christianity. J. C. Russell, *The Germanization of Early Medieval Christianity, A Sociohistorical Approach to Religious Transformation*. Oxford: Oxford University Press, 1994.

[68] See p. 80 above for a discussion of my use of this term.

[69] It would be very interesting to be able to reconstruct the Arian liturgies used by the Goths and Visigoths. It is generally assumed that they would be, to all intents and purposes, just like those of the Catholics but with slight changes in theological emphasis. We actually have very little evidence for this, however, and it is clear that this is one case where the 'victor' has successfully wiped out all signs of their vanquished foe.

[70] The choice of date depends on the reading of Gregory of Tours's History of the Franks, and whether his date for the conversion is accepted. See Wallace-Hadrill, *Barbarian West*, 69.

[71] See Russell, *Germanization*, 146–54 for a wider discussion of the possible motivations of Clovis and of the local Romano-Gallic bishops.

leadership within the local churches as they had done for the previous four hundred years. It was one of these Roman bishops, Gregory of Tours, who wrote the definitive history of the early Merovingian kings and he placed both the conversion of Clovis and his subsequent devotion to Martin of Tours as central to his narrative.[72] It is clear from this writing, however, that Clovis and the early Franks see both the Christian God and St Martin as warrior heroes in the old Germanic fashion and therefore as powerful defenders and supporters of Frankish rights. 'The Franks', according to J. M. Wallace-Hadrill, 'had no hesitation in bringing their thank-offerings to the shrines of the miracle-working Gaulish saints, such as St Martin, under whom they won their battles and amassed their treasures.'[73] Here, however, we do see the beginnings of a distinctly Christian discourse on Frankish history. Whether Clovis or his immediate successors ever really took to Christianity, apart from their devotions at shrines such as those of St Martin and St Denis, is debatable, and it is clear that at this stage in the history, Christian discourses are far from gaining any kind of hegemony.

With the dawn of the seventh century the Merovingians had come to power and a new kind of discourse is introduced. Dagobert, for example, who died at the age of thirty-six in 639, was a particular devotee of St Denis near Paris and established a fair on the saint's feast day that drew traders from across Europe and beyond.[74] It was during Dagobert's time that the Irish missionaries led by St Columbanus moved south through Germany and across France setting up outposts and centres of learning as far south as St Gall in Switzerland and Bobbio in Northern Italy.[75] These monks and missionaries brought with them a Gallican form of liturgy, and some of the best evidence we have for the earlier liturgical practice of the region comes from texts left by the Irish in Bobbio and similar European monasteries.[76] They also brought with them a form of personal confession that had grown up in Ireland but was completely new to much of mainland Europe. This personalising and moralising of Christian discourse was something new and is what J. C. Russell refers to as the secondary stage of Christianisation, going beyond a simple exchange of old pagan Germanic rites with new Christian devotions to a deepening of the specifically Christian discourse of the Catholic populations.[77]

---

[72] Gregory also wrote an influential Life of St Martin. Wallace-Hadrill, *Barbarian West*, 67.
[73] Ibid., 76.   [74] Ibid., 77.   [75] Ibid., 76.
[76] A. Wilmart, E. A. Lowe and H. A. Wilson, *The Bobbio Missal (Ms Paris. Lat. 13246), Notes and Studies.* London: Harrison and Sons Ltd., 1924.
[77] Russell, *Germanization*, 156–65. Russell also refers to the impact that the Irish made on monastic discipline and the understanding of the church under the later Merovingians, and the way in which the Irish ideas laid the foundation for later medieval understandings of death.

All these movements and cross-currents make it very difficult to reconstruct the liturgical life of any region of Western Europe before the reign of
Charlemagne, as the evidence itself is so very patchy and the range of
influences and interconnections makes the likelihood of considerable local
variation very high indeed.[78]

Charlemagne himself inherited a range of different Christian discourses
when he came to power in 768. Not only were different liturgies used in
different regions, but even a range of different liturgies would have been
used in any one region, where Irish, Benedictine and other monastic orders
existed side by side with local liturgical traditions.[79] There were also many
different kinds of Christian discourse at work. Unlike the Merovingians,
who drew primarily on Irish missionaries, the Carolingians who followed
them looked to the Anglo-Saxons for their missionary teams and drew on
the traditions of the York School and the principles laid down by Gregory
the Great in his commission to Augustine. This meant that on the mission
fields of Northern Germany the principal Christian discourse was still one
of power and miracles, transforming local pagan sites and practices into
their Christian equivalents.[80] Within the court, however, and the increasingly educated monasteries of France and Italy, a secondary discourse was
developing with a sophisticated theological base rooted in classical forms of
education. It was a previous member of the York School, the deacon
Alcuin, who built up this educational system under Charlemagne and it
was under Alcuin that the use of liturgy within the developing hegemonic
Christian discourse was developed. The primary aim of Charlemagne and
Alcuin's educational activity appears to be the development of a 'correct'
text of the Bible. However, even this has liturgical implications, as much
of the liturgy, particularly the Office, is biblically based. Wallace-Hadrill
says of the Carolingian renaissance that 'this was no New Athens finer than

---

[78] One area where considerable work has been done is on the Mozarabic Liturgy of Spain. Here the acts
of councils, the writings of church leaders such as St Isidore and others, and the continuing tradition
of the Mozarabic rites in Toledo to the present day mean that it has been possible to reconstruct far
more of the history and form of this rite than has been the case for that of France, Ireland or any
other region of North-Western Europe. Even so, the evidence that we have is primarily a 'reconstruction' based on educated guesswork rather than a clear sense of what the worship of the Christian
churches of Spain might actually have looked like at the time. So much of our knowledge remains so
very partial. See e.g. G. Woolfenden, *Daily Prayer in Christian Spain, A Study of the Mozarabic
Office.* London: SPCK, 2000 and T. C. Akeley, *Christian Initiation in Spain, c. 300–1100.* London:
Darton, Longman & Todd, 1967.
[79] See C. Vogel, *Medieval Liturgy, An Introduction to the Sources.* Washington: Pastoral Press, 1986 and
E. Palazzo, *A History of Liturgical Books from the Beginning to the Thirteenth Century.* Collegeville:
Pueblo, 1993.
[80] Russell, *Germanization*, 192–7.

the Old: it was intellectual reform and textual criticism as the indispens-
able preliminary to the reform of the clergy and to the performance of the
Opus Dei'.[81]

In 783, long before his coronation in Rome, Charlemagne had sent to
Pope Hadrian I asking for a copy of the liturgy written by Gregory the
Great (590–604) and free from all subsequent additions.[82] His aim,
it appears, was to provide a 'pure' text[83] that he could impose as a model
for all the churches of his Empire in order to bring uniformity where there
had previously been diversity. What we see here is a concern not just for
right conduct, doing everything in conformity with Rome, but also, as with
the study of the Bible, for textual accuracy. Hadrian, it appears, did not
really know how to respond to this request, not sharing the Carolingian
scholar's interest in textual criticism, and therefore sent a copy of the only
manuscript that might have met Charlemagne's requirements, a copy of
the Papal festal sacramentary[84] currently in use at the Lateran basilica. This
text is known to liturgists as the *Hadrianum* to distinguish it from other
sacramentaries of the time, but it was from a family of sacramentaries
known as 'Gregorian' after Gregory the Great. Needless to say the
Hadrianum was not a 'pure' copy of a text that was written by Gregory
the Great, even if Gregory had ever produced a sacramentary of his own.[85]
It contains many elements that both contemporary scholars and, it appears,
Alcuin himself knew to be additions.[86] It also, inevitably, missed out many
elements that were familiar to the churches of Northern France. This
meant that the Carolingian reformers had to provide a supplement to
this Roman text before it could be used by the churches of Northern
Europe.

---

[81] Wallace-Hadrill, *Barbarian West*, 102.

[82] A recent scholarly account of this is found in Vogel, *Medieval Liturgy*, 80–92.

[83] The word the pope uses when referring to Charlemagne's request for the text is *inmixtum*. Vogel
translates this as 'free from all additions' (*Medieval Liturgy*, 81).

[84] A sacramentary is a text containing all the prayers needed by the celebrant for the various eucharistic
celebrations throughout the year, along with other rites as appropriate. See Palazzo, *Liturgical
Books*, 21–7.

[85] The Lateran form of the sacramentary is commonly known as the 'Gregorian' and from the eighth
century onwards was thought to be written by Gregory the Great. This is now thought to be very
unlikely and contemporary scholarship suggests that it was probably a compilation of older texts
brought together under Pope Honorius I (625–38). Vogel, *Medieval Liturgy*, 79.

[86] Vogel suggests that Alcuin must have owned an earlier version of the Lateran, or Gregorian,
sacramentary that he possibly brought with him to Tours from York. He certainly shows in his
correspondence a knowledge of such an earlier text and a clear grasp of the liturgical changes that
have taken place in the hundred years or so between Gregory and Hadrian. Vogel, *Medieval
Liturgy*, 101.

Copies of the *Hadrianum* and the supplement still exist and have been the cause of a great deal of controversy within liturgical scholarship.[87] It is unclear, for example, what status the text of the *Hadrianum* itself had for Charlemagne and his reformers. Charlemagne placed it in his palace library in Aachen, and subsequent copies all indicate that this text was to be treated as the 'ideal', the model on which all liturgy was expected to be based.[88] However, was the *Hadrianum* even an accurate description of the rite as it was performed in Rome at the time, or was it a compilation or a summary produced by Hadrian, a document that simply laid out the most important features as the Pope understood them to be? At the very least it was a limited document covering only the main festivals, providing a clear indication that Hadrian did not really understand what Charlemagne was trying to do.[89] Further controversy surrounds the supplement. For a long time it was thought that this, along with a brief introduction explaining its purpose, was compiled by Alcuin of York. In recent years, however, scholars have moved away from this position, preferring to say that Benedict of Aniane, a monastic founder and reformer, assembled the supplement sometime between 810 and 815 during the reign of Charlemagne's successor.[90] Finally there is controversy as to what the Carolingian reformers actually intended local churches and monasteries to do with this new text, how closely they really expected the clergy to follow it. In practice, of course, the local churches and monastic foundations took the text as one among a number of sources that were merged to form a wide range of local variations, or they simply stuck to their older practices because the production of new books was simply too expensive. If the exercise was aimed at creating uniformity in worship across the whole of the Western Empire, then it clearly failed. Having said this, the *Hadrianum* and its supplement proved to be a very significant and influential document in the development of Western liturgy as a whole. By the middle of the ninth century, for example, texts based on this book were being used extensively throughout Western Europe and almost exclusively in Rome itself.[91]

One thing that is clear is that the liturgy used by churches, even before the production of the *Hadrianum*, was already beginning to become more uniform under the influence of texts from Rome. The Anglo-Saxon scholars and missionaries brought into the service of the Carolingian Empire had a lasting commitment for all things Roman, built on their

---

[87] Ibid., 80–92.   [88] Ibid., 81.   [89] Palazzo, *Liturgical Books*, 52.
[90] Vogel, *Medieval Liturgy*, 86.   [91] Palazzo, *Liturgical Books*, 54.

historical links to Rome through Gregory and Augustine. The conflict between the Catholic Franks and the Gothic and Visigothic Arians over the previous few centuries had also led to a natural deferral to Rome among Frankish leaders such as Charlemagne. It is not surprising, therefore, that forms of worship and specific prayers that had a noted connection with Rome were circulating quite widely within the Empire before Charlemagne made his request to the Pope. There is evidence that Charlemagne's father, Pepin III, had also attempted to unify the liturgical life of his empire by commissioning a Benedictine abbey to provide a standard version of what became known as the Frankish Gelasian Sacramentary.[92] This appears, however, to have had little impact and was soon superseded by the more successful reforms of his son. The influence of all these texts was so great, however, that the history of Western liturgy is generally seen to develop as a process of the exchange and transfer of texts between Rome and Northern Europe covering the period from the sixth to the eleventh century.[93]

The traditional liturgical history of the Western rite usually begins with reference to the collections of variable prayers for specific masses (*libelli missarum*) that were collected together by individuals and churches from the first half of the sixth century, at a time when 'the desire to collect all the documents of the Popes was manifesting itself in the Latin church'.[94] The most extensive collection of this kind is the *Veronensis*. This text contains many lists of prayers for use at different masses throughout the year from a wide variety of dates and sources. The copy of the manuscript that has been preserved comes from Verona although it is unclear where the text was compiled. The vast majority of the material that it contains, however, is Roman deriving from Papal worship and, Cyrille Vogel suggests, 'takes us back to the earliest prayer forms of the Roman liturgy'.[95] Many of these prayers appear in later sacramentaries, but the form and content of the *Veronensis*, especially its size, is unique.

As the libelli collections became more organised and the desire for texts from Rome grew, two further families of books developed. The first collections to reflect Roman usage were the Gelasian sacramentaries based on material that was probably drawn together in the seventh century.[96] All the Gelasian-type sacramentaries that have survived come from Northern Europe, and are combinations of Roman and local traditions. They contain a far wider range of prayers than the libelli, including some of the fixed prayers of the mass and other rites as well as the variable prayers for the

---

[92] Ibid., 47–8. [93] Vogel, *Medieval Liturgy*, 3. [94] Ibid., 43. [95] Ibid. [96] Ibid., 69.

year.[97] Liturgical scholars argue over the origins of the various elements of the text, but the general view is that the oldest strata of the documents reflect presbyteral (rather than Papal) practice in the titular churches of Rome and that they were brought to Gaul by individuals who had visited Rome on pilgrimage or for other purposes.[98] The second family of books derives from the Papal liturgy of the Lateran and the various stational churches, and these books are referred to as Gregorian sacramentaries. The *Hadrianum* is the most distinctive of these. Alongside the sacramentaries, however, we must also mention a second series of texts, the 'ordines'.[99] While the sacramentaries contain the texts of the prayers used, the ordines describe the ritual action. Most of the earliest ordines describe the action of the Papal liturgies and hence are extremely complex rites. How far these were ever performed in anything like an accurate fashion in the smaller churches of Northern Europe has to remain a matter for speculation. It is, however, highly likely that a great deal of adaptation was necessary even in the larger cathedrals and monasteries.[100]

In practice the various manuscripts that emerge from the later eighth and on into the ninth and tenth centuries are to a greater or lesser extent mixtures of material from the Gelasian and the Gregorian texts and in most cases either local or other, mainly monastic, material.[101] There is a certain uniformity to the overall shape or structure of the rites, to the liturgical year, and to the content and order of the books. Beyond this, however, there is still a considerable degree of diversity. It is only by going through all the remaining manuscripts that we have and comparing them closely that scholars have been able to build up a picture of the rite as a whole, rather than the rite that might have been used in one particular place at a particular time.

The very fact of writing these texts down, however, and the increasing speed and accuracy of the copyists from the monasteries enabled a growing sense of the desirability for, and even the possibility of, uniformity. This is one case where the changes in information technology of the time were leading to changes in the expectations in the production and presentation

---

[97] Palazzo, *Liturgical Books*, 42–4.

[98] Vogel, *Medieval Liturgy*, 64–78; Palazzo, *Liturgical Books*, 42–8.

[99] Vogel, *Medieval Liturgy*, 135–90.

[100] Alongside the books mentioned a number of other texts would have been needed for any particular act of worship, including books of readings, books of chants and books for other specific liturgical actors. Each of these showed a similar process of dissemination from Rome before being adapted in Northern Europe and brought back to Rome in a highly adapted form. The latter half of this story, however, will have to be told in the following chapter. See ibid., and Palazzo, *Liturgical Books*.

[101] It is clear that the librarians and other scholars of the time were conscious of the differences between these two kinds of books as the manuscripts are generally catalogued under different titles in library lists. Palazzo, *Liturgical Books*, 50.

of worship. Susan White explores this process in much more detail and sees this as one of the most significant driving factors for the growth and stabilisation of liturgical form at this time.[102] The need for uniformity across the Empire, therefore, was not the only pressure on the liturgy leading to a greater sense of uniformity. The ability to impose this uniformity would not have been possible without the greater technological ability that accompanied it. It would also have been impossible if the idea of a set pattern of liturgy had not already begun to emerge.

The real question, however, was not so much the factors that enabled the idea of a uniform liturgy across Western Europe to become a possibility, but more significantly why Charlemagne thought that it might be desirable. What was it about the idea of a uniform liturgy that made it appear attractive to an aspiring Western Emperor? In order to understand this we have to go back to the Christmas Coronation in Rome in the year 800. Owing to their links with Rome, over against the Arians, the Franks had always maintained some kind of contact with, or knowledge about, the emperors of Byzantium. Charlemagne himself was concerned about and, albeit at some distance, involved in the Iconoclast Debates that I have mentioned in the previous section. He was vehemently against all forms of iconoclasm and may even have seen some threat to Rome in the disputes that were going on in Constantinople. However, like the popes, Charlemagne saw an opportunity to make the best of Byzantine weakness during the disputes to assert his own authority in the West. It was, I would suggest, partly with an eye to the activities of the Eastern Empire that Charlemagne sought to provide a definitive, and specifically textual, form for the liturgy of the West.

One force that was growing at this time, and that probably had a much greater influence on the growing uniformity of the rite than has often been recognised, was the Benedictine order and its various offshoots. This grand monastic enterprise with its clear structure, unified pattern of life and sense of independence from both the church and the local secular powers began to have a very significant impact on the religious life of Western Europe from the ninth century onwards. Both the initial attempts at uniformity under Pepin and, in a less direct manner, the production of the supplement to the *Hadrianum* were undertaken within the framework of Benedictine growth and reform. The full impact of Benedictine influence, however, was

---

[102] White, *Technological Change*, 43. White does note, however, that the accuracy and commitment to direct reproduction was never that high in the monastic scriptoria.

not really to be felt for another hundred years or so, and I will come to look at some aspects of this influence in the following chapter.

If we were to ask, therefore, whether Charlemagne's policy actually worked, we might perhaps be asking the wrong question. At one level it clearly did not work. The variety of liturgical activity across the regions covered by the Empire was as diverse after the break-up of the Carolingian Empire as it had been before. The different local rites, especially in France, had certainly taken the Gregorian material seriously and integrated it into their everyday texts. However, each had done something different with it and they had maintained their diversity despite the introduction of this material. Beyond France, the evidence suggests that very little had actually changed. Also, the Carolingian Empire did not really last long enough in its original form for people to claim any real sense of identity with it, or with the material and intellectual culture that became associated with it. Following Charlemagne's death the Empire was broken up and it was some time before a new Holy Roman Empire was firmly established within the Germanic tribes. Regions such as Spain and Lombardy returned to their older identities and moved in a different direction in liturgical terms. However, a start had been made and many of the building blocks on which the Christian hegemony of Western Europe was to be built had been firmly laid. I now need to draw all these ideas together in order to make sense of the various arguments put forward in this chapter.

HEGEMONY, POWER AND LITURGY

All that I have said in this chapter implies that the decision of the ruling authorities to impose a particular ritual activity throughout their Kingdom or Empire has inevitably led to the hegemonic place of Christian discourse within that empire. This is, of course, far from the case, as we have seen more explicitly in the consequences of the collapse of the Carolingian Empire at the end of the tenth century. However, even at the height of the power of a particular Empire and even with the kind of control over the population that we have seen in the case of the Armenian Kingdom, there is no guarantee that the people who are forced to convert or to worship in a particular fashion are either going to take to it willingly, or, more importantly, are going to invest that liturgy with the same meanings as those in authority. This does not matter if the state can also control, to some extent at least, the popular understanding of the liturgy as it did in Byzantium. Such an undertaking is far from easy when the elite is situated at some distance from the majority of the population.

One way to explore this issue is to look at the Central European king-dom of Moravia in the ninth century. If Armenia was the first kingdom to be converted to Christianity, it was certainly not the last. Throughout Central and Northern Europe, kingdom after kingdom, or tribal group after tribal group, was Christianised through the conversion of the king or tribal chief leading to the forced conversion of the people, usually through the work of Anglo-Saxon or, later, German missionaries. The last such conversions in Europe were those of King Mindaugus of Lithuania and his people in 1251.[103] Moravia, a Slav principality, was one such state in which the conversion of the rulers led directly to the conversion of the people. The situation in Moravia, however, was not quite the same as that in many similarly converted kingdoms. Moravia held a position in the centre of Europe between the Frankish Empire to the west and the Byzantine Empire, with its Bulgarian satellite, to the east.[104] This meant that the state was being converted from both directions by two distinct churches, the Latin-speaking church based in Rome but staffed from Germany, and the Greek-speaking church based in Byzantium. This gave the rulers of Moravia an ideal opportunity to play one empire, and one church, off against another. This they managed to do with great success.

Part of this strategy can be demonstrated by the way in which Prince Ratislav approached the question of worship. There were two obvious choices open to him, either to worship in Greek or to worship in Latin. Both of these options would have tied the Moravian church, and with it the state, intimately to the forms and structures of one of the two larger empires. Prince Ratislav, however, was keen to explore the possibility of an independent national church. It was the Byzantine Emperor Michael III who was able to provide a way to do this through a third option in the form of two Greek scholars and diplomats, Constantine (later taking the name of Cyril when he joined a monastery fifty days before his death) and Methodius.[105] These two brothers came from the city of Thessalonica and were fluent in Slav languages as well as Greek. They had already been used by the Emperor as part of a mission to communities in the Northern Caucusus, where they had suggested that it might make sense if

---

[103] Even here it was not until 1414 that some areas of Lithuania and Latvia were finally 'converted'. K. Dowden, *European Paganism, The Realities of Cult from Antiquity to the Middle Ages*. London: Routledge, 2000, 12.

[104] The exact position of Greater Moravia in the ninth century is still a matter of scholarly debate. A.-E. N. Tachiaos, *Cyril and Methodius of Thessalonica, The Acculturation of the Slavs*. Crestwood: St Vladimir's Seminary Press, 2001, 57–60.

[105] See ibid., for many of the details of this mission.

the worship of this new Christian community were conducted in the local language. This was the same policy that, with the Emperor's blessing and Prince Ratislav's encouragement, they brought to Moravia. The only problem was that the Slav languages did not have a written text. The first task, therefore, was to create an alphabet and hence a text. Byzantine scholars had been working on this for some years, but it was Cyril who was to provide the first workable form of what was to become the Cyrillic script. Having developed a working alphabet, Cyril first translated the Evangelistary, or Gospel Book, of the liturgy into a Slav language. The rest of the liturgy followed, using the Byzantine rite as its model, and this became known as the Glagolitic Rite. The Byzantine Emperor Michael III presented the alphabet and the rite as a gift to Prince Ratislav, the ruler of Moravia, and therefore gained the upper hand in the long-running dispute with the German missionaries.

Despite having the liturgy in his own language, Ratislav and his successors continued to play the East off against the West, drawing Rome into the debate as a third player. The German missionaries, following an ancient tradition, claimed that Hebrew, Greek and Latin were the only sacred languages and that it was not possible to celebrate a liturgy in Slavonic. Cyril and Methodius went to Rome to defend their position of translating the liturgy and were hailed in Rome as important figures despite their Greek origins, primarily because they brought with then the relics of St Clement, the 'first Pope', which they had 'discovered' in the Crimea. Cyril died in Rome but Methodius went back to Moravia, and neighbouring Slav states, as Archbishop, this time under the authority of Rome. He continued to have trouble with the German missionaries, being imprisoned by them for two years, but he maintained his fundamental position that the liturgy could, and should, be celebrated in Slavonic and was constantly supported in this by both Rome and Byzantium. This also gave him an unassailable position among the Slav people themselves and helped, without a doubt, to establish the Christian discourse in a hegemonic position within those states.

This was not the last time that the question of language was raised in relation to the liturgy. The Eastern, Orthodox tradition developed by encouraging nations to worship in their own language, but Rome eventually went back to the principle that the language of the church was more important than the language of the people, and Latin remained the language of Western liturgy for many centuries to come. What we do see in this narrative, however, is the central position of textualisation in the imposition of a hegemonic Christian discourse. This is something that we have clearly seen in our discussion of both the Byzantine and the Western rite. While it is clear that in both these contexts, as well as that of the Slavs, literacy was limited to an elite, the very fact that the liturgy and other significant texts existed in literate forms gave them a legitimacy that drew on supernatural authority. The place of literacy within societies and the relationship between literacy, discourse and hegemony have, of course, changed dramatically over the centuries. In the closing years of the first Christian millennium, however, it is clear that there was a direct link between these factors that could not be ignored. In order to explore this further, and to see exactly how it relates to the process of the textualisation of liturgy, much more empirical and theoretical work needs to be done. There is an obvious area of study here that needs much more detailed investigation, but this is not the place to develop these ideas further, as we need to move on to another era and another context.

CHAPTER 4

The dominant discourse of cosmological Christianity, 900–1200

INTRODUCTION: DOMINANT DISCOURSES

As we have seen in the Introduction, discourse is a widely used word that does not have a clearly defined and commonly agreed meaning.[1] In this chapter I want to use the concept of a 'dominant discourse' as a way of expressing the nature of Christian language and thinking within most of the principal Christian societies at the turn of the first millennium.[2] For the first thousand years of their history Christians, or more specifically Christian authors and their literature, understood themselves primarily in opposition to more or less specified others. At its inception Christianity was, of course, a minority religion with a strong missionary zeal. Through the fourth to the seventh century, and within most of the late Roman Empire, Christianity was still battling with various forms of paganism for the hearts and minds of the people. During the following four hundred years the missionary activity of Christianity in Northern and Eastern Europe, the rise of Islam and the internal conflicts within Christianity itself maintained a sense of being one among many competing religious discourses. By the eleventh century, however, especially in Western Europe and, I would suggest, within parts of the Byzantine Empire, the sense of being on the defensive about Christianity had largely disappeared, and Christian discourse had a confidence and sense of 'rightness' that profoundly affected the way in which liturgy was performed and understood.

In using the idea of a 'dominant discourse' to describe the role of Christianity in society at this time I am attempting to find a concept that gets us beyond language. Certainly the language of much of Europe at the

---

[1] See p. 10 above.
[2] See p. 13 above for a discussion of the roots of this term in the work of Gerd Baumann (*Contesting Culture, Discourses of Identity in Multi-Ethnic London.* Cambridge: Cambridge University Press, 1996).

time was saturated with Christian imagery and concepts.[3] The impact of Christianity, however, went much further than this. Christianity was entirely taken for granted by the vast majority of the people who lived within this context. The society was Christian and Christianity was the society. The way in which the world was conceived was determined by Christian reflections, including the taken-for-granted nature of heaven, hell, purgatory, angels and the great chain of being. Art, architecture, music, politics, economics, the agricultural cycle, law, who could marry whom, and the very landscape – all were determined by self-consciously Christian modes of thought. Common sense, and the habitus that reflected it, was Christian in its unthinking ordinariness.[4]

What I have described here may be defined by some as 'culture'. It is certainly true that the culture of much of Europe in the eleventh century was Christian, but I want to say something more than this. I want to be both more precise and more wide-ranging. Culture in its common usage, and even in much anthropological usage, suggests something social, something visible and on the surface.[5] It is the way people do things. I want to suggest that Christianity permeated more deeply than this, into the very fabric of the way people thought of and perceived the world, the way they understood their being and their senses, the way the world was. This reflects, in my view, the absolute domination of a Christian discourse across most of Europe at the turn of the millennium. I also believe that it is in worship that we can see this domination, and the nature of the discourses themselves, most clearly. What is more, it is possible to argue that it was the nature of worship that defined and reinforced the nature of the dominant Christian discourses, and that will bring us back to some of the arguments already raised in the previous two chapters concerning Christianisation and hegemony.

Before looking at the detail of the analysis I need to make two caveats. First, we must realise that there was no one single Christian discourse that was common across Europe at this time. Clearly the Byzantine discourse was different from that of Western Christendom. However, it is also possible to show that a French discourse was different from a German,

---

[3] Even this language, however, had other roots in the philosophies of Aristotle and others, and drew on many local discourses.

[4] See pp. 16–17 above for a discussion of habitus and common sense.

[5] American 'cultural' anthropology from its roots in the writings of Franz Boas and A. L. Kroeber has always tried to include more than surface structures and activities, but this has only rarely been able to be expressed clearly in any study of real people. See T. Ingold, *Evolution and Social Life*. Cambridge: Cambridge University Press, 1986, 33–9.

Spanish or English one, that a noble discourse was significantly different from a peasant one, that a rural one was different from an urban one, that a male one was different from a female one and so on. We could go on and subdivide the discourses even as far as local towns and villages or particular guilds or religious orders. It is also the case that particular individuals may use more than one discourse throughout their lives, switching and changing between them as circumstances demand.[6] This, however, does not detract from the overall thesis in any way. This is a point that I will be returning to in more detail in the next chapter.

The second caveat concerns the place of Judaism within Europe and that of Islam at its edges. There was clearly a sense of otherness against which Christianity could be defined (the Cathars and other 'heretical' groups also contributed to this awareness of otherness from within an essentially Christian discursive field).[7] The difference that had emerged by the eleventh century, I would suggest, comes in the level of self-confidence of the Christian discourse within society. Christian discourse in the eleventh century did not need to define itself over and against these 'others'; rather, it defined the 'other' from within the context of Christianity. What is more, these others had increasingly to define their own discourses over and against that of Christianity. This, I would suggest, is significantly different from many earlier forms of Christian discourse.

Finally, I do need to say that I am not aiming to be too prescriptive in offering the eleventh century as the highpoint of domination of Christian discourse. Again, in different places and at different levels of society this highpoint was reached at different times, and the self-confidence and all-pervasiveness of the discourse may well have ebbed and flowed within different sections of the society. In making these claims I am simply attempting to provide a wider theoretical context within which to discuss the worship of the period, not to make hard and fast historical rules.

In the rest of the chapter I wish to begin by looking at the internal space of Russian Orthodox churches as illustrated by the church of St Sophia in Kiev. This will introduce the concept of 'cosmological' Christianity, a concept that both distinguishes Christian worship in this period from much that went before and is central to the dominance of the Christian discourse. Reading church buildings and the liturgy that they contain as a

---

[6] This is the point that Baumann was making of the people of Southwark who could switch between dominant and demotic discourses at will, what he called dual discursive competence. Baumann, *Contesting Culture.*

[7] Y. Stoyanov, *The Hidden Tradition in Europe, The Secret History of Medieval Christian Heresy.* London: Penguin, 1994.

microcosm of the cosmos is commonly thought to be specific to Eastern Christianities. However, I want to go on to look at the growth and special context of the liturgy at Salisbury in southern England to show that Western Latin worship also had aspects that can be defined as 'cosmological'. It is in this context that I will come back to the questions of 'dominant discourse' raised very briefly in this introduction. Finally, before my conclusion, I wish to look at two other contexts, beyond the bounds of what is normally thought of as 'Christendom', to see whether similar concepts and understandings can be seen here also. I will focus specifically on Georgia in the Caucasus and on Ethiopia, both of which had a flourishing Christian culture in or around the eleventh century.

THE CATHEDRAL OF KIEV AS A COSMOLOGICAL MAP

The kingdom of Rus, based in Kiev, was converted to Christianity in 988 although there is evidence of a Russian diocese from 867.[8] As with so many of the tribal groups of Europe, the official conversion of the kingdom was equated with the conversion of the royal family, and again, as in so many other situations, it was the women in the family who were converted first and who led their menfolk into the faith. Ol'ga, a Kievian princess, was baptised in Constantinople in or around 960. Vladimir, her son, accepted baptism in 988 only after, it is said, seeking advice on all the monotheistic religions of the kingdoms surrounding Kiev.[9] Worship appears to have played a very important part in this decision, as the chronicle recounting the conversion mentions the report of envoys to Constantinople who were taken to the liturgy in the Great Church. They say 'We knew not whether we were in heaven or earth, for surely there is no such splendour or beauty anywhere upon earth.'[10] Rus was at this time a small tribal grouping, part Slav and part Norse, that had come together around Kiev. For a couple of centuries it plays very little role in the wider history of Christianity. It took advantage of the Slav translations of the liturgy made for Moravia and Bulgaria[11] to adopt a liturgy in its own national language but had very little distinctive identity until the beginning of the decline of the Byzantine

---

[8] See J. Fennell, *A History of the Russian Church to 1448*. London: Longman, 1995 for more information on the origins and early growth of this church.

[9] Ibid., 31–4.

[10] Quoted in H. Wybrew, *The Orthodox Liturgy: The Development of the Eucharistic Liturgy in the Byzantine Rite*. Crestwood: St Vladimir's Seminary Press, 1996, 130. Most scholars, however, claim that the account in the chronicle is probably a later elaboration. See Fennell, *Russian Church*, 35–8.

[11] See pp. 117–19 above.

Empire in the early years of the second millennium. In time Rus, or Russia as it was to become, saw itself as the inheritor of the Byzantine mantle both in terms of the political domination of what remained of the Christian East and as defenders of the Orthodox Church. Moscow, the Russian capital from the fourteenth century, was seen to be the 'third Rome'.

By the early eleventh century Kiev was said to have over 400 churches, many built of wood, although this is undoubtedly a gross exaggeration.[12] One of the most significant factors about the early Russian churches in Kiev is just how closely contemporary Byzantine models were followed in terms of art, architecture and liturgy. In art and architecture, however, a significantly Russian slant was added from a very early date. The biggest and most significant churches of the city were eventually rebuilt of stone to Byzantine models and were decorated throughout in an essentially Byzantine style. The basic ground plan of these churches was a Greek cross inscribed in a rectangle and surmounted by a single dome over the crossing.[13] At the west end of the church was a narthex, or entrance porch, and at the east end were one or three apses, of which the central one contained the altar. Adjoining the sanctuary to the left was a recess, known as the *prothesis*, used for the preparation of the communion elements. A similar recess or room to the right served as a sacristy or robing room for the celebrants (the *diakonikon*). The sanctuary was originally set off from the nave by a low railing, which eventually evolved into the icon-ostasis that became particularly elaborate in later Russian architecture. This railing, and the later iconostasis, contained three doors, the middle one of which, known as the royal gate, was reserved solely for the celebrants. In front of the balustrade or screen there was a raised platform with lecterns, known as the *soleia*, which was used by readers and cantors. Galleries for women would have occupied the other three sides of the church, and the nave itself would have been unfurnished apart from benches around the edges for the old and infirm.

The new cathedral of Hagia Sophia in Kiev was begun by Vladimir's son Iaroslav in 1037 replacing an older wooden church, and was consecrated in 1061.[14] The original church differed from the Byzantine model by having five aisles and thirteen cupolas, or domes, symbolising Jesus and the apostles. It was claimed to be the only five-aisled church outside of the

[12] S. H. Cross, *Medieval Russian Churches*. Cambridge, MA: Medieval Academy of America, 1949, 11.
[13] See R. F. Taft, *The Byzantine Rite, A Short History*. Collegeville: Liturgical Press, 1992, 69.
[14] A. Poppe, 'The Building of the Church of St Sophia in Kiev', in A. Poppe, *The Rise of Christian Russia*. London: Variorum Reprints, 1982.

Holy Land, and no other Byzantine churches had as many domes.[15] The symbolism of the domes, however, was not unusual in Russian architecture, with seven-domed churches symbolising the seven New Testament orders of angels and other numbers having similar symbolic interpretations. It has been suggested that this pattern of domes was originally used in earlier wooden structures and subsequently transferred over into the stone buildings.[16] In all other respects St Sophia's was a typical Orthodox church. Having five aisles it had five apses, of which four served as chapels and the fifth – the larger central apse – contained the altar and sanctuary space. The central dome was over the principal crossing and this formed the most significant internal feature. Galleries existed to the south and north, and surrounding three sides of the church there was originally a one-storey arcade. The church was built of red granite fixed in pink cement.[17] The interior of the church would also have been covered in frescos. These were whitewashed during the seventeenth century but were uncovered in restoration work that began in 1848. During this restoration a series of brilliant mosaics in the apses and the cupola were also rediscovered and renewed.[18]

The decoration and distribution of images around St Sophia also follow closely on Byzantine models and norms. In the main cupola is a mosaic of Christ *Pantocrator*, Christ enthroned in majesty blessing the people below. He is surrounded by four archangels, and in the triangular sections between the domes and the arches supporting it are images of the four evangelists 'carrying the gospels to the four corners of the world'.[19] In the roof of the apse above the altar is a figure of the Virgin standing with arms raised in an *orans* pose. Samuel Cross says 'she typifies the church on earth and the eternal intercession of the Immaculate Mother'.[20] This image is of a calm matronly woman in purple standing alone, in her red slippers, against a gold background, with her arms raised in supplication. Below this is a mosaic of the eucharist and, on either side of the arch of the apse, images of the Archangel Gabriel and the Virgin at the annunciation. Many of the frescos in the main body of the church are of saints and stories from the Old and New Testaments. To either side of the nave are images of the founders of the church. Prince Iaroslav and his sons are portrayed in procession on the north wall of the central square of the church; while on the south side

---

[15] Cross, *Russian Churches*, 11.
[16] The first wooden church of St Sophia in Novgorod, which was burnt down in 1045, also had thirteen *vierkhi*, which some people translate as cupolas. Ibid., 12.
[17] This, and the whole of the original structure, has since been encapsulated in a later building finished in the usual white plaster of the Russian Baroque.
[18] Cross, *Russian Churches*, 12.   [19] Ibid., 13.   [20] Ibid.

are his wife Irene and their daughters carrying candles. The family is heading for the west wall where an image of their ancestors Ol'ga and Vladimir on either side of an enthroned Christ once existed. Beyond this wall, in the narthex, were the tombs of the early Christian princes of Kiev.[21] Finally, outside the main church, and up the stairs to the gallery are frescos of hunting scenes and Christmas celebrations in the Hippodrome of Constantinople. It is thought that these staircases once connected the church to the palace of the bishops.[22]

The whole of this space was given symbolic meaning and was seen by the people as a microcosm of the Cosmos itself.[23] The dome at the heart of the church represented heaven with Christ in majesty blessing his people. Below them were the evangelists with books in their hands, 'symbolising the enlightenment of their teaching'.[24] On the church columns were the warrior-martyrs, 'by whose labours faith was fortified'.[25] In the nave the donors symbolised the earthly element and the people on the ground reflected the church and the world as it is. Dimitrii Likhachev takes this principle further by relating the church building to the human person: 'the church was a microcosm, while at the same time representing a macro-personality: it had a head, and beneath the head were the "neck and shoulders" of the column supports. The windows were the eyes of the church (this is shown in the etymology of the word *okno*). Over the eyes were the brows.'[26] Many different symbolisms were possible but the all-embracing sense was of a space designed to represent heaven on earth and to be the meeting place between earth and heaven.

The iconostasis, introduced in a formal sense in the twelfth to fourteenth centuries, came to be seen as the symbolic boundary between earth and heaven within the church. It takes the form of a series of icons in layers from the ground to the ceiling, three layers in most Byzantine churches but rising to five in Russia by the fifteenth century, and going up to eight by the seventeenth century.[27] These icons have a set form that is repeated in

[21] N. Teteriatnikov, 'The Role of the Devotional Image in the Religious Life of Pre-Mongol Rus', in W. C. Brumfield and M. M. Velimirovic (eds.), *Christianity and the Arts in Russia*. Cambridge: Cambridge University Press, 1991, 30–45, 35.
[22] Cross, *Russian Churches*, 14.   [23] Taft, *Byzantine Rite*, 35–6.
[24] T. Vladyshevskaia, 'On the Links between Music and Icon Painting in Medieval Rus', in Brumfield and Velimirovic, *Christianity and the Arts*, 14–29, 16.
[25] Ibid., 15–16.
[26] V. D. Likhacheva and D. S. Likhachev, 'Khudozhestvennoe nasledie drevnei Rusi i sovremennost' (Leningrad, 1971, 54), quoted in Vladyshevskaia, 'Music and Icon Painting', 15.
[27] M. Cheremeteff, 'The Transformation of the Russian Sanctuary Barrier and the Role of Theophanes the Greek', in A. Leong (ed.), *The Millennium: Christianity and Russia (AD 988–1988)*. Crestwood: St Vladimir's Seminary Press, 1990, 107–24.

church after church. There may be some local variations depending on the patron saint of the church or the presence of local saints who need to be commemorated, but the basic structure of the images is always the same. To the right of the main doors, at the centre of the screen, is the image of Christ, to the left is the *Theotokos*, the image of Mary. On the same layer of the screen are icons representing the patron saints of the church and the feasts commemorating the life of Christ. Above this is a row of local and national saints. Above this, the apostles, and at the very top of the screen are icons of the angels. Like the church as a whole, this structure is also seen as something akin to a map of heaven, with the angels at the top, the apostles beneath them and then the ordinary saints. This represents the hierarchy that is believed to exist as a fundamental part of the structure of the universe.

As well as the space itself reflecting the meeting of earth and heaven, the liturgy, as performed within that space, was seen to make that meeting a reality. The singing of the liturgy in particular reflected this merging of heaven and earth. According to Byzantine tradition the singing of the chants of the liturgy not only reflects, but also imitates, the singing of the angels. What is more the angels themselves are understood to partake in the singing, to be present at the worship and to be among the most tangible forms of the relationship between earth and heaven. This simultaneous worship and chant by both the human and the angelic world is reflected in the texts of many hymns and in icons such as that of the 'Intercession of the Mother of God' and others.[28]

The liturgy of the eucharist was also interpreted to reflect the life and Passion of Jesus. Over the centuries in Constantinople commentaries on the liturgy had been written providing a spiritual and symbolic interpretation of every action and event, as we have seen in the previous chapter.[29] The most famous of these were eventually incorporated into the texts of the liturgy itself and were exported, with the liturgy, to the churches of Russia and other Orthodox communities. The incarnation, including the crucifixion, the resurrection and the ascension, was seen as the point at which heaven and earth met most profoundly and in which the permanent links between the two were made. To recreate that moment in the liturgy, therefore, was the ultimate goal. The liturgy expressed this dramatically through its texts and also through a series of movements from the space behind the iconostasis to the nave and back again.[30]

---

[28] Vladyshevskaia, 'Music and Icon Painting', 16.
[29] Wybrew, *Orthodox Liturgy*, see also pp. 105–7 above.   [30] Taft, *Byzantine Rite*, 72–3.

By the eleventh century the liturgy of the Great Church in Constantinople had reached the height of its elaboration, and the understanding of the rite, as contained in the commentaries, was all but fixed. It was this rite that was being exported to, and increasingly imposed on, the churches within the Byzantine orbit and it was this rite, with its interpretation, that was taken up by Russia.[31] The liturgy was preceded by the preparation of the bread and wine at the table to the north of the sanctuary area. This involved the priest in a process of stabbing the bread with a ceremonial spear and then cutting it in a systematic and highly symbolic fashion. The liturgy would then begin with the opening chants, seen to be the prophetic foretelling of Jesus, and leading into the first, little, entrance of the clergy through the north door of the screen and round to the central doors. This represented the coming of Christ into the world in the incarnation. The readings, the sermon and the prayers followed. At this point the great entrance took place as the bread was brought in procession through the north door of the iconostasis and round the nave before coming back through the central doors to the main altar of the church. This was seen to represent Christ's journey to Jerusalem and his entry into the city on Palm Sunday. The doors of the iconostasis were closed and the anaphora was said by the clergy beyond. This was interpreted in relation to the crucifixion and the resurrection, as the consecration of the elements was seen to be a process of breathing life back into them and bringing them back to life within the church. It was the life-giving body that was received by the people, not the dead flesh of Jesus. Communion, therefore, acted as the final movement of the liturgy with the chants after communion being seen in relation to the ascension.[32]

What is important to note here was the way in which the liturgy was interpreted in terms of a dramatic re-enactment of the life of Jesus. That very re-enactment was the action that made that life a reality for the people taking part and their role was to be caught up into that life through the actions of the liturgy. There was little if any active participation by the congregation in the actions of the liturgy itself, except to pray, to adore and on occasion to receive communion. The liturgy was seen to be an end in itself, a means for achieving the unity of heaven and earth, the action that enables people to touch heaven even if only for a moment. The liturgy took on cosmic proportions. It was done because it had to be done, not because there was any specific benefit for those who took part. This attitude was also taken over into the other worship of the church as the round of offices

[31] Wybrew, *Orthodox Liturgy*, 129–30.   [32] Ibid., 182–3.

was matched to the round of the sun during each day, and the round of the seasons over the year. The celebrating of the liturgy was a way, the primary way for most, of tuning in to the cycle of the world and the way in which the world was. It was a means of entering into the cosmic pattern of creation.[33]

For some, however, it was more than this. It was a way not just of enabling a meeting between heaven and earth, but of becoming one with heaven. It was a way of bringing the earthly into the heavenly realm, of making the mundane and the ordinary into something special, something cosmic. This was particularly true of the human participant. The liturgy was seen as providing a channel by which the ordinary human person could partake in the life of heaven, or more specifically in the life of Christ. This was part of a process that the Orthodox described as 'deification' or *theosis*: bringing the life of the individual on earth into union with the life of Christ in heaven, entering into Christ and becoming one with him.[34] The sense of a mystical union between Christ, creation and the individual human being has been a far more significant element of the Eastern way of thinking than it ever was in the West. It originated in the monastic traditions where contemplation and solitary prayer were focused on the achievement of deification, but soon spread into the ordinary churches and into the way of thinking of many, if not all, Orthodox lay people. This kind of mysticism became particularly strong within the spirituality of the Russian church and was developed by a long line of thinkers from the fourteenth century on.[35] It is also a process that is central to the specifically Russian understanding of the liturgy.

SALISBURY AS A POWERHOUSE OF FAITH

When we move to the Western church we can see many of the same kinds of features that we have already identified in the East. It is possible, for example, to see the cruciform shape of the Western cathedral as in some senses a map of the cosmos, this time mapped onto the body of the crucified Christ. We can also see devotional literature that presents the mass as a re-enactment of the crucifixion and the sacrificial act of Christ's

---

[33] See N. Arseniev, *Russian Piety*. London: Faith Press, 1964, 28–47 and J. Meyendorff, *The Orthodox Church, Its Past and its Role in the World Today*. Crestwood: St Vladimir's Seminary Press, 1981, 190–207.

[34] V. Lossky, *In the Image and Likeness of God*. London: Mowbray, 1974.

[35] V. Lossky, *The Mystical Theology of the Eastern Church*. Napierville: Allenson, 1957.

death.[36] The mystical element is not really present in Western thought until some two hundred years later, but the principles are already beginning to develop.[37] In the Western church, however, we can perhaps go a little bit further than we were able to do in Kiev. We have far more information; many more texts survive concerning the management of cathedrals and the organisation of worship. We can also see the Western cathedral within its wider socio-political context more easily than we can in the East, and trace the impact of the close association between church and state. In order to investigate this further, therefore, I wish to focus on the cathedral at Salisbury in southern England, and what became known as the Sarum rite.

Salisbury is an interesting place to look at in detail. This is first because we have a very wide range of material from different periods of the history of the church.[38] Secondly, it is because Salisbury was a secular cathedral and did not have to conform in any direct way to any monastic order in terms of its worship or organisation. Finally, it is because the liturgy that was developed at Salisbury became the standard rite for much of the rest of England and was extremely influential in Archbishop Cranmer's revision of the English rite at the Reformation. Other cathedrals in England originally had their own rites, which varied in minor details from that of Salisbury, and the monastic foundations clearly followed monastic practices. Sarum, however, had royal approval and, because of its inherently secular nature, was used very widely in parish and collegiate churches across the country. It was this rite, therefore, that became the archetypal English liturgy.[39]

The bishop's seat in the region under the Saxon rulers had been at Sherborne in Dorset, and the bishop had also been Abbot of the Benedictine monastery at Sherborne.[40] Following the invasion of the

---

[36] M. Rubin, *Corpus Christi, The Eucharist in Late Medieval Culture.* Cambridge: Cambridge University Press, 1991, 106–8.

[37] D. Turner, *The Darkness of God, Negativity in Christian Mysticism.* Cambridge: Cambridge University Press, 1995.

[38] See the 'Introduction' to W. H. Frere, *The Use of Sarum, vol. I. The Sarum Customs as set forth in the Consuetudinary and Customary, The Original Texts edited from the Mss. With an Introduction and Index.* Cambridge: Cambridge University Press, 1898, x–lviii.

[39] The place of the Sarum rite in the history of English liturgy goes well beyond the Reformation, as it was picked up again during the later nineteenth century by those who wanted a Catholic liturgy that was not Roman. There was a strong movement to re-establish elements of the Sarum rite in Anglican liturgical use. See M. Dalby, *Anglican Missals and their Canons: 1549, Interim Rite and Roman.* Cambridge: Grove Books, 1998.

[40] For a brief summary of this history see P. Baxter, *Sarum Use, The Development of a Medieval Code of Liturgy and Customs.* Salisbury: Sarum Script, 1994.

Normans, William, the new king, set about a major reorganisation of the English church. William knew the importance that was attached to the authority of the church and had gained the blessing of the Pope before setting out on his invasion. He also headed to Canterbury before marching to London after winning the battle at Hastings. We can see here the use of a dominant discourse of Christianity playing a central role in the legitim-ation of William's claims. The reorganisation of the church was part of the same process, and within William's ecclesiastical reorganisation in 1075 the episcopal seat of Sherborne was moved to a hill fort some ten miles north of the current town of Salisbury called Sarisberie or Sarum. The fort was already on land controlled by the Bishop of Sherborne and here a castle and a cathedral were built within the grounds of the old fort. This site was close to the royal palace and hunting lodge at Clarendon and hence retained a central role within the running of the country for much of the following century.

The Saxon Bishop and Abbot of Sherborne was transferred to the new diocese at Sarum in 1075 and remained in post for a couple of years.[41] He probably brought some of the monks and their liturgical practices from Sherborne with him, although he would also have been influenced by the traditions of the Norman church. The first liturgy in Sarum, therefore, would have been a mixture of Saxon (that is Roman with some Celtic elements), Benedictine and Norman styles.[42] In 1078 William appointed his kinsman Osmund to the see, the first of only three bishops who were to hold office in Sarum for the next hundred years. This established a level of stability that was central to the growth of the Sarum rite. What is more, all three of these bishops were political appointments and entirely uncon-nected to the monastic institutions, so setting a strong secular tradition within the development of the worship and organisation of the church. Each of the bishops also added their own layer of organisation and liturgical development that can be traced in the various extant manuscripts still kept by the cathedral.

Following the completion of the cathedral in 1092 Osmund prepared a charter that allowed for a dean, three archdeacons and between thirty and thirty-five canons.[43] These canons were each endowed with money from land owned by Osmund or the cathedral and were commissioned to sing the offices and say the masses in the cathedral. In Osmund's cathedral a semi-circular apse provided the space for the meeting of the officers of the cathedral, with Osmund on the chair at the east end and the dean and

[41] Ibid., 10.   [42] Ibid.   [43] Frere, *Sarum Use*, xiv–xv.

canons to either side. The high altar was placed in front of the apse and would have been surrounded by candles (nothing being allowed to rest on the altar itself at this time). Above the altar would have been a beam on which the relics were kept and from the beam a pyx containing the reserved sacrament would have hung over the altar.[44]

Osmund's successor, Roger of Caen, took on significant posts within the government, rising eventually to being vice-regent to King Henry I.[45] Because of his governmental duties Roger developed the hierarchy of the cathedral by appointing four officers to overlook the running of the building and the worship. The dean remained the principal officer. Then there was a precentor to take control of music and worship, a chancellor to look after the business of the cathedral, including the choir school, and a treasurer to take charge of finances.[46] Bishop Roger also adapted the east end of the cathedral, removing the apse and adding a rectangular structure and increasing the size of the choir. This also meant that he had to add a separate chapter house for the canons and officers to meet to undertake their business. Roger fell out of favour with Henry's successor Stephen, and Stephen confiscated the Castle at Old Sarum and threw Roger into prison. Finally Jocelin de Bohun succeeded Roger in 1139, built himself a new palace in the grounds of the old fort and prepared a series of texts on the organisation of the cathedral including an *Institucio* and an early form of what became the *Consuetudinary*.[47] Jocelin died in 1189 and the next couple of bishops began the process of moving the cathedral to its new site in the valley below the fort.

Most of the scholarship on the Sarum rite has tended to look at the library of books that was developed over time within the cathedral and its precincts and to treat each book as a distinct text or as part of a historical sequence.[48] One major concern has been to show the earlier influences of French texts on the Sarum rite and then, subsequently, to see how the Sarum rite influenced Cranmer and those who came after him. Other scholars are interested in the way in which Sarum differs from other English and French rites and many are interested in the details of specific prayers and orders of worship.[49] What we must do, however, if we wish to

---

[44] Baxter, *Sarum Use*, 14.   [45] Ibid., 16.   [46] Ibid. Frere, *Sarum Use*, xv.

[47] Baxter, *Sarum Use*, 20–2.

[48] See for example the way in which Frere presents the texts in *Sarum Use*.

[49] See for example E. Bishop, 'Holy Week Rites of Sarum, Hereford and Rouen Compared', in E. Bishop, *Liturgica Historica, Papers on the Liturgy and Religious Life of the Western Church*. Oxford: Oxford University Press, 1918, 276–300. For a more recent and somewhat different approach see A. Dawtry, 'The Decline of the Cult of Old English Saints in Post-Conquest England: A Case of

gain a picture of what the liturgy of the cathedral actually looked and felt like, is not to take each book one at a time, but rather to bring them all together and to try to gain an overall picture of the worshipping life of the cathedral. If we begin to do this then the first thing that will strike us is the sheer quantity of worship-related material that is available. Everything is carefully controlled and noted in one book or another, but it is only when we bring the whole together that we begin to see just how much was going on, even on an ordinary weekday, not to mention Sundays or feast days.

If we try to follow through an average kind of day then we must note two kinds of liturgical activity that are standard for every day of the year. The first is the cycle of offices, beginning just before dawn and lasting through to the evening. These offices derived from the original daily worship of the church as it interacted with the monastic round of prayer.[50] The form of office that became standard in the Western churches by the turn of the first millennium was heavily influenced by Benedictine monastic spirituality. By this date all clergy would be expected to say the seven offices of the monastic order, usually privately and within their own parish churches. At a cathedral or large church, such as Salisbury, the offices would be sung in choir with a permanent group of singers and a regular clergy. The canons appointed by Osmund were established primarily for the purpose of providing a choir for the regular recitation of the office. As the post of 'canon', and the 'prebend' or income that went with it, was increasingly offered on an honorary basis to non-residents such as the abbots of Bec and Montebourg in Normandy, the canons were expected to provide vicars choral to take their place in the daily office.[51] Each office would also involve some element of ritual activity, either a procession through the church or a censing of the altar and other significant points around the sanctuary. The core of the office, however, was the singing of psalms and canticles with readings and prayers.[52]

The *Consuetudinary* for the cathedral outlines the rota by which each canon knew whose turn it was to lead each office.[53] The canons would sit in order in choir, each individual placed within a very strict hierarchy. Minor orders and choristers would also form part of the regular personnel and would be expected to be present for all worship within the cathedral. For most of the offices the clergy would stand, as would any members of the

Norman Prejudice or of Liturgical Reform?' in M. Dudley (ed.), *Like a Two-Edged Sword, The Word of God in Liturgy and History, Essays in Honour of Canon Donald Gray.* Norwich: The Canterbury Press, 1995, 61–8.

[50] R. F. Taft, *The Liturgy of the Hours in East and West, the Origins of the Divine Office and its Meaning for Today.* Collegeville: The Liturgical Press, 1986.

[51] Baxter, *Sarum Use,* 20.   [52] Taft, *Liturgy of the Hours,* 211–13.   [53] Frere, *Sarum Use.*

laity who happened to gather in the nave. Clergy would wear thick robes, white surplices and, for most of the year, heavy cloaks with hoods.[54] It would have been very cold within the church for much of the year and there was no regular heating. There was no procession at the beginning of an office and the clergy would have gathered informally either before or during the singing of the office itself.

The day would begin with Mattins just before dawn, followed immediately by Lauds.[55] This would be followed through the day by the minor offices of Prime, Terce, Sext and Nones. The day would then conclude with Vespers, or 'Evensong' as it came to be known at Sarum. Compline, which is not one of the seven prescribed offices, would also be sung just before dusk. Each day would be the same except for festivals and Sundays, although there were a considerable number of these (182 in the Sarum Kalendar) and a highly elaborate hierarchy of special days was established. On these days the same offices would be sung but the number of psalms and antiphons sung during the office, as well as the number of readings, would be increased, and the level of ritual and ceremonial associated with each service, especially Mattins and Vespers, would be far more elaborate. On some feasts through the year there would also be a vigil lasting into the night, or beginning very early on the morning of the feast. On ordinary days the singing of the offices may have taken a couple of hours in total; on principal feasts and Sundays this could very easily be doubled or tripled as nine lessons with full psalmody and extensive processions came into play.

Following Terce there would be a meeting of the chapter followed by the main celebration of the eucharist within the cathedral.[56] Once again a canon would be designated to celebrate mass formally each day and the entire choir and clergy would be expected to attend. On most days the ritual of the mass would be fairly limited, but again on Sundays and feast days it would be highly elaborate, involving a wide range of clergy and other officiates. The preparation for the mass would begin before Terce with the blessing of water and salt on the steps of the rood at the west end of the choir.[57] The altars and statues within the choir would be sprinkled in blessing. A procession would then leave the choir by the north door and move clockwise round the inside of the cathedral sprinkling all the altars on the way. It would go down the south aisle and up the centre of the nave to

---

[54] Baxter, *Sarum Use*, 42.   [55] Ibid., 59.   [56] Ibid., 53.
[57] The full English translation of the 1526 edition of the rite can be found in F. E. Warren, *The Sarum Missal in English*. London: A. R. Mowbray & Co., 1913. While there were clearly changes in the rite between 1000 and 1500, the basic structure remained the same.

the west front of the choir where the rood screen was set up. Here the celebrant would conduct the bidding prayers in English before entering the choir.[58] Some of the clergy would then go to bless the priests' cemetery and others would go to the sacristy to prepare for the mass, and those who remained would sing Terce. The mass itself, with full choir and ceremonial, could take up to two hours, or even longer on festivals, and immediately following the mass the clergy would begin the office of Sext.

This brings us to the second cycle of rituals that took place within the cathedral each day. Not only was there one main mass, usually celebrated at the high altar at the east end of the cathedral. Each of the canons in residence, and any other priests associated with the cathedral, were all expected to celebrate their own masses.[59] A communal rite where all the clergy concelebrated was unheard of at this time and so each of the clergy had to celebrate their own mass at an appropriate time at one of the chapels or smaller altars of the cathedral. However, as it was a rule that only one mass could be celebrated at any one altar each day, there was a proliferation of altars around the cathedral. These masses would be said rather than sung, and were usually attended by a single server. The priest and server would leave the sacristy in procession, arrive at their designated altar, celebrate mass and then return. It was at these masses that the clergy and those members of the laity who so wished would receive communion. The whole event would probably take less than half an hour.

There may have been as many as twenty such masses each day, all of which would have had to be said before the main mass following Terce. What this meant in practice, therefore, was that throughout the morning there would be a continuous sequence of masses being said, often more than one at a time. There would inevitably have been continuous movement throughout this time; small processions leaving the sacristy or returning to it at regular intervals through the morning, and the quiet mumbling of Latin at a range of altars throughout the cathedral. This along with the daily singing of the office meant that at any one time, especially during the morning, if a member of the public were to wander into the cathedral, some form of worship would be going on somewhere and in some way.

What I have described so far is what might be called the formal or official worship of the cathedral. Other members of the public would be using the

---

[58] T. Bailey, *The Processions of Sarum and the Western Church*. Toronto: Pontifical Institute of Medieval Studies, 1971, 13–16.

[59] A number of the canons and minor clergy would have had responsibilities at other churches served by the cathedral and may well have said their masses in these other churches.

building for many other purposes. Whether courts or fairs actually took place within a building such as the cathedral at Old Sarum is difficult to determine; we certainly have records of this kind of activity taking place in similar buildings across Europe. What I am thinking about here, however, were the more devotional activities as individuals came in to pray and light candles or to fulfil vows of one sort or another. Sarum, like so many cathedrals, was also a site of pilgrimage. There was no formal shrine until that of St Osmund was set up in the new cathedral at Salisbury. However, an altar was dedicated to St Thomas Becket within a few years of his death in 1170 and this must have attracted considerable devotion, as did his main shrine at Canterbury.[60] Other images and shrines within the cathedral would also have drawn their own devotees. Some of the pilgrims may have arrived as part of a party and would move through the cathedral in an official pattern with prayers, masses and other devotions being conducted at set intervals.[61] Others would arrive alone and pass through the nave of the church up to the shrine of their choice for private devotions, perhaps taking in a mass as it was happening on the way. Once again, therefore, this kind of devotion adds to the overall sense of movement and activity taking place within the cathedral day in and day out.

On feast days, however, and during the major festivals of the church's year everything would be increased manifold and the cathedral would be a hive of constant activity. The various books used for the saying of the liturgy outline a whole series of distinct rituals that were to take place on and around the high festivals.[62] The offices would be expanded with further psalms and antiphons, as I have already indicated. The canons would probably all be in attendance and involved in the worship in different ways. The best copes and other vestments would be used and the whole church would be decorated for the feast. The colours of the vestments and the hangings within the cathedral would change with the season, so creating a visual sense of the changes of the year. Sarum had its own distinctive 'use' in terms of liturgical colours that was derived in part from its Anglo-Saxon roots.[63] By contrast with many other cathedrals of the time, Sunday was given a distinctive feel with red vestments outside of the main festivals.[64] Lent would also have been very distinctive, with the

[60] Baxter, *Sarum Use*, 21.
[61] See R. C. Finucane, *Miracles and Pilgrims, Popular Beliefs in Medieval England*. London: J. M. Dent & Sons, 1977 for later discussions on pilgrimages in England.
[62] See for example the texts quoted in Bailey, *Processions*.
[63] W. S. Hope and E. G. C. F. Atchley, *English Liturgical Colours*. London: SPCK, 1918.
[64] Most other uses at this time would have had green vestments outside of festivals. Ibid., 162.

veiling of statues and crosses in unbleached cloth from the very first Sunday of Lent, unlike other uses where veiling, usually in red or purple, would have only happened from Passion Sunday. On the highest festivals, Easter, Christmas and so on, the colour of the vestments gave way to jewels and embroidery that lent a richness and opulence to the proceedings that would have thrilled all those present.

Within the texts are also short dramatic interludes that were to be said or more usually sung within the round of worship, often by boys from the choir.[65] The texts specify both what was to be sung and where it was to be sung, whether on the altar steps, from the rood loft or at the great west door. Each of these short dramatic elements added something distinctive to the feast and illustrated an important part of the wider narrative of salvation. They were not dramas as such; those may have been performed outside in the cathedral grounds. Rather, they were liturgical elements that attempted a brief dramatisation of a particular story. Each element, therefore, added something new to the whole, and the experience of the day would have been one of constant music and light as services merged into each other from dawn to dusk.

What is important to note, however, through all these different liturgical activities is the role of the laity. The vast majority of the worship that was taking place within the cathedral would have been conducted without a congregation of any sort. Even the high masses of the primary festivals did not need a congregation for their performance, although the laity were obliged to attend. The people came into the building to be caught up in the constant round of the worship. Men would have stood on the south side of the nave and women on the north, with their heads veiled. Only the infirm would have sat on the benches around the walls. They may not have stayed for the whole service and they would certainly have moved around and engaged in conversation during the liturgies. They probably did not understand exactly what was going on (although familiarity would have given many of them a very fair idea). The members of the congregation were, to a very large extent, spectators to the main event. It is very unlikely, however, that they were simply passive.

There is considerable evidence that ordinary lay people had a profound and active devotional life.[66] For those who were educated, books of devotion were beginning to become available by the end of the twelfth century. For ordinary lay folk the images and statues adorning the cathedral itself would have provided their own form of prayer book. All churches at this time

---

[65] Bailey, *Processions*, 12–26.   [66] Rubin, *Corpus Christi*, 98–108.

would have been brightly painted. It was not just the windows that provided images. The walls themselves would have been covered with frescos, often with a less rigid scheme than those found in Russia. For example, the chancel arch 'was viewed as the great door of heaven, and so naturally had displayed above and around it the drama of the Last Judgement, as intervening between Time and Eternity, or between this world and the next'.[67] Most of the paintings would have been of stories from the life of Christ, representations of liturgical feasts, or the legends of the saints. Other images such as the virgin and child or the Jesse Tree (a family tree of Jesus) were also traditional.[68] These would provide the focus for the devotion of the people, as would statues of individual saints and shrines containing the relics of other saints or perhaps of the true cross or some similar item.

More important than these acts of devotion to individual images or statues was the way in which individuals immersed themselves into the life of the church through the understanding of the mass. As with the Eastern tradition of the liturgy as a re-enactment of the life, death and resurrection of Jesus, so the Western mass was also understood as a re-enactment of the crucifixion.[69] Different elements of the rite were associated in devotional material with different points of the Passion narrative and the individual was able to become present at the Passion in all its glory by being present at the mass. The evidence suggests that this was very important to people at the time. Attendance at mass was high, but more than that, the pictorial evidence suggests that people did not keep a safe distance, engaged in private devotions in the centre of the nave.[70] Rather they began to move forward, to crowd around the sanctuary and the altar in order to see and to be present at the action. In the later years of the first millennium eucharistic devotion had not developed in the highly elaborated forms that it was to take from the twelfth century onwards. Elements such as the elevation of the host or specific devotion to the bread and wine did not come in until much later.[71] It was still the case, however, that the mass was the most important ritual act conducted within the cathedral and was still the principal focus for the devotion of the laity.

Finally, as with the liturgy of the cathedral, so with personal devotion: people would become tuned to the cycle of the year. In so many ways this

[67] E. W. Tristram, *English Medieval Wall Painting, the Twelfth Century*. New York: Hacker Art Books, 1988, 9.
[68] Ibid.   [69] Rubin, *Corpus Christi*, 106–8.   [70] Ibid.
[71] Ibid. For a discussion of the development of eucharistic devotion through the Middle Ages see C. W. Bynum, *Holy Feast, Holy Fast, The Religious Significance of Food to Medieval Women.* Berkeley: University of California Press, 1987, 48–69.

cycle of rites mirrored and highlighted the cycle of the seasons and the crops. Many of the extra rites, and particularly the processional elements that became part of the liturgy, had their origins in agriculture and the need to bless and to bring the crops before God. The presence of the Christmas celebrations in the depths of the winter, the association of Lent with the last days of want before the first harvests could begin again in the spring, and the association of Easter with the new life of nature were expressed in many of popular rituals of the seasons. The rogationtide processions on the three days before Ascension were perhaps most closely associated with the agricultural cycle.[72] These processions had their origins in late Roman Gaul and were widely established by the beginning of the tenth century. The later Sarum processionals indicated a procession in which the entire staff and congregation of the cathedral came out into the town, going to the north of the cathedral on the Monday and to the south on the Tuesday.[73] There is no doubt that something similar would have occurred from the old cathedral at Old Sarum, probably taking in some of the fields and crops as well. The whole round of liturgies reflected both the dependence of ordinary people on the agricultural cycle and the perceived need for this liturgical activity in order for the crops to grow, for the cattle to fatten and for all to be well with the world. The two were intimately connected and one could not be seen to happen without the other.

It is this that I am referring to when I want to talk about the worship of the church at the turn of the first millennium as 'cosmological Christianity'. The Christian community had come a long way from the small group of Spirit-filled individuals meeting in Corinth under Paul's leadership. Here was a Christianity that spoke less about individual conversion and concerns about the end of the world, and more about the maintenance of the world and being drawn up into the glory of God. If we were to ask the citizens of Salisbury in 1100 what their worship was about they would be hard pressed to provide an answer that went beyond the rote learning of the catechism. However, if we were to push them, they would probably begin to talk about the need to worship, the importance of the worship for the maintenance of the world. They would say that this is what God desires, that we are here to worship God, that the representation of the mass, the crucifixion of Christ, is the deepest mystery in all creation.

The kind of approach to the worship of God in a cathedral such as Salisbury is much the same as the approach to the worship of the gods of Egypt at Harnack or the gods of the Aztecs at Mexico City. This is worship

---

[72] Bailey, *Processions*, 25.   [73] Ibid.

undertaken by a clerical elite, worship with fully detailed and carefully controlled ceremonial and ritual, worship whose sole function is the maintenance of the world as it is. Without this worship, demanded of us by God, then the whole of creation would groan and grind to a halt. Along with this cosmological understanding of worship came a sense of the punishment of God in plagues and famine, a close link between the fortunes of the nation and the worship of the people, and a realisation of the vagaries of nature. All of creation is brought into the worship and that worship provides the powerhouse of faith that maintains the world in its course.

It was not just Sarum that acted to maintain this kind of cosmic worship. Sarum was just one of many cathedrals across Western and Eastern Europe where similar understandings were expressed. Even each and every parish church, in its own way, was seen to be part of something much larger, part of a cycle of nature and part of the power and beauty of God expressed to the people. Some places, such as the great pilgrimage shrines of Rome, Compostela and Canterbury, became even more important and a focus for cosmic intervention, and acted as magnets for people from across the Continent. They were, in a true sense of the phrase, powerhouses of faith, places where the faithful went to experience heaven and to renew their very beings.[74] This was a world that was saturated by faith, by the expectation of God, by an understanding of the cosmos that placed Christianity right at its heart. Sarum was just a small part of something much, much larger.

ALTERNATIVE CENTRES ON THE MARGINS

It was not only the major centres of Christendom that built and maintained what I have just called 'powerhouses of faith'. The same principle can be seen beyond the boundaries of what we might today define as Christendom. In some ways the religious centres of the smaller Christian nations, surrounded as they were by Islamic or pagan peoples, became even more clearly 'centres' of the spiritual life of the nations concerned. There was never a full sense, either in the West or in the old Byzantine Empire, that the fortunes of the nation depended directly on the correct or continued worship of the churches, although this idea was always present in an indirect way. In terms of smaller Christian kingdoms, somewhat cut off

[74] M. Dunn and L. K. Davidson (eds.), *The Pilgrimage to Compostela in the Middle Ages.* New York: Routledge, 1996.

from the mainstream of Christendom, then we can see a much closer association in play. In this section I wish to look more closely at two such kingdoms that undertook considerable building work in the years just after the turn of the millennium, Georgia in the Caucusus and the Zagwe kingdom in Ethiopia.

The kingdom of Kartli, a predecessor of contemporary Georgia sited in the centre of the present country, was converted to Christianity only a few years after Armenia to the South.[75] There had been Christians in Georgia for many centuries. Graves exist that can be dated to the second and third centuries, and there are suggestions that the Jewish community of Kartli was profoundly influenced by Christianity.[76] The legend recounting the conversion, first recorded in 403, tells of King Mirian, who was converted through the ministrations of St Nino. Nino, a Christian from Cappadocia, had been taken to Georgia as a slave woman and became a healer and confidante to the queen.[77] The king, however, refused to fully accept the Christian message until he was alone and lost in the woods whilst out hunting. He called on the name of Nino's God and consequently found his way home.[78] From that time on Kartli became a Christian nation. The spiritual heart of Kartli was the town of Mtskheta. This was a cosmopolitan city with large Greek and Jewish communities where the king had his main palace.[79] On the conversion of the king to Christianity the city was moved across the river away from the old pagan centre to an area of land surrounding the new Christian church. The site of the church itself was determined as the place where the robe that Jesus had worn at his crucifixion was said to be buried.

The story goes that following the crucifixion and the casting of lots for the robe it passed into the hands of Elias, a Jew from Mtskheta, who subsequently took it home with him. On approaching his home he was met by his daughter, Sidonia, who was so overwhelmed with emotion at the power of the robe that she died on the spot clutching it to her breast. It was impossible for anyone to prise it from her arms and so she was buried at the same spot still clutching the robe. A cedar of Lebanon grew on the site of the grave, which was removed and transformed into a miraculous pillar

[75] See my discussion of Armenia on pp. 92–5 above.
[76] K. Lerner, 'Georgia, Christian History of', in K. Parry et al. (eds.), *The Blackwell Dictionary of Eastern Christianity*. Oxford: Blackwell, 2001, 210–14.
[77] Later versions of the story state that Nino was the daughter of the Patriarch of Jerusalem but this is highly unlikely. Ibid., 211.
[78] D. Marshall Lang, *Lives and Legends of the Georgian Saints*. London: George Allen & Unwin, 1956, 13–19.
[79] M. Bulia and M. Janjalia, *Mtskheta*. Tbilisi: Betania Centre, 2000.

within the new church owing to the intervention of Nino herself.[80] Around the church, however, known locally as the 'holy of holies', many other churches and monasteries came to be built with titles alluding to the life of Christ (e.g. Gethsemane, Golgotha, Bethany, Olivet and Tabor),[81] and the town of Mtskheta became the holiest site for the Georgian church even when the capital itself was moved downriver to Tbilisi in the early sixth century.

The history of the church of Georgia, and its worship, is difficult to piece together. In the fourth and fifth centuries it came under the patriarchate of Antioch and looked to Syria for support. The so-called 'Syrian fathers' are highly venerated throughout the country and particularly in the East where they set up monasteries and founded churches.[82] These monasteries functioned in a typically Syrian fashion with small cells scattered around an inhospitable landscape, and maintained links through to the wider church. In the late fifth century the king declared the church to be independent under a Catholicos based in Mtskheta. In subsequent centuries the church joined with that of Armenia and other Caucasian churches but finally split with the Armenians in the 720s and allied itself to Byzantium whilst retaining its autocephalous nature. Throughout its history the Georgian church has also had very close ties with Jerusalem, with Georgian monks maintaining a house in Jerusalem from the fifth century. Much of our evidence for the liturgy in Jerusalem actually comes from Georgian manuscripts and it is very likely that the liturgy of the Georgian church from the fifth to the tenth century was based closely on that of Jerusalem, although from the fifth century worship had always been in the Georgian language.[83]

By the tenth century, Georgia had refocused its political and ecclesial life on Byzantium and had come within the Orthodox fold. The nation, however, retained a certain level of independence in appointing its own Catholicos rather than looking to the Patriarch of Constantinople for guidance. It is even told with pride in Georgia itself that it was Georgian bishops who maintained the orthodoxy of the area round the Black Sea during the Iconoclast Controversy.[84] The highpoint of the Georgian kingdom came in the period from the eleventh to the thirteenth century when Byzantium was under pressure from Latin invasions. This was the time when the nation was brought together through the skill and influence of

[80] Ibid., 26–9.   [81] Lerner, 'Georgia', 210.
[82] Z. Skhirtladze, *Desert Monasticism, Gareja and the Christian East: Papers from the International Symposium, Tbilisi University, September 2000.* Tbilisi: Gareja Studies Centre, 2001.
[83] Lerner, 'Georgia', 211.   [84] Personal communication while visiting the country in 2002.

King David the Builder and Queen Tamar. This was also the highpoint for the Georgian church. King David, in an attempt to draw together the disparate elements of his kingdom, chose to build three grand and imposing cathedrals, one in the west at Kurtasi, one in the east at Telavi, and one to replace the original cathedral at Mtskheta. It was within this kingdom that Mtskheta, once again, became the spiritual powerhouse of the nation, the focus for the liturgical life and the centre for all ritual activities. This influence survived even after the later Arab invasion and the decline of the Georgian kingdom.

The central church of Mtskheta, the cathedral of Svetitzkhoveli (literally the 'life-giving pillar') that had originally been built over the shrine of the Robe, was always the holiest church of the land. It was destroyed a number of times and finally rebuilt by Catholicos Melchisedec I between 1010 and 1029.[85] In the fifteenth century a chapel was installed in the south aisle of the church that was supposed to be a symbolic copy of the shrine of the Holy Sepulchre in Jerusalem. This was not simply an attempt to copy something of central importance to the Christian world, both architecturally and spiritually; it was also an attempt to bring something of Jerusalem to Georgia and to reinforce the ancient link between Mtskheta and the Holy City. This reconstruction set up a small part of Jerusalem, with all that it stood for, at the heart of the Georgian church and once again established Mtskheta as the spiritual home and centre of the nation. Similar copies of the shrine at the Holy Sepulchre were built in other sites across Europe, most commonly in Western Europe, but these had a far more direct link to the crusades than that of Mtskheta, and were seen in relation to the Western interests in the Holy Land. In Mtskheta the shrine continued a long tradition of linking Jerusalem to Georgia and of situating the cathedral at the heart of the worshipping life of the nation.

In a very real sense, therefore, the churches of Georgia provide a concrete map of the Christian cosmos, with Mtskheta, the symbolic Jerusalem, at their centre. The liturgy also reinforces this sense of the cosmic in its use of the buildings and in its central place within the life of the nation. Here we see a clear dominant discourse wielded by those in authority, most significantly by the reformers and uniters of the country in the tenth and eleventh centuries, that is rooted in the daily worship of the people and manifested in the architectural forms of the nation's churches.

If we now turn to Ethiopia, we will find a story remarkably similar to that of Georgia. According to Acts, the eunuch who met Philip was the first

---

[85] Bulia and Janjalia, *Mtskheta*, 89.

Christian missionary to Ethiopia.[86] There is, however, no direct evidence that this encounter had any impact on the religion of the nation. The first historical account of conversion comes, as with Armenia and Georgia, in the fourth century and is attributed to a merchant, Frumentius, who was abandoned on the coast of the Red Sea following a shipping accident. This merchant became very significant at court and converted the king, his queen and their son, the future King Ezana.[87] This was at the old royal site of Aksum in Northern Ethiopia. Ezana sent Frumentius to Alexandria to ask for a bishop to be sent to Aksum. Athanasius, the Patriarch of Alexandria, ordained Frumentius and sent him back as the first bishop. Aksum soon became a Christian capital, although the church there was never entirely independent, as the *abun*, or head of the church, was always appointed by the Patriarch of Alexandria and was a Copt rather than a native Ethiopian.[88] As in Georgia, the growth of monasticism was attributed to roving Syrian monks who came to the country in the fifth century and set out monasteries along Syrian models in the lands surrounding the capital of Aksum.[89]

The distinctive style of worship in Ethiopia is generally attributed to the Aksumite period, with the chant of the church being attributed to Yared, a musician at the court of Gabra Masqal in the sixth century. Yared is supposed to have introduced 'African' elements into the music and into the worship, including the use of drums, lyres, tambourines and other percussive instruments along with the distinctive dances that are undertaken by deacons before the *tabot*, or ark, at festivals.[90] The art of the Ethiopian church, both in churches and in manuscript form, is also attributed to this period and follows a remarkably consistent pattern through the following centuries up to the present day.[91] Finally the so-called 'Jewish' elements of Ethiopian spirituality and practice also appear to date from the Aksumite period, although this is disputed. The Ethiopians themselves place a strong emphasis on the Old Testament and their own supposed association with the Queen of Sheba. The practices of circumcision, the keeping of the Sabbath, and Jewish-style food restrictions,

---

[86] Acts 8:26–40.

[87] S. Munro-Hay, *Aksum, An African Civilisation of Late Antiquity.* Edinburgh: Edinburgh University Press, 1991, 204.

[88] Ibid.   [89] Ibid., 207–8.

[90] Ibid., 208, 251. More could probably be said about the traditions of the ark in Ethiopian tradition and faith. Much of this would support the kind of argument I am making in this chapter. Unfortunately, however, much of this material is so shrouded in myth and legend that it is very difficult to distinguish fact from fiction. See R. Grierson, 'Dreaming of Jerusalem', in R. Grierson (ed.), *African Zion, The Sacred Art of Ethiopia.* New Haven: Yale University Press, 1993, 5–17.

[91] Grierson, *African Zion.*

however, appear to have derived from a literal reading of the Old Testament rather than through any direct Jewish heritage.[92] A final feature of Ethiopic religious practice that probably dates back to Aksum, and maybe even beyond, is the use of magical inscriptions. These were vellum scrolls on which texts from the Bible were written and illustrated. The resulting objects were used both to ward off evil spirits and as part of healing rituals overseen by the clergy.[93]

With the decline of the Aksumite Empire in the seventh century the history of Ethiopia and its church begins to become very hazy. It only surfaces again in the records some two to three hundred years later with the rise of the Zagwe kingdom, which was focused on an area south of Aksum. A Zagwe queen, Gudit, was thought to be responsible for the complete destruction of all older churches. Whether this is true or not, most of the churches and monasteries currently seen in Ethiopia, Tigray and Eritrea date from the thirteenth century or later.[94] Many of these new churches are cut directly out of the stone, the most significant group of which can be seen at Lalibela. The churches were probably built over a number of centuries but were brought together and given symbolic significance in the reign of King Lalibela in the thirteenth century. They are interesting for what they can tell us of the aims and spirituality of their builders.

We have no written records, but the churches themselves are laid out in such a way that it is clear that two distinct things are going on. First, these churches are obviously aiming to recreate the glory of Aksum itself with its great Cathedral of Mary in Zion. The largest of the churches at Lalibela, Medhane Alem (The Saviour of the World), is thought to be an exact copy, carved in stone, of the Aksumite cathedral as it was at that time.[95] More significantly for our purposes, however, it is clear that these churches aimed, in some way, to reproduce biblical symbolism at the heart of the Ethiopian kingdom. A canal, known locally as the Jordan, divides two sets of churches. A hill on the edge of the complex is known as the 'Mount of Transfiguration', and the church known as 'Bethlehem' is about the same distance from Lalibela as the original is from Jerusalem.[96] Alongside Medhane Alem are churches dedicated to Mary, St Michael, Golgotha and the Trinity. In the church of Golgotha are two tombs, one of Lalibela

---

[92] It has also been suggested that these practices came from Jewish influences in the Yemen but this hypothesis is dismissed by most contemporary scholars. Munro-Hay, *Aksum*, 209.

[93] J. Mercier, *Art That Heals, The Image as Medicine in Ethiopia.* Munich: Prestel, 1997.

[94] D. W. Phillipson, *Ancient Ethiopia, Aksum: its Antecedents and Descendants.* London: British Museum Press, 1998.

[95] Ibid., 133.   [96] Grierson, 'Dreaming', 13.

and the other attributed to Christ.[97] The positioning of a Holy Sepulchre at the heart of this complex reflects a strong interest in the Holy City, and it could be argued that these tombs are designed specifically to bring the spiritual power of that city into the heart of the Ethiopian kingdom. Interestingly, the Zagwe dynasty is the only line of kings in Ethiopia who do not claim descent from Solomon and the Queen of Sheba, and Roderick Grierson argues that Lalibela is, in part, an attempt to claim an association with Jerusalem at a time when the nation was in flux and looking in on itself. This claim had to be made in stone, as the more usual symbolic claims were not open to the rulers.[98]

Like the Georgians, the Ethiopians had maintained a monastery in Jerusalem even when the country itself was almost impossible to reach.[99] A strong sense of the importance of the Holy City was a part of the spiritual life of the Ethiopian church and nation, including the significant secular role given to those who had made the pilgrimage to the City within the national government.[100] It should not surprise us, therefore, to see attempts at the reconstruction or representation of that most holy of centres within the holiest centre of the nation itself. This is true of both Georgia and Ethiopia by the turn of the millennium and is part of an attempt to build up a Christian nation with a significant powerhouse of faith. Both Ethiopia and Georgia, however, are situated on the margins of the Christian world, and their architecture and worshipping life have to reflect their own particular attempts to maintain their marginal position. The importation of symbolic structures related to Jerusalem is a significant part of these attempts, and their realisation in stone establishes a clear sense of the kind of cosmological Christianity that I have already outlined for Kiev and Salisbury. Each society provides a symbolic map of the whole of creation with the Christian church and worship at its heart. Each would also be meaningless without the worship that it supported and it is to this that I must return in the conclusion of this chapter.

COSMOLOGICAL CHRISTIANITY AS A DOMINANT DISCOURSE

Throughout this chapter I have talked of Christianity as providing the 'dominant discourse' for the societies that I have been discussing. This

---

[97] Phillipson, *Ancient Ethiopia*, 135.   [98] Grierson, 'Dreaming', 12.

[99] K. S. Pedersen, 'The Qeddusan: The Ethiopian Christians of the Holy Land', in A. O'Mahony (ed.), *The Christian Heritage in the Holy Land*. London: Scorpion Cavendish, 1995, 129–48.

[100] Munro-Hay, *Aksum*, 204.

dominance is seen particularly, I have suggested, in the forms of worship espoused by the official churches and by the buildings that were constructed to house that worship. I have also described this as 'cosmological Christianity'. In this concluding section of the chapter I want to come back to these ideas and draw some of the various threads together. I wish to begin, however, by questioning my own use of Gerd Baumann's idea of the dominant discourse.[101] It is clear from what I have written that my understanding of this term is very different from Baumann's. For Baumann, the dominant discourse is that used by the political elite and is the discourse that everybody has to learn if they wish to engage successfully with that elite.[102] There is some element of this in my own use of the term, although it depends on a close and significant relationship between the political and the ecclesial elites in each of the societies that I have been discussing. My own idea of a dominant discourse, however, goes much further than Baumann's discourse of the elite.

In order to understand this we need to go back to my discussion in Chapter 2 where we looked at the concept of Christianisation. This was a process by which Christianity, in whatever form, became the taken-for-granted, commonsense, discourse of the society. In this chapter we have seen, in some sense, the end point of that process within the societies that I have been looking at. Christian discourses are dominant not simply because they are espoused by the elite, political or ecclesial, but because they form the commonsense, everyday, cosmological discourses within which everybody has to function. Christianity, by the eleventh century, had for most of Europe, and for a few places beyond, formed the basic cosmology or worldview of the vast majority of the population. This cosmology was fundamentally different from that of the pagan societies that it had usurped, and it differed subtly from one society to another. This cosmology, however, this commonsense view of how the world worked and what the world consisted of, was fundamentally Christian.

What I have tried to show in this chapter is the way in which this Christian cosmology, or dominant discourse, was central to, and rooted in, the official forms and structures of worship as practised at this time. Time was dominated by liturgical events, be they the offices of the day or the festivals of the year. The passing of time was recalled and responded to by the tolling of the bell or the call to worship. Even for those people who did not participate greatly in the worship of the church, days and seasons were

---

[101] Baumann, *Contesting Culture*.   [102] Ibid., 10.

known by their Christian, liturgical, names.[103] Space was also determined by worship: the space within the church, the place of the churches within the cities, villages or towns, and the place of Jerusalem at the centre of the world and other pilgrimage sites at its periphery. As people moved through time and space they moved through a Christian cosmology punctuated by Christian symbols and Christian rites.[104] This was unavoidable and went principally unquestioned. Even the models of the society, with their emphasis on hierarchy and the place of the individual within that hierarchy, were reflected in worship and in the official forms of worship of the churches. Hierarchy was a dominating principle of many, if not all, of the major discourses of this time, and worship was no exception. The sense of order and the place of the individual within that order were central.

This brings me back to a point that I made in my Introduction and to one of the central problems we face in understanding the worship of this particular period. In my Introduction I introduced the concept of 'habitus' as that which mediates between worship and discourse.[105] Habitus was a term drawn from the work of Pierre Bourdieu and rooted in the kind of commonsense cosmological understanding of the world that I have been developing in this conclusion.[106] Habitus, however, also brings an element of the unconscious and the bodily into the discussion. For Bourdieu habitus refers, among other things, to the way in which the person holds and uses the body in relation to a specific commonsense discourse. Within the various settings I have explored within this chapter, therefore, worship provides its own habitus. This habitus is central to the habitus of all social action, sacred and secular. Both sacred and secular, as I have just explained, are rooted in hierarchy and both involve a series of overlapping postures and actions that are expected of each person in their particular status in life. It is this habitus, I would suggest, rooted in the dominant cosmological discourse of worship, which underpins the whole hierarchical structures of society, and embodies that hierarchy in the physical practices of the people. It flows out from the primary context of worship into the world of economics, politics and kinship and it flows back from these contexts into the forms of worship. It is that which shows the Christian discourse to be most dominant.

---

[103] S. J. White, *A History of Women in Christian Worship.* London: SPCK, 2003, 220.

[104] I could also talk about the rites associated with birth, marriage and death that were also a part of this dominant Christian discourse of time and space. See the many examples in White, *Women.*

[105] See pp. 16–17 and the references to P. Bourdieu, *Outline of a Theory of Practice.* Cambridge: Cambridge University Press, 1977.

[106] Bourdieu is particularly concerned with questions of time and space within his book and relates habitus to these directly. See ibid.

The notion of habitus, however, also answers the problem that I have hinted at in various ways throughout this chapter: the problem of participation. Liturgy at this time, for almost all traditions, and certainly for all those I have looked at in this chapter, was primarily a clerical activity. It is certainly true that the definition of 'cleric' went far beyond the narrow confines of priesthood as we understand it today, and in all these traditions there were many different people involved in one way or another in the performance of the rite, especially in the grand cathedral churches. There were, however, always many others, including practically all the women, who had no formal or prescribed role in the liturgy at all. This did not mean, however, that they were inactive, or that their position was non-participatory.[107] Lay people may have wandered in and out of the churches while the worship was going on, but they were not unaware or ignorant of that worship; they participated in it, but in their own fashion. There were actions, postures, part of the habitus of the people, that were central to devotion: lighting candles to saints or icons, praying in various ways, following private meditative practices, and so on. This habitus was the form of worship of the ordinary lay man or woman of the time and a central part of their being. Christianity was the dominant, cosmological discourse; worship was the primary activity of practically all people, and Christian devotion of the kind I have just alluded to was central to life from kings and popes to the poorest of the beggars on the streets. This devotion came to play an ever-increasing part in the day-to-day lives of laity and it is to this that I wish to turn in my next chapter.

---

[107] Susan White offers a number of clear examples of this drawn from the writing of women at the time, or the reports of court cases in which women gave oral testimony. White, *Women*.

CHAPTER 5

Accessing the demotic discourses of devotion, 1200–1500

INTRODUCTION: DEMOTIC DISCOURSES

At the end of the previous chapter I referred in passing to the concept of 'devotion' in relation to lay participation in medieval liturgy. I suggested that ordinary worshippers might be engaged in their own form of devotional habitus while the official, dominant, cosmological discourses were being presented in the liturgy itself. Up to this point, however, I have hardly explored the distinction between liturgy and devotion at all. This is partly because for much of the first thousand years of Christian history official liturgical worship and lay devotion were largely indistinguishable; each fed off and into the other. To some extent this is also true of the medieval period. A hard and fast distinction is impossible to make and each one would not exist without the other. In this chapter, however, I do want to focus more closely on this particular distinction and I want to relate it to the understanding of discourse that I have developed throughout the book. More specifically, I want to explore the distinction between 'dominant' and 'demotic' discourses within later medieval Christianity and explore how this relates to understandings of worship at this time.

Gerd Baumann introduced the concepts of 'demotic' and 'dominant' discourse in his discussion of the role of religion and community in a contemporary West London suburb.[1] Baumann was primarily interested in the way in which the different religious 'communities' of Southwark represented themselves and how this played within a larger political discourse within the suburb as a whole. Baumann discovered that he had to listen very carefully, not just to what was being said by the different communities, but also to how they said it and the meaning that each group gave to significant terms such as 'religion' and 'community' in

[1] G. Baumann, *Contesting Culture, Discourses of Identity in Multi-Ethnic London.* Cambridge: Cambridge University Press, 1996.

different contexts. What each group was doing, Baumann argues, was to use a range of different discourses that changed depending on whom they were talking to and what they were talking about. A discourse that was suitable for internal consumption, within a particular religious or social group, was different from that which was used for outsiders, or between groups, or by the political establishment.[2] This led Baumann to introduce the distinction between 'dominant discourses', those of the political establishment, that everybody had to engage in if they were to gain political ends, and 'demotic discourses',[3] or the internal discourses of the different religious communities. Baumann then went on to develop the idea of 'dual discursive competence', the idea that each individual was able to switch between two or more different discourses at will, depending on context.[4]

Where this analysis has an impact on my own study is in the way in which this kind of thinking allows us to readdress an old debate about the relationship between 'religion' and 'superstition', or between 'official' and 'popular' religion. This distinction has been used by scholars in many different contexts, but has been most widely applied to the situation in late medieval Western Europe.[5] One reason for this, undoubtedly, is that this is a distinction that was common at the time and was used extensively, especially by those holding ecclesial authority. This distinction also became one of the major foci for the Reformation and was used widely, as a means to condemn Catholics, by Reformed thinkers.[6] More recently, however, scholars with an interest in the late medieval period have been challenging the use of this distinction.[7]

It has been argued, for example, that the distinction is merely a part of the dominant discourse of the time, a means by which the church authorities maintained their control by condemning or dismissing the activities of the non-elite as 'superstition'.[8] This was not, however, how the situation looked from the perspective of those for whom the discourse labelled as 'superstition' formed the popular devotion of their faith. It has been difficult, however, for contemporary scholars to find other terms in which to interpret this debate without also falling into the traps set by

---

[2] Ibid., 10.   [3] Ibid.   [4] Ibid., 34.
[5] See for example the discussion in R. N. Swanson, *Religion and Devotion in Europe, c. 1215–c. 1515*. Cambridge: Cambridge University Press, 1995, 184–90.
[6] See pp. 179–83 below.
[7] See W. A. Christian, *Local Religion in Sixteenth-Century Spain*. Princeton: Princeton University Press, 1981.
[8] See the references in ibid.

the dominant discourse of the time.[9] One way in which this can be done, I would suggest, is to draw on Baumann's work and to apply the concepts of 'dominant' and 'demotic' discourses to the period under investigation. So-called 'superstitions' and other popular devotions then become the expression of religious faith within the demotic discourses of the period. What is more, such an analysis would recognise that the people of the time, whether peasants, nobility or even bishops, could easily move between the two discourses, demotic and dominant, at will and therefore function within a dual discursive competence of their own.[10]

This kind of language enables us to go further than the scholars of the period have tended to go. To talk of 'dominant discourses' in a Baumannian sense immediately raises the question of power.[11] For whom are these discourses 'dominant', and how is that dominance maintained? We have looked at these kinds of questions before in Chapter 3, but there we were talking of empires and obvious sources of power and authority. What is interesting about the late medieval period was the way in which these traditional sources of power were under threat. In many ways the authority of the emperors was stronger than ever. Increasingly this authority was breaking free of its traditional roots in the church and becoming something of an end in itself. At exactly the same time, however, other sources of power, and therefore alternative possibilities for authority, were arising among the merchants and guilds within the cities. This was leading to a period in which power was contested and religious language was central to the way in which that contest was expressed.

We begin to see at this time something of the rise of powers that have been explored and elaborated in the work of Michel Foucault.[12] Foucault was talking primarily of the nineteenth and twentieth centuries, when different dynamics of power were at play. Many of his concepts and ideas, however, can be taken back into the later medieval and early modern periods. In particular we have to note the way in which Foucault sees power not as a single entity that is wielded by one person, or one group of people, and imposed on another. Rather, for Foucault, power is part of a relationship and both parties to that relationship have some power over the other.

---

[9] Changing the term 'superstition' to 'popular religion', 'peasant devotions', 'rural cults' or any other term merely perpetuates the dualisms implicit in the original term. I will discuss this in the conclusion of this chapter.

[10] Christian makes this point in relation to late medieval Spain but does not use these terms. See Christian, *Local Religion*.

[11] I use this to distinguish it from the dominant cosmological discourses discussed in the previous chapter, although there is undoubtedly a power factor involved in these kinds of discourse as well.

[12] M. Foucault, *Discipline and Punish, The Birth of the Prison*. London: Penguin Books, 1977.

The way in which this works out in practice, however, depends entirely on the local circumstances. An important part of this relationship of power, according to Foucault, can be seen in the play of language, in the relationship (although he did not use these terms) between the dominant and the demotic discourses involved.

If we turn this kind of discussion to the subject of worship, we can see quite clearly how the ideas of liturgy and devotion can be mapped onto those of dominant and demotic discourses. Devotion, as I have introduced it, relates to local activities that are undertaken by ordinary people as a regular part of their everyday spirituality, while liturgy is the official worship of the church. Whether all devotion is what some would like to call 'superstition' is an entirely different discussion, but once again we can see that talk of demotic and dominant discourses allows us to avoid this question. The issue is not one of right or wrong. Rather it is a question of context and, by implication, of power. The church controls devotion as much as it controls the official liturgies. However, devotion is usually individual in practice and it is often local in character. This is not true of liturgy. Occasionally, however, liturgy and devotion do overlap, when individuals draw on liturgical motifs and themes for their devotion or when local, popular devotions become so widespread that they are drawn into the official liturgy of the church as a whole.

As I have implied, the relationship between devotion and liturgy also involves a relationship of power, and a relationship of the Foucaultian kind where it is not always clear which has power over the other. In some places it is popular devotion that appears to be taking the upper hand, and the liturgy of the church is almost seen to be at the service of local devotions. We will see examples of this in India, Spain and Northern Italy in the text that follows. This, however, can only ever make sense when the situation is viewed from the local point of view. It is only within demotic discourses that devotion can ever be seen to have primacy. When viewed from the perspective of the Catholic Church in Europe, or even the Syrian Church as a whole, the local manifestation of devotion is obscured by the liturgy of the church and, if it is to be tolerated at all, it is tolerated as a minor player in the larger dominant discourse.

This situation, however, leads me to my final point in this introductory section. Where devotion is seen to be demotic from the point of view of a wider dominant discourse, it can also be seen as dominant from the perspective of a local community. If, therefore, that local community is placed into a position where it is isolated from the sources of authority associated with the dominant discourses of the liturgy and the official doctrines of the church, the demotic discourses of devotion can begin to develop unchecked and become a form of dominant discourse of their own within a very specific locality. This is exactly the situation we see when we begin to look at local cults. In this chapter, for example, I wish to look first at the situation in South India, where the local church was isolated from any central authority, in any meaningful sense, for many centuries. Here the local Christian devotions interacted with the devotions of other religious traditions to form a syncretic mixture of their own. In the second section I want to begin by looking at a study of small, isolated communities in the Italian Alps and to see that here too, in communities cut off from the sources of power of the dominant discourse, the local demotic discourse begins to claim dominance. In the final example, that of the rising Italian cities of the thirteenth and fourteenth centuries, we see a different way in which the dominant discourse is challenged, this time for political reasons rather than because of isolation. Here Foucault's analysis becomes even clearer as we see the dominant discourses having to adapt and change to accommodate devotional activities of local demotic discourses.

This will inevitably lead me to look at worship from the position of the ordinary Christian, that is from the bottom up. It will provide a useful foil, therefore, to the essentially top-down perspective of the previous chapter. What did late medieval worship look like from the ground? In order to answer this I will explore the specific situation of South India and then move on from this to an analysis of popular devotion in rural and urban areas of Western Europe. This will lead me back to the principal theoretical interest of the chapter, and the concept of demotic discourse, in my conclusion.

POPULAR CHRISTIAN DEVOTION IN SOUTH INDIA

South India may seem a very strange place to begin an analysis of Christian popular devotion. However, there are elements of that situation that make it an ideal starting point for this chapter. According to local legends the church in South India was founded by the apostle Thomas when he arrived in Malankara in December c. 50. The stories tell us that Thomas preached in the area for some time before being martyred by a Brahmin with a lance in Mylapore, where his tomb was to still to be seen.[13] There is, however, no hard evidence to support this claim. Similarly, there is no solid reason to

---

[13] L. W. Brown, *The Indian Christians of St Thomas, An Account of the Ancient Syrian Church of Malabar.* Cambridge: Cambridge University Press, 1956, 49–50.

reject it. Leslie Brown notes that 'We cannot prove that the Apostle worked in south India any more than we can disprove that fact.'[14] He goes on to note the possibility of Persian Christian traders on the Malabar Coast carrying the Thomas tradition in the first three centuries. The recorded history of the church in India, however, begins in the sixth century when Cosmos Indicopleustes describes the church in his *Christian Topography* (c. 535).[15] By this time the church appears to have been already well established.

The church had always looked to Syria and the Church of the East for its authority and for its bishops, although there were times through the centuries when the links were cut and the patriarchs were unable to consecrate bishops for the church. The official liturgy of the South Indian church, however, remained essentially Syrian in shape and form, while being translated into a local dialect, Malayalam. Vestments were a little different to suit the climate and local traditions, and the wooden churches were clearly built to a local style. However, the form of the liturgy would have been as recognisable to a visitor from Persia as it was to the local people, their clergy and the monks. As with so many of the Eastern Churches, liturgy was an area in which tradition came first and very few changes were ever made.[16]

Between the fifth and the thirteenth century Kerala was ruled by Hindu rajahs with the impact of Muslims from the North being very strong from the tenth century on.[17] On the coast, however, the mix of religions had been common for many centuries, as in many trading centres. As elsewhere in India, this mixture existed in an essentially peaceful and non-threatening fashion, with each community maintaining their own traditions while respecting the traditions of others. By the time the Portuguese arrived in Goa in the fifteenth century they found Christians, Jews, Muslims and Hindus living and working alongside each other in the ports and, up country, Hindus and Christians maintaining traditions that had gone back hundreds of years.[18] While this was something of a shock to the visiting Europeans, it was taken as completely normal by the local religious communities.

---

[14] Ibid., 59.

[15] J. Fenwick, 'India, Syrian Christianity in the South', in K. Parry et al. (eds.), *The Blackwell Dictionary of Eastern Christianity*. Oxford: Blackwell, 2001, 251–6, 251.

[16] See Brown, *Indian Christians*, 213–88 for a full account of this liturgy.

[17] J. Keay, *India, a History*. London: Harper Collins, 2000, 167–79.

[18] D. Mosse, 'The Politics of Religious Synthesis: Roman Catholicism and Hindu Village Society in Tamil Nadu, India', in C. Stewart and R. Shaw (eds.), *Syncretism/Anti-Syncretism, The Politics of Religious Synthesis*. London: Routledge, 1994, 108–26.

When we look more closely at what was going on in the part of India where the earliest Christians settled, we find something very interesting. It is clear that each religious community maintained their own rituals and their own identity as Christian, Hindu or whatever. These were rooted in tradition and belonged to the community as a whole. Within these traditions, and surrounding them, however, was a range of other activities that were either social, relating to weddings, funerals and the like, or which could probably be best described as devotional or 'superstitious'. These latter included the celebrations associated with the major festivals of the different religions and the devotion that was shown to the shrines of local saints. It also included the attitude to priests and the use of charms, astrology and other divination methods common to all the communities of the area.

George Joseph claims that 'customs and rules, heavily influenced by high-caste Hindu practices, relating to food, occupation and rites of passage emerged to define Syrian Christian identity'.[19] Concepts of pollution, particularly in relation to the eating of food and in maintaining physical distance, became an important part of the life of the community. Rules relating to the keeping of distance appear to have been particularly strong in Kerala. 'A custom that still survives among some [churches] is that during the Easter service street procession, shouts of "*poyin, poyin*" (go away, go away) are heard.'[20] Christians were called upon by the higher castes of the majority Hindu community to purify objects touched by lower-caste people. The Christians also maintained the customs of horoscopes, the tying of a pendant (*minnu*, although with a cross rather than the traditional Hindu motif) at marriage, ceremonial bathing and vegetarianism following death, and the celebration of the first feeding of rice to newborn children (*annaprasanam*).[21]

Another way in which the community adapted to their local context was to place an increased emphasis on family ties. A story is told of St Thomas converting thirty-two Brahmin families, with two in particular being designated as priests.[22] The importance of family was retained over the centuries. The community was endogamous: that is, they never married outside of their own community, and they discouraged evangelisation and conversion particularly from lower-caste communities. Despite this, it is clear that a number of the practices and cults introduced by the Christians

[19] G. Joseph, 'India, Syrian Christian Community', in Parry et al., *Dictionary*, 249–50.
[20] Ibid., 249.   [21] Brown, *Indian Christians*, 167–208. See also Joseph, 'India', 249.
[22] Brown, *Indian Christians*, 51.

were also taken over by the local Hindu population. The cult of St George, for example, was probably brought to the Malabar coast by Syrian merchants and the current legends combine both Latin and Syrian versions of the story.[23] St George was called on particularly for his power against snakes, and both Hindus and Christians visit his shrines following snakebites. Local tradition even suggests that the St George associated with a particular church in Puthupally is related to the local Hindu goddess Bhadrakali as a brother to a sister. The bells of his church, it is said, 'sweetly awaken Bhadrakali each morning'.[24]

What also becomes clear from the evidence that we have is that even in the fifteenth century, before the arrival of the Portuguese, when the region was far more isolated from the roots of their traditions, the different communities stuck rigidly to their own identities and did not mix their religious activities in an entirely syncretic fashion. The official worship of the church, as we have seen, remained recognisably East Syrian, and the Indian Christians always appeared to have made a clear and conscious distinction between that official worship and all other practices. Nothing was allowed to change the worship, and other rites and devotions were conducted outside of, and often separated from, those of the official church. Clearly in the context of weddings and funerals much of the Indian cultural elements and the official liturgy of the church did get mixed, and it is very likely that the people themselves would not have seen an obvious distinction between the two, but in practice the two elements appear to have been kept strictly apart.

When we look at the local traditions themselves, therefore, we see some interesting features. Brown informs us that many of the rites related to weddings and similar social events were granted to the Christians as special privileges and were shared either with local Brahmins (the right to ride an elephant to church for example) or with local Nayars (Indians of a different caste).[25] These distinctions and similarities are remembered and spread from ritual behaviour to elements of dress and the style of building houses. This, along with the emphasis on endogamy within the community, indicate that these rites and practices said as much about the identity of the people over against their neighbours as it said about the similarities in

---

[23] See C. G. Dempsey, *Kerala Christian Sainthood, Collisions of Culture and Worldview in South India.* Oxford: Oxford University Press, 2001.

[24] Many of these local traditions can only be uncovered through contemporary ethnography. However, the churches, the stories and the relationships clearly predate the arrival of the Portuguese in 1500. Ibid., 49.

[25] Brown, *Indian Christians*, 187–99.

some religious discourses. This can be seen most clearly in Brown's account of the two communities of Indian Christians. It appears that even before the Portuguese arrived the community was divided into two, the Northists and the Southists.[26] Each group was endogamous and members of each community would never marry members of the other. Local legends tell of the later arrival of the Southists, or their purer 'Syrian' ancestry, but the fact that the local Brahmins also divided into similar communities with identical names suggests that this might have been a more local development. As with the situation between the Christians and the Hindus, it was the differences in social and ritual practices associated with weddings, dress and other minor everyday activities that distinguished the communities most clearly. Their liturgy and official Christian practices were identical, although each community refused to worship in the other's churches. Devotions, and the local demotic discourses that encompassed them, therefore, were intimately tied up with identity for each of these various groups.

This sense of maintaining a deep-rooted tradition within an alien landscape was not the only way in which Christians isolated from the rest of the church developed. The situation in India was, of course, distinct, primarily because of the tenuous nature of the links that were maintained with the Persian church and the sheer depth of the tradition that was being retained. If the authority of tradition had not been so deep-rooted behind the liturgy, then we might ask what would have happened to it. Would the devotion and the festivals have come to define the tradition itself? Would the demotic discourse have become dominant? One place where we may get a fleeting glimpse of this is in the kingdom of Kongo in Central Africa.

During their travels the Portuguese had landed off the Zaire River in 1483.[27] Here a local king sought conversion, introduced Christian practices and learning, and maintained contact with Portugal and Rome, sending his son to be consecrated as a bishop. This kingdom, however, never entirely rejected the local religious traditions on conversion. Rather, it appears, they managed to internalise much of what they had learnt from the European visitors and combined this with local traditions in an utterly unique way. This process was made easier because the Kongo kings themselves defined the local form of Christianity and used local words with religious association as translations for priest (*nganga*, a traditional religious specialist) or religious objects, such as medals, crucifixes or rosaries (*nkisi*, a term

---

[26] Ibid., 175–8.
[27] J. Thornton, 'The Development of an African Catholic Church in the Kingdom of Kongo, 1491–1750', *Journal of African History*, 25 (1984), 147–67.

originally used for a material object which houses spiritual forces). The Christian nganga 'performed all the public and private roles expected of such practitioners in the Kongo'[28] including the provision of charms for luck and the performing of public ceremonies to appeal to earth spirits in case of drought 'with penitent processions and self flagellation'.[29] Meanwhile the traditional Kongo nganga were condemned as witches.

The kingdom had a troubled history with constant incursions by slave traders, wars with Portuguese Angola and local uprisings. Many visitors to the court comment on the corrupt nature of the Christianity there but never condemn it as paganism. It was only after the collapse of the kingdom in 1665 that the Portuguese hierarchy left and a series of female prophets arose, among other religious developments.[30] Some form of Christianity was, however, maintained by the local nobility and in many of the villages. An account from 1780, for example, talks of well-kept chapels and teachers who were fluent in Portuguese.[31] It is clear that some elements of Christian tradition were transplanted and retained by the Kongo, while others were dropped and other local traditions were incorporated. What exact form the worship of this community took after the Portuguese clergy left is almost impossible to determine. When other missionaries came up from Angola the first request that was made was for baptism.[32] What is clear, therefore, is that local, demotic and devotional forms of Christianity were retained in the heart of Africa for two centuries, before the missionary movements of the nineteenth century onwards arrived and destroyed them.

DEVOTION AND IDENTITY IN RURAL EUROPE

It was not only in India and Africa that the question of local, demotic, devotional discourses took on a local flavour while the official discourses of the liturgy were maintained by the authority of tradition or the church. The same situation was true of much of Europe. In 1913 Robert Hertz wrote a paper on the contemporary pilgrimage activities in a series of Alpine valleys.[33] This was one of the first attempts to apply anthropological

---

[28] Ibid., 157.   [29] Ibid.
[30] E. Isichei, *A History of Christianity in Africa, From Antiquity to the Present*. Grand Rapids: Eerdmans, 1995, 66.
[31] Ibid., 67.   [32] Thornton, 'African Catholic Church', 166.
[33] R. Hertz, 'St Besse: A Study of an Alpine Cult', reprinted in S. Wilson (ed.), *Saints and their Cults, Studies in Religious Sociology, Folklore and History*, Cambridge: Cambridge University Press, 1983, 55–100.

methods to the study of European cults. In this particular case, what is described is a series of devotions to a local saint that were focused on an annual pilgrimage and the collection or rocks or stones with supposedly healing powers. What Hertz goes on to show is the way in which the rivalry apparent in the devotions, the pilgrimages and the legends surrounding the saint highlight the rivalries between different valley communities and between the valleys and the city on the plains. These devotions were both a statement of local identity and a means for establishing the primacy of one community over another. They played a very similar role, albeit within an entirely different Christian discourse, to the pilgrimages and festivities of the different religious communities in Kerala.

This should not really surprise us, because we see in this paper the outlines of a principle that is universal among human communities of many different religious traditions. The fact that people use devotional activities as part of a demotic discourse of identity, especially when these can be set against the devotional practices of others, is a general principle and can be demonstrated in many different circumstances.[34] What is of far more interest at this point in our discussion is why certain kinds of devotional activity are chosen as symbols of this identity and not others. Throughout Western Europe it appears that the cult of the saints, and the subsequent use of pilgrimages, shrines and relics became the standard currency, or vocabulary, of identity.

The first point to note is that the use of shrines and pilgrimages does not occur only at the local level, and many different kinds of identity can be generated through the use of shrines. We have the local cults, such as that of St Besse as outlined by Hertz, which have a currency within a valley or two on the border between France and Italy. At a wider level, we have regional cults that can draw together a number of different communities and help to define a regional identity. Beyond this we have the national cults, such as that of St Thomas at Canterbury for example, that draw on national symbols and define the identity of the nation.[35] Above the national shrines are those centres of pilgrimage that could be said to define the identity of the whole of Western Europe. The most obvious of these is St James of Compostela, but others also emerged, including the various shrines of Rome itself. Finally we have the ultimate centre for pilgrimage and the

[34] Richard Werbner was one of the first to identify this in his work on regional cults in Southern Africa. R. Werbner, 'Introduction' in R. Werbner (ed.), *Regional Cults*. London: Academic Press, 1977.
[35] R. C. Finucane, *Miracles and Pilgrims, Popular Beliefs in Medieval England*. London: J. M. Dent & Sons, 1977, 121–6.

ultimate shrine, complete with relics and symbols of identity, in Jerusalem, a shrine for the whole Christian world, as we have seen in Chapter 2.[36]

Outlining this pattern, however, does nothing to answer the question of why these particular shrines and cults are chosen over others. One answer to this question can be developed through detailed historical analysis. We can look at the histories of the different shrines, look at who supported them and who provided relics for them, place them within a network of economic and political relations, and hence understand why, for example, Compostela became the central shrine for European identity.[37] This can be done, and can provide very fruitful answers. One or two points, however, are likely to be missed in such an analysis. Why, for example, do shrines exist at the margins, and not at the centre of the area being defined? Again we could take Compostela as our example. North-Eastern Spain is hardly central or easy to get to for thousands of pilgrims a year from across Europe. This, however, is part of the point. It is the very inaccessibility that turns the location into something important, as well as its association with the apostle James, Charlemagne and many others. As practically all analyses of pilgrimage tell us, the site of pilgrimage must be at the margins for it to be truly effective.[38] So, while Rome, the centre, is an important part of European spiritual geography in the Middle Ages, Compostela gains on Rome by its sheer remoteness. The same can be seen in the relationship between Canterbury and the Shrine of Our Lady at Walsingham in England.[39]

This, however, does not provide the final answer to my question. There are other sociological and anthropological factors that are also at work. Some have suggested, for example, that the important factor about practically all these shrines is that they exist on the sites of earlier pagan worship. Some even suggest that they are a direct and continuous link to the pagan past within late medieval Christianity. As in pagan Europe, many people had worshipped at local (and isolated) sites, whether trees, springs or rocky outcrops,[40] so this pattern of the local worship of nature continued by transferring the power of the sites from a nymph or local god to a saint or

---

[36] See p. 74 above.
[37] See e.g. A. Ferreiro, 'The Cult of the Saints and Divine Patronage in Gallaecia before Santiago' in M. Dunn and L. K. Davidson (eds.), *The Pilgrimage to Compostela in the Middle Ages.* New York: Routledge, 1996, 3–22. For recent work on the pilgrimage see M. Dunn and L. K. Davidson, 'Bibliography of the Pilgrimage: State of the Art' in the same volume, xxiii–xlviii.
[38] See the discussion of the geography of pilgrimage in Finucane, *Miracles and Pilgrims*, 152–72.
[39] Walsingham is situated in a remote part of Norfolk in eastern England but became the principal shrine of Our Lady for the whole country. See ibid., 196.
[40] K. Dowden, *European Paganism, The Realities of Cult from Antiquity to the Middle Ages.* London: Routledge, 2000.

relic. Hertz, for example, implies this in his study of the devotion to St Besse.[41] The unusual rock under which the chapel of St Besse is built is presented as having been a site of worship long before Christianity came into the valley. There is probably some truth in this, and it is very difficult in many cases for us to get beyond the local peasant religion of the later medieval period. However, as we shall see, the assumed link with pagan rites does not exist in many shrines where we do have the evidence we need.

One place where we might be able to 'get beyond', as it were, is in Central Spain. William Christian, writing in 1981, draws our attention to a series of unique documents produced for the Spanish government in 1575 and 1578.[42] These took the form of a printed questionnaire that was sent round to every town in New Castile and answered by local townspeople. Many of the questions are of an economic or political nature, but Christian draws particular attention to two questions towards the end of the questionnaire that ask about relics, shrines, miracles and holy days associated with local vows.[43] Christian uses the answers to these questions as the basis for his wider analysis of local religion in Spain in the late sixteenth century.

A number of points come out of this analysis. The first reinforces the point that I have already made; that shrines, on the whole, tend to be on the periphery of the towns in question. Christian claims that this is in deliberate opposition to the parish churches at the heart of the town. Images, he claims, are held at the shrines on the periphery while relics are held by the parish churches and monasteries in the towns.[44] He goes on, however, to make a number of other points that are interesting for my analysis. The first is the fact that the kind of saints being called upon, either in the shrines or on the holy days (most of which are instigated because a particular saint is seen to answer the prayers of the villagers during some kind of crisis), drift over time. Prior to the eleventh century there were a series of traditional shrines throughout Northern Spain associated with the relics of local saints. From the thirteenth century on, and coinciding with the reconquest of Southern Spain from the Moors, there was a shift in dedication and devotion from local 'Spanish' saints to Our Lady.[45] Alongside these shifts, Christian illustrates a growth of devotion to particular non-Spanish saints associated with specific illnesses, or with plagues of locusts and the like,

[41] Hertz, 'St Besse'.   [42] Christian, *Local Religion*.
[43] See ibid., 6 for the specific questions.
[44] The relics held by the town-based churches and monasteries tended to be those recently bought in Rome or acquired from the wars in Northern Europe rather than the relics of ancient Spanish saints. Ibid., 93.
[45] Ibid., 123–4.

such as St Gregory and St Sebastian.[46] At the time of the census, Christian also shows that local devotions were again in the process of changing from those associated with Our Lady and the Saints to those associated with the Passion, although this was only going to become really fashionable in the following century.[47]

Each of these phases of devotion was instigated and supported by the 'discovery' of new images or relics, usually by poor peasant children or other marginal figures. Christian shows how the evidence from the questionnaires can demonstrate the process by which the legends surrounding the founding and popularising of devotion to a particular image may have developed, from simple stories of healing through to full-blown archetypal founding myths.[48] What is clear, however, is that while these images and relics are almost all discovered in the countryside, outside the town, there is no real evidence that each new 'find' is associated with an ancient pagan shrine. What Christian proposes is that these rural shrines actually reflect the association that the contemporary people held between the sacred and the landscape; they are a means of sacralising that landscape in a way that is constantly shifting and redefining itself. Once again the association with local identity is clear, but Christian's local religion spreads that identity out of the town or the local community to encompass the rural landscapes surrounding them. Festivals, processions, shrines and images, all help to reinforce the sacred environment in which the people of the towns live and work. It must also be remembered that this sacred landscape has a temporal as well as a spatial dimension. The festivals and holy days, with their processions out to the shrine and all-night feasting there,[49] are spread throughout the agricultural year as well as across the local landscapes surrounding the town.

Underpinning these festivals, images and shrines, however, is another series of discourses that are just as important. Elsewhere I have written of Edward Tylor's working out of the animist idea in his two-volume work on *Primitive Culture*.[50] I have suggested that Tylor, in presenting his evidence

---

[46] Ibid., 42–7.   [47] Ibid., 181–208.   [48] Ibid., 83–4.

[49] All-night feasting at shrines during festivals, along with all-night vigils by individuals seeking healing at the shrine, appear to have been a feature of the religious activities of Central Spain that was being suppressed at the time of the questionnaires. This suppression was being instigated primarily as part of an increasing attempt to bring such devotion under the direct authority of the church and went alongside the suppression of local lay hermits and the choosing of May queens and May kings. Ibid., 163–7.

[50] M. D. Stringer, 'Rethinking Animism: Thoughts from the Infancy of our Discipline', *Journal of the Royal Anthropological Institute*, 5:4 (1999), 541–56, referring to E. Tylor, *Primitive Culture: Researches into the Development of Mythology, Philosophy, Religion, Art and Custom.* London: John Murray, 1871.

for the evolution of religious ideas, actually shows us that within all societies various layers of religious discourse will exist side by side. By providing evidence for the existence of each layer of his evolutionary schema in each kind of society ('primitive', 'barbarian' and 'civilised'), Tylor has demonstrated that all societies have some recourse to discourses on local spirits and/or saints, all societies see certain sites or objects as centres of spiritual power, and all societies respond to the presence of 'demons' and maintain some kind of relationship with those spiritual forces which can provide for healing and security in an unstable world. All societies also engage in devotions to higher forces and ultimately, to a greater or lesser extent, to God, and some individuals in all societies speculate on the origins of life and the meaning of existence.[51] What changes from society to society is not the range of responses to the spiritual as outlined by Tylor, but rather the specific content of the discourses within which this range of responses is expressed.

If we focus back on late medieval Spain, therefore, the dominant discourse was clearly that of the Catholic Church, with its reinforcement in the liturgy. Alongside this was a growing critical discourse rooted in the works of Erasmus and other humanist thinkers.[52] The local demotic discourses, however, could take many different forms, from the language of saints and devotion to particular images, to those of spiritual powers, local healers, and debates about the role of any number of local sprites, goblins and others. Christian emphasises the way in which the discourses related to vows, festivals and images tended to deal with the day-to-day life of the community. The questions in the government questionnaire did not ask about specific individual devotions; rather, they concentrated exclusively on the communal. At this level, however, vows were instigated following times of crisis within each town, be that illness or blight on crops. Saints were turned to in order to help the town to rid itself of these evil forces and to provide protection for the future. The continuation of the feast ensured the continuing support of the heavenly protector.[53] Much the same occurred in relation to shrines, images and the questions asked about miracles. It is clear that the saint associated with each shrine or image was seen as a source of power for the healing of the members of the community and for their protection from disaster. This is a very specific and very pragmatic kind of discourse that in its structure has lasted for centuries, even though the specific focus on Mary and the increasing popularity for images of the Passion and processions of flagellants that embodied this

[51] Stringer, 'Rethinking Animism'.   [52] Christian, *Local Religion*, 158–61.   [53] Ibid., 23–69.

discourse at the time of the questionnaires was specific to late sixteenth-century Spain.

Each level of religious discourse clearly interacts, to a greater or lesser extent, with all the others, but need not overlap in terms of perceived contradictions or tensions. Most ordinary people can have dual or even multi-discursive competence, and can switch from discourse to discourse depending on circumstances. It is for this reason that it is impossible to define the discourses of shrines and miracles as in any way 'popular' religion, with the assumption that this is a discourse that is specific to the peasants while other, higher, discourses are engaged in by townspeople or the nobility in society.[54] As Christian proves, exactly the same discourses are engaged in by urban communities, clergy and nobles within late medieval Spain. In fact, King Philip II himself, who called for the questionnaires to be undertaken, was a keen advocate of these kinds of demotic discourses.[55] Some individuals, more often those with a higher stake in one of the more academic discourses, may find this switching difficult, disturbing, or even dangerous, and may, for reasons of their own insecurity, set out to destroy the alternative discourses. Ultimately, however, this is unlikely to happen, as we will see in the following chapter, when the 'Reformation' went some way to redefining the range and content of some of these discourses, even if it did not finally destroy them.

DEVOTION AND THE BATTLE FOR PUBLIC SPACE IN THE EMERGING CITY

The kind of devotions that I have been discussing in the previous section relate primarily to the rural areas of Western Europe and could in many ways characterise these areas from the fourth to the nineteenth century. The very fact that we are dealing with marginal sites means that these must be situated within the rural areas. Towards the end of the Middle Ages, however, a new process was beginning to gather momentum; this was the rise in importance and independence of the urban communities. Here we find popular devotions being used for political purposes, closely associated with the ideas of power and identity that I have already looked at, but functioning in a very different way.

---

[54] Ibid., 178. This is also the mistake that Tylor made in placing his discourses within an evolutionary frame. He, like most academics, wished to see the most civilised members of the society rejecting the more 'superstitious' discourses, but in reality this has never been the case.

[55] Ibid., 148–53.

In the West of Europe the power of the church and the state had seldom been combined under one single system as in the Eastern Empire. In many cases the civil power and the religious power had been locked into conflicts with the Pope having access to land and secular power while the emperors and other rulers had been attempting to distance themselves as far as possible from any dependence on the spiritual powers of the Pope. Within this context spaces were left for other forms of authority to arise in particular circumstances and with allegiances of their own to both the secular and the spiritual powers. In most cases these other bodies arose within the cities and towns, primarily of Northern Italy but also in Germany, the Netherlands and elsewhere. Within the cities the old structures of feudalism had already begun to break down and a new merchant class, with money but without ancestral ties, was growing to fill the spaces of power. As cities developed with their own independence, it was the merchant classes who often took control, either through elected councils of one sort or another, or through the wealth and patronage of specific families. It is within this kind of context that the devotional life of the late medieval city has to be understood.

The wealthy families had long been supporting the building of churches, and the guilds, having formed around particular trades, followed in this kind of patronage. The building of churches, as well as being a physical sign of the wealth of the donor, also provided a space where the priests employed by the church could say mass for the departed, whether members of a family, a guild or a confraternity. This was the principal activity of many of the clergy employed within the towns. The late medieval period was one in which death was an ever-present reality, and this in its turn was accentuated by the urban communities themselves. Wherever people gather together in close proximity, as in a city or a town, lack of space and unsanitary conditions allow for the rapid spread of diseases of all kinds and make the city a far more dangerous place to live than the rural hinterlands. The spread of the Black Death and other major epidemics in the fourteenth and fifteenth centuries took the cities by storm and killed up to half the population of many communities, a third of the population of Europe as a whole. Added to this were the regular threats of fire, siege, earthquakes and the collapse of buildings, all of which conspired to focus the minds of many citizens on the subject of death. The focus on death within Northern Italy, however, had actually begun some decades before the Black Death first hit in the 1340s.

In order to understand this development more closely we need to go back to the thirteenth century and the trends that led to, or derived from, the emergence of the mendicant orders such as the Franciscans. To some extent the growth and influence of the friars, with their emphasis on poverty and personal devotion, can be seen as a rejection of the growing urbanism, or at least a rejection of the accumulation of wealth that was at its heart. Alongside the growth of the Franciscan movement, however, other devotional groups began to emerge. Initially they were popular movements, but with time they became organised orders, communities and confraternities. They took a number of different forms and this is not the place to explore them. There are two, however, that have a special impact on the form of worship and devotion at this time. The first is the growth of communities of women who set themselves apart for the sole purpose of prayer. The second was the growth of male-only lay fraternities devoted to charity, prayer, flagellation and the commemoration of the dead. It is the male communities that are perhaps better known, but it is impossible to fully separate out these two trends.

The rise of independent orders for women began in Northern Italy in the early years of the thirteenth century.[56] The initial impetus appears to have been a drive towards radical poverty and the desire on the part of a few wealthy women to endow communities for themselves and their companions. These slowly came under the control of the church, through association with the Franciscan foundations of the Clares or the Damianites. This did not, however, stop the upsurge of popular female devotion and it appears that many new, local and relatively small communities of women continued to form through the next century, often referred to by the collective title of the *sorores minores*.[57] Many of these communities did not live by any particular rule, although there was always an attempt to bring them under control. Many of them did not form a convent as such and did not, as almost all earlier women's orders had, cut themselves off entirely from the world. Rather, they were often heavily engaged in worldly affairs, albeit of a charitable and caring nature. The majority of these communities also maintained a deliberate control over their own spiritual lives, engaging in their own popular devotions and employing their own priests under their own control rather than placing themselves under the authority of a bishop or religious order. Some of these small communities remained in the towns, taking over the residences of wealthy widows or

---

[56] See L. Pellegrini, 'Female Religious Experience and Society in Thirteenth Century Italy', in S. Farmer and B. H. Rosenwein (eds.), *Monks and Nuns, Saints and Outcasts, Religion in Medieval Society, Essays in Honor of Lester K. Little*. Ithaca: Cornell University Press, 2000, 97–122.
[57] Ibid.

heiresses; others moved to hermitages in the countryside. The movement as a whole, however, was extremely significant in terms of the number of women involved, and slowly spread beyond Northern Italy to other parts of Europe.[58]

If we now turn to the confraternities, we see a very similar devotional attitude but turned in a slightly different organisational direction. In 1260 a certain Fra Ranieri in Perugia led a revival of lay people, men and women, older people and children, tradespeople and nobility, in a series of devotional processions through the streets accompanied by flagellation.[59] This continued for some years and spread to other cities of Northern Italy, especially to Bologna. Raffaello Morghen argues that the cause of this outburst was the desire, on the part of the ordinary people of the town, to engage in penitential acts in the hope of bringing peace to a region that had been racked with wars for the previous hundred years.[60] In Bologna this movement was organised into lay, male-only, confraternities, and these spread to many of the cities of Northern Italy. As the confraternities spread, however, the purposes behind the penitential devotion also changed, with less emphasis on communal peace and more on individual salvation. These flagellant communities formed just one of a series of confraternities devoted to prayer, penance and charity at the time.

James Banker outlines three different types of lay confraternity in the small town of San Sepolcro on the Tuscan/Umbrian border and claims that these would be typical of many towns in the region.[61] The oldest confraternity began in the thirteenth century as a society that dealt in charity and the commemoration of the dead. It accepted both men and women as members and eventually formed a central part of the town's elite institutions, especially when the townspeople began to take control of their own affairs from the early fourteenth century. Over time the confraternity became very wealthy through money left to it on the death of its members, and its officers spent almost all of their time administering their wealth and the conditions of the various bequests left to them.[62] The second type of

[58] This movement has also been associated with what has been described as the 'feminisation' of sanctity in the late Middle Ages, that is the growth of devotions to, and canonisations of, female saints during this period. Pellegrini points out, however, that the vast majority of the new women saints were not members of any religious community, not even of these informal kinds, and that this shows a rise in popular female piety of a very different sort. Ibid., 121–2.
[59] See J. Henderson, 'The Flagellant Movement and Flagellant Confraternities in Central Italy, 1260–1400', *Studies in Church History*, 15 (1978), 147–60.
[60] Quoted in ibid., 149–51.
[61] J. R. Banker, *Death in the Community: Memorialization and Confraternities in an Italian Commune in the Late Middle Ages.* Athens: University of Georgia Press, 1988.
[62] Ibid., 38–74.

confraternity, which emerged as the town became self-governing in the 1300s, also began as a popular movement and, like the first, it ended up simply administering significant wealth and bequests from influential townspeople. What distinguishes the second type, however, was that it was rooted socially among rural labourers who lived in the town and emerged with the desire to engage in processional singing on all major feasts of Christ and of Mary. The processional singing did not entirely cease, but it came to play a very minor role in the activities of the confraternity, and other similar confraternities that began to grow at the same time all died out when the Black Death struck the town in the 1340s.[63]

The final type of confraternity was related to the flagellants.[64] These confraternities emerged at about the same time as the second group but only began to be popular following the plague of 1342 and an earthquake in 1352. Banker shows that these groups were not interested in bequests or public charity as such, although two of the five such confraternities in the town did run hospitals. Their purpose appears to have been solely for the good of their members, to provide sickness benefits during life and proper memorialisation on death including a suitable funeral and masses for the dead in subsequent months and years. The flagellation or whipping was seen as part of the discipline of the confraternity rather than as a penitential rite as such, and Banker argues that the confraternity went to some lengths to distinguish the discipline meted out by the prior of the confraternity for the breaking of its own rules from sin and ecclesiastically imposed penance.[65] This was a lay community that wished to maintain control entirely in lay hands, electing new priors (a lay post) and other officers every six months. It was a community controlled by the middle-ranking figures of the town, neither the political elite nor the poor. It was also a community dedicated to the achievement of holiness throughout life and to the sanctification of its members. What is more, in San Sepolcro, it appears that in 1400 practically every male in the town belonged to one of the five flagellant confraternities that were available.

It is the male-only nature of these flagellant confraternities that links them to the situation we saw among the communities of women. Banker argues that it was because alternative avenues for intensive personal devotion were already available to women that the confraternities became male-only, offering the working men of the town an outlet for their own

---

[63] Ibid., 110–44.   [64] Ibid., 145–73.   [65] Ibid., 150.

devotional needs.[66] Whether this is borne out in other towns of the region is difficult to say.

In San Sepolcro the establishment of the confraternities clearly went hand in hand with the increasing political power of the lay government at the expense of the abbey within the town and the diocese. San Sepolcro was not alone in this. Towns and cities across Europe were experiencing the same kind of transformation and the changes in devotion clearly followed as they had in San Sepolcro. This was not, however, simply a matter of political determinism. There were at least two distinct forces at work in this process. The first was the laicisation of the city governments, with power being placed increasingly in the hands of the guilds or similarly organised political groups. The second was the increasing concern on the part of lay people to claim control over their own devotional life for themselves. These two movements are not necessarily the same thing, nor are they necessarily causally linked; they simply appear to have been two parts of a wider process that was occurring across Europe at the time. The consequences are also not always the same in each and every city either. In San Sepolcro and other cities of Northern Italy the consequence appears to have been seen in the rise of the flagellant communities and other confraternities. In northern England it was the rise of vernacular drama that, among other things, resulted from a very similar transformation.[67]

Within the northern English cities the Wars of the Roses and other political upheavals had combined with a growing confidence among the laity to bring control of cities such as York, Chester and Coventry out of the control of the abbeys and into the hands of the lay people of the cities, most significantly of the various trade guilds. This led to a number of changes in the devotional life of the cities and in particular to the rise of religious, or more specifically biblical, drama. It has been argued that the vernacular drama of the fourteenth and fifteenth centuries developed through a smooth evolutionary path from the older liturgical dramas that we looked at in relation to Sarum in the previous chapter.[68] Lawrence Clopper, however, argues that this is not the case.[69] The new city leaders of the fifteenth century were not simply trying to bring the Latin ecclesial dramas to a wider audience. They were, he suggests, trying to do something

[66] In 1300 there were 150 women in such communities in San Sepolcro out of a total population of just over 4,000, while only 50 male clerics lived within the town, although it is impossible to say how many of these were priests. Ibid., 34–5.
[67] L. Clopper, *Drama, Play, and Game, English Festive Culture in the Medieval and Early Modern Period.* Chicago: University of Chicago Press, 2001, 138–59.
[68] See p. 137 above.   [69] Clopper, *Drama*, 142–3.

very different. In part these cycles of vernacular drama, based primarily on biblical themes, were a way of bringing the Bible to the people in a relatively uncontroversial way, at a time when the translation of the Bible itself was banned. They were also a way of developing, or perhaps of tapping into, the increasing lay spirituality of the time that we also saw in the confraternities of San Sepolcro.

One of the points that Clopper makes is that these dramas were performed, not in the churches, but on the streets of the city.[70] They were not exactly banned from the churches but represented in some ways an anti-clerical, or more specifically anti-abbey, position; the abbeys had often been the main source of political power within the cities up to this point. The lay authorities of the city did not have access to the churches; they did, however, have access to the streets and they began to use these for the kind of spectacle and entertainment that had, up until this point, been the responsibility of the church, or the kind of 'play' that was risqué, lewd, violent and antithetical to all that the church stood for. The city government was not, therefore, simply substituting an existing popular 'secular' discourse for that of the church; they were creating a new 'Christian' discourse that was aimed as much at educating the mass of the population as it was at providing entertainment. The rise of morality plays alongside the biblical cycles makes this situation very clear. This new vernacular drama was part of a process that would ultimately lead into the Reformation; it was part of a moral crusade on the part of the religiously orientated laity aimed as much against the mass of the population and their own demotic discourses as against the official discourses of the Church. It is an application of power in the arena of the city streets but not a simple imposition of authority.

Another example of the use of demotic discourses of devotion for wider political ends can be seen if we go back to Northern Italy and the cult of St Anne in Florence.[71] On St Anne's day, 26 July 1343, the Florentines rose against Walter VI of Brienne, who had established a despotate within the city. There was no obvious link between the uprising and St Anne apart from the coincidence of the date. However, as Roger Crum and David Wilkins show, this led to a rapid rise of the cult of St Anne within the new republic.[72] On 12 January 1344 the city government declared the feast of

[70] Ibid., 159.
[71] R. J. Crum and D. G. Wilkins, 'In the Defense of Florentine Republicanism: Saint Anne and Florentine Art, 1343–1575', in K. Ashley and P. Sheingorn (eds.), *Interpreting Cultural Symbols, Saint Anne in Later Medieval Society*. Athens: University of Georgia Press, 1990, 131–68.
[72] Ibid., 131–3.

St Anne an official holiday with processions and offerings in honour of the saint. An image of the saint was also set up in the Orsamichele. This building was in part a church, financed by public taxes, and also a grain store and market place, the front of which contained niches with statues for all the major trade guilds of the city. This was one of the most important communal buildings in Florence. In 1349 a separate oratory was built and dedicated to the saint opposite the Orsamichele and the veneration of St Anne, along with processions through the streets, became one of the most significant religious events of the city.

Crum and Wilkins show, through a study of the iconography of the paintings of St Anne produced during the fourteenth and fifteenth centuries, how the saint became a potent symbol of the republic and republicanism within Florence. St Anne was shown as originally the liberator, and later the protector, of the city. Her grandmotherly care of the Christ child was transferred to the city itself and its particular form of government. The image took on a series of different meanings during the political turmoil that followed over the next century until the return of the Medici to Florence in 1512 and the fall of the republican government. The Medici, it appears, were then able to claim the image of St Anne for themselves, as one of their own family saints, and so to break the symbolic association of St Anne with republicanism while still retaining her protective role in relation to the city itself. Within this history we can see the way in which a number of different discourses, of power, of devotion and of display, come together and interweave to capture the identity of the city community. None of these discourses could normally be counted as 'dominant', although for a time, within the city itself, that of republicanism and the association of St Anne with the ideals of the Republic clearly were. The association and interaction of discourses, including the demotic discourses of devotion, are in fact far more complex in this kind of situation and need to be recognised as such.

This discussion of St Anne shows how, towards the end of the fourteenth century, new devotions were beginning to develop, often linked with the growing lay interest in religion. These again had political roots as different communities vied to get their particular devotion recognised by the church and into the dominant discourses. They also had a great deal to do with fashion as devotions spread from city to city, each one trying to outdo its neighbours in keeping up with the latest trends. It is within this context that we need to see the rise of importance for the feast of Corpus Christi, perhaps the most significant of the new feasts at this time.

The devotion to Corpus Christi originated in Liège, in what is now Belgium, where a rapid growth in the number of women wanting to leave society and enter religious communities, similar to that of Northern Italy, led to a growth in the first half of the thirteenth century of what were known locally as the *béguines*.[73] Among the beguines there was an established tradition of visions and a strong sense of eucharistic devotion, which Miri Rubin argues was one of the few ways in which the women concerned could make actual physical contact with Jesus.[74] In 1208 one of the beguines, Juliana of Cornillon, had a vision in which she believed Jesus himself encouraged her to establish a feast of the eucharist. The local bishop and the Dominican order supported Juliana's proposals and the feast was established in Liège in 1246.[75] However, the feast began to get lost in local and international politics after Juliana's death, and it was not until it was established by Pope Urban IV in a Papal decree of 1264 that it began to spread beyond its original setting. This was the first universal feast that had been established by Papal decree and it is not insignificant that Pope Urban had been present, as an archdeacon, in Liège when the feast was first celebrated in 1246.[76]

The feast grew and spread very rapidly across the whole of Western Europe, partly because of fashion, and partly because of its official support and the office written for it by St Thomas Aquinas. We also have to realise, however, that this was a devotion that all people could take part in; it was not in any sense a local cult, and yet contained the most important relic of all, the body and blood of the Lord. It was also a feast that quickly took on many of the elements of popular demotic devotional practices including regular processions, confraternities and cycles of religious drama. The feast of Corpus Christi in many ways became the distinguishing feast of the period, drawing to itself all the different demotic discourses of devotion and yet having the full backing of the most powerful official discourses of the church and the local authorities. Finally, the feast provided one of the most important contexts for display within the late medieval cities of Western Europe.

The question of display highlights one of the most widespread and significant forms of devotion in the late Middle Ages, the procession. I discussed processions in some detail in previous chapters in relation to

[73] M. Rubin, *Corpus Christi, The Eucharist in Late Medieval Culture.* Cambridge: Cambridge University Press, 1991, 167.

[74] Ibid., 169; see also C. W. Bynum, 'Women Mystics and Eucharistic Devotion in the Thirteenth Century', *Women's Studies*, 11 (1984), 179–84 and the wider discussion of medieval women and food in C. W. Bynum, *Holy Feast, Holy Fast, The Religious Significance of Food to Medieval Women.* Berkeley: University of California Press, 1987.

[75] Rubin, *Corpus Christi*, 174.   [76] Ibid., 176.

Constantinople, Jerusalem and even Rome.[77] However, it was only in the late Middle Ages that the procession began to be an important arena for the combining of demotic and dominant discourse, and of power and devotion through much of Western Europe.[78] A procession could establish and sustain the political authority both of those who took part (who comes before whom in the order of the procession) and of those who sponsor the procession (there are regular accounts of fights between members of competing processions in many major cities). In Coventry, for example, in central England, the procession came to define the corporate bodies within the city and helped to establish the social hierarchy.[79] Many of the processions were made up of the laymen of the city, but these were divided into craft guilds and religious confraternities. The confraternities had a significant control over the city government, with the Master of the Corpus Christi guild becoming Mayor, and then, on leaving office, the Master of the Holy Trinity guild. It was in the Corpus Christi procession that this political allegiance was shown, with the order of the procession being determined by membership of the guilds and confraternities and the contributions these bodies made to the expenses of the feast.

Once again, as with rural demotic discourses and the situation of the Northern Italian cities, we find issues of identity at the heart of this politicking in relation to the procession. Within the procession individuals could assert their identity by the position they held within the procession. Also a guild, a family or even a city could assert their own identity, over against others, by the flamboyance and display of their processions. These were devotional, and highly liturgical activities, part of the dominant discourses of the church, but their popularity, I would suggest, came as much from their political value as from their religious content. It is utterly impossible, as we have seen, to distinguish political from devotional discourses within the demotic practices of the period.

DISCOURSE, POWER AND THE DRIFT INTO CORRUPTION

At this point in the chapter, therefore, we need to get back to my initial discussion of demotic and dominant discourses and to ask whether this can

[77] See pp. 64–74 and 98–101 above.
[78] See the various essays in B. A. Hanawalt and K. L. Reyerson (eds.), *City and Spectacle in Medieval Europe.* Minneapolis: University of Minnesota Press, 1994.
[79] C. Phythian-Adams, 'Ceremonies and the Citizen: The Communal Year at Coventry 1450–1550', in P. Clark and P. Slack (eds.), *Crisis and Order in the English Towns 1500–1700.* London: Routledge and Kegan Paul, 1972, 57–85.

shed any light on what was happening in relation to worship and devotion as Western Europe approached the Reformation. There are two issues that I wish to look at. The first looks back to the conclusion of the previous chapter, where I talked about the power of the dominant 'cosmological' discourses, and the second looks forward and raises questions about the growth of corruption within the Western Church, or at least at the growth of discourses about corruption by those who were dissatisfied by that church.

At the end of the previous chapter, I argued that the cosmological nature of the dominant Christian discourse, associated with the worship of the grand cathedrals of East and West, provided a way of understanding the lack of direct participation in the rite by the majority of the laity, especially the women.[80] This led me into a discussion of devotion and so onto the issues of this chapter. Another way of looking at this situation is to suggest that the context of the cathedrals in the eleventh century was the last point at which something very specific within Christian worship, which emerged during the third century, could be seen in Western Europe. This was the idea that in some way the worship, or spiritual discipline, of a small group within the Christian community could be taken as the worship of the whole. This idea was alien to the very earliest Christianity and even Tertullian and others in the third century would not have recognised it. For many authors at this time the very matter of debate was how far one had to enter into continuous worship and spiritual discipline before being called a Christian. Tertullian was very strict with his Montanist background; others argued for a far more lax approach.[81] It was only after the monastic tradition had been under way for some time that certain individuals, monks, hermits and other ascetics were recognised as taking on a spiritual discipline far greater than, and in some ways on behalf of, the ordinary Christian.

With the increase in the number of Christians through the fourth century, and the growing Christianisation of society, the possibility of vicarious worship became ever more significant. It was not possible to expect every member of society to become an ascetic; society itself would collapse if this were to happen. The conversion of the barbarian kingdoms, and the mass baptisms that followed, only reinforced this view that somehow the mediation between the human and the divine worlds could, and perhaps should, be undertaken by the few on behalf of the many. This was the role of the priest, and more specifically the role of the monk or the nun.

---

[80] See pp. 148–9 above.   [81] See pp. 54–5 above.

What had been true of spiritual discipline began gradually to be true of all worship, such that the offices and the masses said by the clergy with their regular round of devotion were enough for all, and it was only important for most lay people to know that this was taking place for them to gain the benefit. This was the situation we saw in the case of Salisbury and Kiev in the previous chapter.

Of course, ordinary devout lay Christians have always engaged in their own forms of devotion and spiritual disciplines throughout the fourth to the fourteenth century as we have seen. It is the dominant trend, however, that concerns me here, and that I would argue was firmly rooted in the vicarious tradition. Elements of this continued through the thirteenth and fourteenth centuries and on beyond the Reformation to the present day. It has never been entirely lost within the worship of the Eastern churches, where the idea of the liturgy being celebrated for all, irrespective of their presence, still prevails. With the growth of the women's devotional orders and the lay confraternities of the thirteenth and fourteenth centuries, however, we begin to see a subtle change within the Western church. Whether this is simply the final stages of Christianisation, the point at which truly Christian discourses finally become accepted across society, or whether it has more to do with the rise of individualism and the desire for people to take responsibility for their own destiny is difficult to say, and probably beyond this text. The result was the kind of situation we saw in San Sepolcro, where the vast majority of the men were members of lay confraternities, a significant number of women belonged to women's orders, and the whole population appears to have been engaged in some kind of personal devotional activity and spiritual discipline of one kind or another.

One way of looking at this situation, therefore, is to talk about the 'monasticisation' of society, a situation in which the ideals of spiritual discipline and continuous worship of the monastery are taken out into the streets and houses of the entire community. This, as we will see, begins to lay the foundations for the next stage, that of the German and Swiss Reformations.[82] What is difficult to determine, however, at this point in the church's history, is the way in which this made people feel about the religious orders themselves. There is no obvious sense of the decline of the orders before the Reformation, although the disconnecting of the abbeys from political power in the cities that we saw in the previous section may have raised questions that made Henry VIII's dissolution of the

---

[82] See pp. 183–8 below.

monasteries in England easier to accept for the majority of the population. It is one thing for the laity to take responsibility for their own devotion and salvation; it is quite another to accuse the whole clerical class of corruption.

One of the questions that is inevitably asked, therefore, given the date of these different popular devotions, is 'does this kind of demotic discourse of power and religion lead inevitably to accusations of corruption on the part of those who support the dominant discourse?' Related to this question are others previously discussed. What, for example, is the relationship between devotion and superstition? What is the relationship between demotic discourses of devotion and dominant discourses of doctrine? One of the reasons why I believe that a discourse of corruption was allowed to develop takes us back to the fact that the spiritual and secular powers were increasingly held by different institutions in Western Europe and that these seldom worked in harmony.

It was clear in the later medieval period that the sacred power was invested in an institution that also demonstrated secular power. This was as true of the Papacy at an international level as it was of the abbeys and other ecclesiastical powers in the cities. It was this close association of the two distinct kinds of power, and the challenging of this association by the laity, that led ultimately to the debate about corruption. When it is clear that it is the secular powers that are benefiting from the mishandling of sacred sources of power, then this can be dealt with through primarily secular means: the dominant sacred discourses, and those who control them, can lay claim to their rights to exclusivity over sacred sources of power and condemn the secular intruders. When the sacred power, however, does not have this kind of secular scapegoat then it is in deep trouble, and that, I would argue, was the case towards the end of the fifteenth century with the Catholic Church in Western Europe.

Many of the ordinary devotional activities had, at least in the cities, been taken under the control of city leaders, guilds or local families, and were clearly being used for their own purposes. At times the church had fought back through specifically spiritual means, as with the rise of the public sermon and the claiming for the dominant discourse of significant popular elements of the demotic, such as Corpus Christi. However, this was not enough for the influential city leaders. Alongside the positive work that the mendicant orders were doing, and the great spiritual renewal of the other monastic orders, there was also the experience of the inquisition, or at the very least the rumours of the inquisition that were beginning to circulate, and the growth of the wealth of the Papacy at the clear expense of ordinary worshippers through the imposition of indulgences and other forms of tax.

178   *A Sociological History of Christian Worship*

This set the local city authorities, who wished to lay claim to some of this income, against the Papacy itself. Where the bishops associated themselves with local feeling, as in Northern Italy, the church retained its integrity. Where the bishops were too distant, and associated themselves too closely with the Papacy or the imperial government, as in Southern Germany and Switzerland, then the local representative of the dominant discourse was seen as part of the problem.

It was possible for the church, with its dominant discourses, to condemn many local and particularly rural devotional activities as 'superstition' in order to retain at least some power over these practices. This, however, only heightened the problem, as it was often the popular devotional activities of the laity, and the demotic discourses that went with them, that were so condemned. It was difficult at times to see where the secular powers ended and those of the church began, and this made the whole situation very dangerous. The church needed to maintain its own discourse as dominant, especially among the poor and the rural populations. However, its increasing attempts to dismiss the demotic discourses of these areas as 'superstition' only heightened the problems. Linked with this was the growth of the merchant class, who distrusted both the traditional secular authorities rooted in the nobility and the power of the church, based as it often was on the blind devotion of the workers and the peasants. The merchant classes had a vested interest in dismissing the popular devotions of the mass of the population as 'superstition'. These maintained the power of the church over the people who performed them, and yet denied these people access to the new demotic discourses of personal spirituality and salvation that the merchants were advocating.

The merchant class, therefore, was caught; they had no obvious place within the old order and had no obvious means of changing that order to their own advantage apart from the complete overthrow of that order. Where they could, they managed to control the cities and adapt the devotional life of the cities to their own ends, as we have seen. However, even here they had to acknowledge the greater sacred power of the church and often came into dispute with the wider church in relation to their own devotional lives. The stage was set, therefore, for some kind of change, and that was to come in the Reformation. However, this political analysis was not the only factor involved in the origins of the Reformation, and the other elements, more closely associated with worship, are the issues that I will move on to explore in the following chapter.

CHAPTER 6

Worship and the rise of humanistic discourses, 1500–1800

INTRODUCTION: 'DE-CHRISTIANISATION'

It is possible to see this chapter, at one level, as simply a reversal of Chapter 2. In that chapter we looked at the way in which the gradual Christianisation of the late Roman Empire affected the development of worship, and how the increasingly public nature of that worship contributed to the process of Christianisation. In this chapter, we could argue that, beginning with the Reformation in Western Europe, we will be looking at the gradual process of de-Christianisation and the impact this has had on liturgy and worship. We could also argue, fairly convincingly, that this process of de-Christianisation was helped by the increasing privatisation of worship from the fourteenth century onwards. To look at the situation as simply and as starkly as this, however, would be a mistake.

The first question we have to ask is what, if anything, performed the role of the Christian discourses in the process of Christianisation: what was it that was driving Christianity out of its role as the dominant discourse in society? The obvious answer might well be 'science', or 'modernism' or even 'rationalism'. These have all, in their different ways, become central parts of the dominant discourse of the Western world today. I would want to suggest, however, that neither science in itself, nor modernism, nor rationalism, are the discourses that have been driving Christianity out of its previous position of dominance. Science is only part of a wider discourse; it is not all-encompassing enough to become an alternative dominating discourse on its own. The same is true of rationalism, and, I would suggest, of modernism. In the Introduction I proposed the title of 'humanism' for the alternative discourse that has taken over from Christianity, and stressed that this is not one specific thing, but rather, like the Christian discourses before it, a series of attitudes and assumptions, of which science, modernism and rationalism, as we know them today, are simply various elements.[1]

In using the word 'humanist'[2] here to describe the discourse that has taken over from Christianity in the Western world, I am not simply referring to the technical use of the term as applied to the writings of Erasmus and others in the sixteenth century.[3] However, I do wish to pick up one particular element of their writing and thought that I would want to argue has become dominant in Western thinking. This is the focus on the human person over against, or at the very least in preference to, the divine. If I go back to the four features of Christian discourse I discussed in the Introduction,[4] then humanist discourses clearly relate to these in very different ways from the Christian discourses. Time, for example, is understood in the humanist discourses as either limited to the human span, or stretched into geological vastness, neither of which equates with the eternity of Christian discourses or the cyclic nature of pagan time. Many humanist discourses talk of the absence of God rather than an intimacy with the divine. However, the deist views of the eighteenth century and the idea of the divine spark within the human soul are both, in different ways, variations on humanist understandings of the divine, placing the human person higher in our system of values than any kind of divine element. This is also true in human-to-human relations, where the language of 'rights' probably characterises the humanist approach better than any other. However, Communist or Fascist totalitarianism can both be considered as 'humanist' in the terms I am using, as they have no place for the divine in human relationships. Finally, the question of truth, for humanist discourses, is rooted in what human beings can discover for themselves, whether that is the deductive logical truth of rationalism, the hope of final teleological truth as specified in modernist and some forms of scientific discourse, or the abandonment of any possibility of ultimate truth as we see in post-modernism. All of these approaches limit the possibility of truth to that which can be gained by humanity alone and all, in their different ways, are humanist in the terms that I am using.

If this is the case, then what we should be talking about is not a process of 'de-Christianisation' as such, which presents the process of change in a

---

[1] See p. 18 above.

[2] In so doing I recognise that 'humanist' may not be the best choice of words and I would be open to other alternatives. Having said that, however, I am convinced that something of the kind of discourse I am describing has become dominant in the contemporary Western world.

[3] B. Hall, *Humanists and Protestants, 1500–1900*. Edinburgh: T. & T. Clark, 1990.

[4] See pp. 19–23 above.

negative fashion; nor should we be talking about a process of 'secularisation', which has similar overtones and focuses on what I think is the wrong element;[5] rather we should be looking at the way in which the various discourses of humanism have slowly, but surely, become the dominant discourse in the West from its origins in the fifteenth century to the present day.[6] Just as the Christianisation of the Empire in the fourth to the eighth century was not really a process of de-paganisation, but rather the growth of something new that slowly, but never completely, displaced an earlier discourse, so the growth of humanist discourses does not set out to de-Christianise as such; rather it displaces, and more importantly transforms, the earlier dominant discourses of Christianity into something new.

In order to look to the origins of humanism we need to go back to medieval philosophy and the rise of the mystical tradition as well as to the rediscovery of classical discourses in the Renaissance, the rise of rational science and many other causes. If we focus on the mystical tradition, it may seem odd that a tradition so solidly rooted in the spiritual should form the basis for a series of discourses many of which ultimately rejected any form of spirituality or transcendence of any kind. However, this is where many forms of humanism do appear to have their origin. The mystical traditions spoke of spiritual discipline and the relationship of the individual to God. They questioned whether it was ever possible to speak in positive terms about God at all and settled on negative language as the primary mode of discourse about the divine.[7] We can never say what God is, but we can say what God is not. This discourse of negativity is only a short step from a discourse of denial. Linked with this tradition was a growing focus on the individual and the individual's own spiritual development that we have also seen within the women's orders and lay confraternities of the later Middle Ages.[8] Here again the idea of the individual soul seeking its ultimate union with God is only a small step, intellectually, from the idea of humanist individualism, the individual person alone against the

---

[5] The 'secular' is very difficult to define; it is a lack of something rather than a thing in itself. For this reason the growth or infringement of the secular in society is, almost by definition, the decline of the religious. However, secularisation does not define what replaces the decline of religion. Hence my own preference for 'humanism': despite all its faults, it does at least specify something about what has taken the place of Christian discourses.

[6] I would also claim that humanism is becoming a dominant discourse in many other parts of the world, but this is a much more complex situation, as humanist and Christian discourses arrived in many places together under the form of colonialism and have engaged with many other local discourses. I have more to say about this in the final chapter.

[7] D. Turner, *The Darkness of God, Negativity in Christian Mysticism.* Cambridge: Cambridge University Press, 1995.

[8] See pp. 165–70 above.

world, and René Descartes's 'I think, therefore I am'. It would simply be a matter of laying out those steps in order and seeing where the various discourses are leading, but such a task is beyond the scope of this particular text.

It is clear, therefore, that contemporary humanist discourses were already at work within the Reformation. Ulrich Zwingli was happy to acknowledge the importance of humanism to his own intellectual development.[9] To suggest that the Reformation could be the consequence of the rise of humanist discourses alone, however, would undoubtedly be very controversial and probably wrong.[10] I have already looked, in the previous chapter, at the increasing 'monasticisation' of the laity, at the role of corruption within the church, and at the economic and political impact of the rise of urbanism in relation to the origins of the Reformation, and all these factors must also be borne in mind.[11] No historical process can ever be reduced to a simplistic analysis of cause and effect. All I am trying to propose in this section, therefore, is that the Reformation demonstrates one element of the rise of the humanist discourses as I have defined them, albeit a very significant one. As I will show below, the kind of humanism espoused by the Reformation thinkers still had a very strong role for the divine and focused much more on the individualist elements of the discourse than the atheist elements. Later in the seventeenth and eighteenth centuries, however, with the Enlightenment and the growth of rationalism, another element of humanist discourses, we can see the atheist strands coming to the fore, while the individualist elements sometimes appear and at others are submerged beneath the language of scientific rationalism. All of this, however, I would want to argue, is part of a single set of discourses that was slowly becoming central to the thinking of the Western European elite from the fifteenth century onwards. It was inevitable, therefore, that this discourse was going to have an impact on the worship of what, until well into the twentieth century, remained the dominant religious expression of Western Europe.

In order to see this at work we need to look at the way in which humanist discourses impacted on Christian worship, paying particular attention to questions such as the privatisation of worship. I want to do this by focusing on three specific areas. I will begin with the Reformation itself, understood as part of the initial stages of the rise of humanist discourses and their interaction with Christianity. I will then focus on what has variously been called the Counter-Reformation or the Catholic Reformation, although it is probably best seen as the response of traditionalist Christianity to the humanist

---

[9]   See W. P. Stephens, *Zwingli, An Introduction to His Thought.* Oxford: Clarendon Press, 1992.
[10]   See the discussion in Hall, *Humanists and Protestants.*   [11]   See pp. 176–8 above.

discourses in Western Europe and beyond (that is, in both Russia and China). Finally, I will come back to the Reformation and the impact of privatisation on what has been called the 'radical reformation' and some of its offshoots in Europe and the New World, with a particular emphasis on the role of music in the worship of these communities.

ICONOCLASM AND CREATIVITY

In trying to understand the impact of the European Reformation on the history of worship I could begin to lay out all the different changes to the liturgy that took place across Europe between 1500 and 1700.[12] To do this, however, would be very complex, take far too long and provide a far greater sense of diversity and discontinuity than was perhaps the case. What I wish to do, therefore, following on from my discussions in the first section of this chapter, and following a pattern I have used throughout the book, is to outline the changes, along with their possible causes and their consequences, in one particular community before making some more general comments about the subsequent changes across Europe.

The phrase 'stripping of the altars' has been used by Eamon Duffy of the English Reformation in the middle of the sixteenth century.[13] The phrase is a deliberate attempt to link the iconoclasm of the English Reformation with the Latin liturgical rite of Maundy Thursday, during which all the decorations and other movable objects were removed from the church before Good Friday. There have been questions asked, however, as to how far the English Reformation actually led to the destruction of the 'old religion' with all its imagery and ceremonial during the sixteenth century.[14] It was perhaps only during the Commonwealth, a hundred years later, and the civil war that preceded it, that the final stripping of the altars in England was achieved. I want to transfer Duffy's idea, therefore, to another context where, I feel, it is far more apt: that is, to Zurich towards the beginning of the sixteenth century.[15]

---

[12] See the references quoted in D. H. Tripp, 'Protestantism and the Eucharist', in C. Jones et al. (eds.), *The Study of Liturgy*. London: SPCK, 1992, 294–308.

[13] E. Duffy, *The Stripping of the Altars, Traditional Religion in England c. 1400–c. 1580*. New Haven: Yale University Press, 1992.

[14] Ibid.

[15] Zurich was not the first place to experience iconoclasm. That occurred in Wittenberg, where Andreas von Karlstadt preached against idolatry and led an iconoclastic campaign in 1521 while Luther was in hiding from the authorities. Zurich was, however, the first place in which iconoclasm became the official policy of a legitimate authority and therefore fits better into Duffy's image of the 'stripping of the altars'. See C. M. W. Eire, *War Against the Idols, The Reformation of Worship from Erasmus to Calvin*. Cambridge: Cambridge University Press, 1986.

Zurich was one of the birthplaces of the Reformation and one of the communities where the Reformation took most hold. In order to understand what was going on in Zurich in the early years of the sixteenth century, however, we need to look at a range of different phenomena. From the point of view of worship, the most obvious and the starkest change that took place was in the space of worship. The space was cleansed of all the paraphernalia of medieval worship: the relics, the ornaments, the colour, and the smells. The church was quite literally stripped and, as we saw with the Byzantine iconoclasm of the eighth century, the churches were whitewashed and left no distractions for the congregation.[16] This, however, was a relatively minor change in relation to the full range of transformations that were going on. Within three years from 1522 to 1525 the ceremonial and pomp of the mass was replaced with a form of worship in German, based firmly on the word, in both a theological and a textual sense. The old monastic office that had dictated the times of day, along with much of the calendar that had determined the seasons, had been swept aside. The processions, along with the devotion to images, relics and the sacrament, had all been abandoned with nothing to replace them. Finally, all instrumental music had been silenced, seemingly forever, within the churches.[17]

Whether this new form of worship reflected humanist principles is a matter for debate, but the process is one in which the beginnings of the humanist discourse can clearly be seen. The question remains, however, of why a community such as Zurich was willing and able to apparently throw off so many centuries of tradition and such deep-rooted spirituality within such a short space of time. What were the continuities, and what were the changes that made such a radical transformation possible? In order to understand the changes that occurred in Zurich we need to understand the situation from the perspective of three different groups within the city. The first is that of the intellectual and theological elite, not always led by Ulrich Zwingli, the principal pastor of the city, but certainly including him. The second are the city leaders, the authorities that made up the council and who, thanks to Zwingli's careful politicking, actually made all the decisions. The third are the ordinary people who ultimately supported and encouraged the changes imposed by the council. It is in the interrelation between these three groups, and the discourses that they were developing and negotiating, that the Reformation in Zurich needs to be seen.

---

[16] See pp. 101–3 above.
[17] For a good summary see C. Lindberg, *The European Reformations*. Oxford: Blackwell, 1996, 169–98.

Let me begin, however, with Zwingli himself.[18] Ulrich Zwingli was not unique among the intellectual elite of Zurich. He had come to Reformation ideas in his own time and in his own way, through the study of Erasmus and other humanist thinkers, but also through a thorough conversion to the idea of a personal relationship with God.[19] Zwingli was not, however, the only one to have followed this path among the Swiss clergy. When he came to Zurich as pastor to the Great Church in 1518, he found a community of thinkers within the city that already wanted to reject all that the Roman Church stood for on the basis of Gospel teaching.[20] Zwingli himself was a great biblical scholar, and it was his reading of the Gospels, associated with his personal faith in a direct and personal saviour, which had tempered his humanism and led, in turn, to the tenets of Reformation thinking. Others among the intellectual elite of Zurich had wanted to move much further in a humanist direction, questioning even the Gospel texts. Others again focused more on the Gospels and wanted to impose what they understood as a 'biblical faith' on the people of Zurich. Zwingli was careful not to ally himself too closely with either party. He was not among the most radical of the thinkers in the city, nor did he reject the radicals entirely. Above all he placed a major emphasis on the need to teach the ordinary people about the Gospel before implementing any radical changes.[21]

Practically all of those involved in the radical party within the city had been led to their position through intellectual activity and the reading of the Gospels. They were convinced of the literal words of the text and they wished to implement those words in the spiritual and devotional life of the citizens. It is undoubtedly the case that the Catholic Church had moved a long way in its thinking and its worship from the situation described in the Gospels and Epistles. However, it is also the case that the reformers of Zurich were still reading the texts from within their own context and reading into them the kind of individualist, evangelical theology that they wanted to see. It was a particular reading of the text, not a literal reading, that was being propagated and this was as true for Zwingli as it was for his more radical opponents. In fact, it is probably this realisation that led Zwingli himself towards a more moderate line. He was above all else a teacher, and began a series of series of public sermons on the day after his appointment to the post at the Grossmünster in January 1519. This preaching was based on the Bible and, beginning with Matthew's Gospel, he took the citizens through the text verse by verse.[22] Zwingli was also a linguist and understood the Greek behind the text, including many of the difficulties of

---

[18] See Stephens, *Zwingli*.   [19] Ibid., 13–15.   [20] Ibid., 16.   [21] Ibid.   [22] Ibid.

interpretation that this must lead to.[23] His teaching makes the textual questions clear and refuses to be drawn into a dogmatic fundamentalism. His approach, therefore, while being literalist in many respects, has more of the humanist scepticism in it than that of many of his opponents.[24]

On regular occasions from the 1520s onwards Zwingli and various opponents, either more radical or more Catholic, were invited to come before the City Council to dispute matters of discipline and worship.[25] The Council was reluctant to act until it had been convinced by the arguments of those it listened to. Was it, however, intellectual debate that was ultimately driving its actions? There were, of course, as there inevitably are in all political bodies, questions of personality and local individual political motivations involved. These could be worked out and presented in any detailed exploration of the situation if all the relevant documentation was available. We must remember, however, that this was also a city-state with other allegiances and a wider political context to take into account.[26] The Council members were, within reason, all members of the merchant classes within the city and they had their own motivations as members of that class that we began to see in the discussion of the Italian city-states in the previous chapter.[27] The city, however, also had alliances with other cities, should have paid allegiance to the Holy Roman Emperor, and was part of one of the largest dioceses in Europe at that time, with a bishop who lived in Constance, some fifty miles away. These other factors must also have played a part in their decisions.

The other major group within the city of Zurich was the general population. If we have little written evidence for the real motives of the members of the City Council, we have even less for the majority of the population, except for the evidence of their actions as recounted by the major players. It is clear that the population, on the whole, went along with the reformers, or even pushed them on. There was opposition, that is clear, but not as much as might be expected when we think about how much of the ordered way of doing things was being destroyed. There are various possible reasons for this. Part of the reason may be associated with the very intensive teaching that Zwingli was offering. Part may have been due to the fierce loyalty of the people of Zurich to their city and its leaders, especially in the face of

---

[23] Ibid., 31.

[24] This can be seen particularly in his non-literalist interpretation of the last supper. Zwingli was the first person to present the phrase 'this is my body' as a symbolic statement so leading to the complete rejection of the real presence in the Eucharist. See ibid., 94–110.

[25] To distinguish the Council from the people too much is probably to give the wrong impression. At times the Council meeting consisted of over 900 people, a significant proportion of the population at the time. Ibid., 24.

[26] Ibid., 7–11.   [27] See pp. 165–74 above.

opposition from others outside the city. The people may even have preferred
the new regime and the new forms of worship. It may not have been all that
different in essence from the developing lay spirituality of the confraternities
that we looked at in the previous chapter.[28] What this worship lacked,
however, was any clear reference to healing, financial security, fertility and
so on that had been part of the demotic discourses of popular religion for
centuries.[29] These were only slowly reintroduced into Reformed worship as
the forms settled down over the decades.[30] At the time, however, such
discourses and the issues that concerned them were of less importance. It
was clearly enthusiasm that inspired the people initially and this enthusiasm
made sure that whatever was being done in the short term, even the
destruction of the cosmological system as they knew it, was seen as possible
and even desirable. Enthusiasm, however, can only last so long without some
form of continued external motivation.

What, then, were the changes that the reformers brought into play within
Zurich through the various means and motivations that I have just outlined?
Essentially they consisted of the dismantling of the old Catholic devotions
and the building of an entirely new form of worship. In practice, however,
things were not quite as simple as this. The first move was against what had
been defined as 'superstitions', activities that had no obvious purpose and no
biblical warrant, such as the fast in Lent and the devotions to shrines and
statues. Certain radical intellectuals began to eat meat during the fast in
March 1522, and while Zwingli did not join them he did preach in favour of
religious liberty and gave his explicit support to them.[31] This led on to the
destruction of images and decoration within the churches by the radicals in
October 1523 (a move made officially by the council in June 1524)[32] and finally
to a rejection of Latin and all ceremonial within the eucharist by Easter 1525.
On Maundy Thursday 1525 a table with a clean cloth, wooden platters of
bread and wooden beakers of wine was set up between the choir and the nave
of the Great Church and, with women on one side and men on the other, the
Lord's Supper was celebrated in Swiss German for the first time.[33] With each
of these steps the radicals wished to move on their own at a much more rapid
pace. In each case Zwingli advised waiting for the Council and proceeded to
argue their case before the Council. In each case, therefore, it was the City
Council and not the church authorities that actually initiated the changes.

---

[28] See pp. 168–9 above.   [29] See pp. 163–5 above.
[30] See S. G. Karant-Nunn, *The Reformation of Ritual, An Interpretation of Early Modern Germany.*
London: Routledge, 1997 for an account of this process in Germany.
[31] Stephens, *Zwingli*, 18.   [32] Eire, *War*, 76–83.   [33] Stephens, *Zwingli*, 24–5.

More significant changes, however, followed in arenas where neither the Council nor the church had any authority. I have already mentioned Zwingli's own attempt to introduce the teaching of the Gospel to the people. In June 1525 Zwingli began to hold public meetings in the town square to which he gave the title of the *Prophezei* or prophecy.[34] This was an open meeting and not under the control of either the Council or the church, but ultimately of far more influence in the changes that took place, and much more reminiscent of the new forms of worship that were to be introduced than any of the formal, agreed changes. In this preaching Zwingli expounded the scriptures in their original Greek and Hebrew and called for sweeping moral changes within the city. This led directly to reforms in marriage laws, the care of the poor and a moral mandate from the council in May 1530.[35] Zwingli wrote many of the new acts of worship for the city, and it was ultimately his ideas that found their expression in these rites.[36] Part of what he was attempting to do, both in his preaching and in his liturgy, was to try to draw the whole population together into a closer spiritual community, perhaps even a city monastery, in which every individual was expected to be devout and personally committed to piety and individual morality. For the ordinary members of the population, however, who were not versed in the details of theological discussion, the minutiae of the arguments were probably lost and what they were left with were long, powerful and often extemporary sermons surrounded by readings and prayers. Even the Lord's Supper began to be celebrated with increasing infrequency.

One of the elements that went completely, of course, was that of music, driven out with the decoration and the smells, and for much the same reason. There was something of a drive towards simplification, or perhaps we should say purification, about the process of reform, and music was seen as one of those elaborations that was unbiblical and irrelevant, leading people into sin. It was therefore banned in all public worship.[37] This demand for biblical purity made great demands on the individual members of the community and, in its Zwinglian rigour, could not have survived for very long. Following Zwingli's death, therefore, on the battlefield at Kappel in October 1531, the task of revising the rites yet again, in a form that was ultimately more user-friendly, fell to Zwingli's successor, Heinrich Bullinger.[38]

---

[34] Ibid., 25.   [35] Ibid., 26.

[36] For details of the eucharistic rite see Tripp, 'Protestantism and the Eucharist', 300.

[37] P. Westermeyer, *Te Deum, The Church and Music.* Minneapolis: Fortress Press, 1998, 149–53.

[38] Stephens, *Zwingli*, 29.

Not all the reformers were as against music as those of Zurich. Martin Luther was a great believer in the power of music to transmit his new doctrines to the population at large and he drew on Gregorian chant and popular dance tunes to help this process.[39] John Calvin allowed the simple melodies and unaccompanied singing of psalms,[40] and in England the choral tradition of the cathedrals continued through the early years of the Reformation, even if the words were now to be in English as opposed to Latin.[41] In each country or region the principles of liturgical reform were very similar, but the contexts and the results were very different. In neither Germany nor England were the particular influences of a city-state at work, and more compromises were needed for the population at large to accept the changes. Most of the leaders of the English or German Reformations were also less radical in their thinking than those of Zurich. This was as true for the forms of worship that were produced as for their theologies.[42]

The German reformers and the followers of Luther always tended to be more traditional in their development of the liturgy than the Swiss. Germany, however, was a very complex society in the sixteenth century and it is very difficult to generalise. Peter Matheson stresses the creative elements of the German Reformation rather than the destructive themes of iconoclasm. He talks of Luther's ideal of the Gospel being preached, painted, sung and rhymed (*gepredigt, gemalt, geschrieben und gesungen*).[43] He tells of Thomas Müntzer, who prepared a vernacular liturgy for his village of Allstedt in 1523 in order to allow the congregation to sing along to the old plainchant melodies.[44] Luther, on the other hand, appears to have been more reluctant to prepare material for worship, not because he thought that the Latin rites would suffice but because he did not always believe that he was the person to do it. Eventually, however, friends and colleagues did manage to persuade him to write liturgies for most occasions. Even at this stage he primarily noted only what was happening in his own city and allowed considerable freedom to others to do what was right for them. For Luther it was important not to alienate the population and so, in many cases, his own proposals are less radical than those of Zwingli or other German colleagues. As Susan Karant-Nunn says, 'By the time Luther prepared his "*Deutsche Messe und Ordnung Gottesdiensts*" in 1525,

---

[39] Westermeyer, *Te Deum*, 141–9.   [40] Ibid., 153–8.
[41] See P. le Huray, *Music and the Reformation in England 1549–1660*. Cambridge: Cambridge University Press, 1978.
[42] Lindberg, *European Reformations*.
[43] P. Matheson, *The Imaginative World of the Reformation*. Edinburgh: T. & T. Clark, 2000, 25.
[44] Ibid., 26.

others had paved the way.'[45] She goes on to say, 'One of Luther's chief concerns in bringing the Mass into German was to render the often traditional words well sung. For to Luther the Mass was a musical event, and it would be so all over Lutheran Germany by mid-century.'[46]

There was a strong sense of the relationship between worship and society within the Lutheran tradition that maintained a feeling for tradition while rejecting all those elements that led to superstition and corruption. This also led, as with Zwingli in Zurich, to an increasing sense of control by political leaders over all aspects of individual and social life, an increase in what I began to describe in the previous chapter as the monasticisation of society.[47] Births, marriages and deaths were all more highly controlled, with the beginnings of mass registrations. The elaborate rituals that surrounded these periods were discouraged, although never fully removed, and the church, usually in the form of prayers and a sermon by the minister in the church building, took a much more active role.[48] This had the unforeseen consequence of reducing even further the role of women in worship and society. While at the beginning of the Reformation women had a visible and active part in the public sphere,[49] as in most reform and revolutionary movements, by the end of the sixteenth century in much of Germany their position had been reduced dramatically to the domestic sphere of life, a sphere that had been shorn of much of the daily ritual of popular devotion so common in the later Middle Ages.[50]

Further north the Lutherans of Scandinavia maintained far more of the basic structure and ceremonial of the liturgy and retained the eucharist at the heart of their spirituality. The church in Sweden proclaimed independence of Rome following a rebellion against the Danish King Christian II in 1523, although the hierarchy was continued and the exact relationship with the Roman Church remained a matter of dispute for some decades. The various kings of Sweden during the sixteenth century appear to have had different views of the church and the relationship between the church and state, and therefore supported different factions within the church from those who wished simply to reform the older Catholic forms to those who wished to depose the whole hierarchy and to implement a full form of German Presbyterianism. Through all this, the stabilising factor was the figure of Laurentius Petri of Nerike who in 1531 was consecrated as Archbishop of

---

[45] Karant-Nunn, *Reformation of Ritual*, 118.	[46] Ibid.	[47] See p. 176 above.
[48] Karant-Nunn, *Reformation of Ritual*.	[49] Matheson, *Imaginative World*, 101–18.
[50] Karant-Nunn, *Reformation of Ritual*.

Uppsala at the age of thirty-two.[51] Petri held on to the post of archbishop throughout his life, despite a number of attempts to oust him from both the Romanisers and the more radical reformers. He died in October 1573, having won over all opposition and established the continuation of the hierarchy within the Swedish church. It was also Petri who provided the basis for the vernacular Swedish liturgy. This was very conservative by German standards and Petri provided a biblical explanation for much of the ceremonial that was continued. It was, however, his Church Order of 1571 that provided texts for the worship of the church that would last into the future.[52]

In England the liturgy underwent a series of transformations at the hands of Thomas Cranmer, Archbishop of Canterbury from 1532 to 1556.[53] Little was possible during the reign of Henry VIII (1509–47) although some vernacular elements were introduced into the mass as a preparation for communion. It was the death of Henry and the accession of Edward VI in 1547 that allowed the reform of worship to become state policy. Cranmer produced two books within the short reign of Edward. The first, in 1549, was essentially a translation into English of the Sarum rite, suitably adapted where necessary to reject elements that reformers objected to such as eucharistic sacrifice and prayers for the dead. The second, in 1552, was a much more thorough-going reform and restructuring along more radical reformed principles.[54]

It was Cranmer's view, as it was that of Luther, Zwingli and the majority of other reformers, that the eucharist should have been retained as the central and most frequent rite. However, over time this was displaced in England by the beautiful liturgies of Morning and Evening Prayer and the Litany. The writing of the books was accompanied by state orders to destroy images and ceremonial items and by a radical restructuring of the chancel area of each church.[55] The altar was no longer to be at the east end of the chancel; rather, a table with a clean white cloth was to be placed lengthwise in the middle of the chancel and the priest was to celebrate the Lord's Supper standing on the north side. Where this was implemented the visual impact on the population, who on the whole were far less prepared through preaching than those of Switzerland and Germany, must have been highly dramatic. Nothing, it appeared, was ever to be the same again. The Reformation, however, was brought to an abrupt end by the succession of

---

[51] E. E. Yelverton, *An Archbishop of the Reformation, Laurentius Petri Nericius, Archbishop of Uppsala, 1531–73, A Study of His Liturgical Projects*. London: Epworth Press, 1958.
[52] Ibid. [53] G. J. Cuming, *A History of Anglican Liturgy*. London: Macmillan, 1969.
[54] Ibid., 66–116. [55] Duffy, *Stripping the Altars*, 445–77.

Mary in 1553 and the reintroduction of Latin and the full accompanying ritual. When Elizabeth I came to the throne in 1558 she arranged for a compromise position and, although Cranmer's *Book of Common Prayer* was reintroduced, many of the radical ceremonial aspects were dropped.[56]

In Switzerland the iconoclasm of Zurich spread rapidly through the German and French speaking regions of the north: Bern and St Gall 'cleansed' their churches in 1528, Basel and Schaffhausen in 1529, Neuchâtel in 1530 and Lausanne and Geneva in 1535.[57] In each case the reformers met considerable opposition but eventually won the day through a combination of debate and public violence. When John Calvin came to prominence in Geneva he appears to have tried to follow Martin Bucer in Strasbourg by developing something of a compromise between the Lutheran traditionalism and Zwinglian radicalism in his liturgical efforts.[58] Bucer, however, was far more traditional in his approach, and had a significant impact on the English tradition. Calvin, on the other hand, was much more radical, and could not ultimately deny his own highly sophisticated theological position.[59] Calvin himself was, like Zwingli, more of a theologian and a preacher than a skilled composer of worship, and his legacy was ultimately to lead to a tradition of Church Orders with considerable freedom for the minister to develop through extemporary prayer. This eventually became the custom in Scotland and in other places where Calvinism had a significant impact.[60] I will pick this story up again in the fourth section of this chapter below. First, however, we must look at how the Catholics responded to all this destruction and creativity in worship in their own parts of Europe and beyond.

FEEDING THE MIND AND THE HEART

In 1534 a Catholic student in Paris founded a religious order with six of his friends that was going to change the nature of the Catholic Church for the next four hundred years. The student was Ignatius Loyola and the order was the Society of Jesus, or the Jesuits. In founding this order Loyola was already beginning to introduce elements of the humanist discourse into Catholic thinking.[61] The Ignatian Exercises on which the spirituality of the

---

[56] Cuming, *Anglican Liturgy*, 120.   [57] Eire, *War*, 107.   [58] See ibid., 197–228.

[59] B. A. Gerrish, *Grace and Gratitude, The Eucharistic Theology of John Calvin*. Edinburgh: T. & T. Clark, 1993.

[60] See the essays in D. Forrester and D. Murray (eds.), *Studies in the History of Worship in Scotland*. Edinburgh: T. & T. Clark, 1996.

[61] See W. W. Meissner, *Ignatius of Loyola, The Psychology of a Saint*. New Haven: Yale University Press, 1992.

order was based are firmly rooted in an individualist spirituality that places the imagination of the individual at its heart. In their intellectual practice also the members of the order, like all other intellectuals of the time, embraced a number of the growing humanist discourses of the day. When it came to liturgy and worship this interaction with humanism can also be seen, particularly in the order's relationship with 'the other'.[62]

For many Jesuits the order was first and foremost a missionary order, a body of priests who devoted their lives to the spreading of the Gospel in the newly discovered territories overseas. The Jesuits had a very significant impact on the history of the Catholic Church in Latin America, India and China, and in each of these areas the way in which members of the order responded to not only the people they encountered but also the ways of life these people held dear was highly distinctive. In India and China, for example, the Jesuits realised the depth and profundity of the religious and intellectual traditions of the people they were engaging with and they wanted to learn from these traditions and to incorporate aspects of them into their own presentation of the Gospel. Even among the native peoples of Latin America the Jesuits found much of value and refused to see these people simply as 'savages' fit only for slavery, and were among the first to make serious studies of the indigenous ways of life.[63] They attempted to incorporate elements of many different local traditions into the theology and worship of their churches. This was a relatively new approach and one that was seen to be very controversial in Rome.[64]

It was in China that this practice became most significant with what became known as the Chinese Rites Controversy.[65] The Jesuits in Macao, like other European missionaries, had been trying, unsuccessfully, for some time to make inroads into Mainland China. It was the new provincial, Alessandro Valignano, who in 1577 realised that if Christianity was to find a permanent home within Chinese culture and tradition then it had to engage with that tradition and possibly even to incorporate elements of

---

[62] See R. F. Taft, 'Liturgy in the Life and Mission of the Society of Jesus', in K. Pecklers (ed.), *Liturgy in a Postmodern World*. London: Continuum, 2003, 36–54.

[63] J. Hemming, *Red Gold, The Conquest of the Brazilian Indians*. London: Macmillan, 1987, 98.

[64] We could argue that the mission of Augustine to Canterbury and other examples of Christian mission in history had also adapted local traditions to the theology and worship of the church. The basic underlying principles, however, were very different. The work of the Jesuits was underpinned by Enlightenment thinking and the origins of what was to become anthropology. The local 'cultures' were beginning to be granted an integrity and coherence of their own, rather than being seen as a series of pan-pagan practices that needed to be adapted to Christianity, and this changed the nature of the interaction. See ibid., 97–118.

[65] G. H. Dunne, *Generation of Giants, The Story of the Jesuits in China in the Last Decades of the Ming Dynasty*. Notre Dame: University of Notre Dame Press, 1962.

that tradition into itself.[66] Christianity would never survive as a foreign import that was unable to engage creatively with the intellectual and cultural world of the Chinese. Michele Ruggieri was sent from Europe with the explicit task of learning the Chinese language and customs. This enabled him to develop good relations with the Chinese and eventually to build a small mission at Chaoching on the mainland close to Macao. Ruggieri moved into this mission with another Jesuit, Matteo Ricci, on 10 September 1583.[67] This was the beginning of a long and successful relationship between the Jesuits and the Chinese authorities.

There were many controversies, as the Jesuits aimed to make Christianity acceptable to the Chinese, not least around the appropriate word to use for God.[68] Ricci and the other Jesuits became significant scholars of Chinese custom and traditions and were well versed in Confucian classics. They aimed to understand the way in which these determined the lives of the Chinese, especially of the scholarly classes that they hoped to convert. It was in this context that the question of 'Chinese Rites' first emerged. There were a number of rites that any Chinese person from the scholar class would have to engage in. These all related to Confucian traditions and concerned the passing of exams and veneration shown to ancestors. These rites, for the Chinese, had no specific religious connotations, although some involved offerings and sacrifice that looked very 'religious' to European eyes. The Jesuits, from their scholarship, recognised the distinctions and allowed converts to continue with some of the rites (while banning those that were thought to be too controversial). In the case of the use of the *k'o-t'ou* at funerals (kneeling and performing a profound bow in which the forehead touched the floor) the Jesuits themselves also engaged in the practice, recognising it as a sign of respect for the dead rather than the worship of ancestors.[69] The Jesuits were unaware that what they were attempting would be in any way controversial; it appeared to be the natural response to a culture with the history and traditions of the Chinese. Others, however, had other ideas.

In 1639 the Dominican Juan Bautista de Morales reported the situation to the local Catholic authorities and, at the same time, directly to Rome.[70] The local authorities, on hearing the arguments of the Jesuits, supported the Jesuit position, but de Morales travelled to Rome in order to make the case directly to the *Propaganda Fide*. Rome, far from the situation on the ground, and with its own concerns for the maintenance of order and

[66] Ibid., 17–18.   [67] Ibid., 21.   [68] See ibid., 282–301 for a full discussion of the dispute.
[69] Ibid., 290.   [70] Ibid., 298.

practice in Europe, had other ideas and the Congregation banned these 'Chinese Rites' as unchristian in September 1645. The Jesuits arrived a little later and explained their position, so getting the decision overturned in 1656. This, however, only led to a bitter philosophical dispute that rolled on through the next century before Benedict XIV in 1742 forbade any toleration of the rites and banned any further debate.[71] This severely restricted the work of the Jesuits in China and brought about the end of the first significant attempt at what was later to be called 'inculturation' within the Catholic Church.[72]

Back in Europe it was not the case that the liturgy of the Catholic Church was remaining static; if anything, the Catholic liturgy was adapting much more rapidly to the 'culture' of humanism than it had ever been allowed to do with the culture of China. Following the various upsets of the Reformation and the religious wars that followed, the Catholic Church had to reassess its position and its various practices. In some ways the Church was caught. If it recognised that it had been at fault and that certain practices were superstitious or corrupt, then the reformers had, in effect, won. If, however, it did nothing, the situation would only get worse and it appeared that more and more regions of Europe would go over to the Reformation. It was the task of the Council of Trent, opened in December 1545 by Pope Paul III, to tackle this question and this was done in relation to church order, doctrine and liturgy.[73]

The Council of Trent appears to have begun in a spirit of reconciliation, with the hope that its actions could bring the Church back together again. As time went by, however, and as politics began to infringe on the debates, the Council took a conservative turn. It could not really have done much else. It reinforced the truth of the doctrines that the Catholics held over and against the Reformers and it set in stone many of the practices that the Reformers had objected to (although often with subtly different justifications). The Council did manage to remove some of the worst excesses when these were blamed on regional churches rather than the position in Rome. For the most part, however, the Council did little more than reinforce the status quo. This is exactly what it did, for example, in the area of worship.[74] Sacraments were discussed in the seventh session in March 1547 just before the Council disbanded for four years. The eucharist, penance and extreme

[71] Ibid., 299.   [72] See pp. 225–6 below.

[73] D. A. Withey, *Catholic Worship, An Introduction to Liturgy.* Bury St Edmunds: Kevin Mayhew, 1990, 86–96.

[74] C. Howell, 'From Trent to Vatican II', in C. Jones et al. (eds.), *The Study of Liturgy.* London: SPCK, 1992, 287.

unction were discussed in sessions XIII and XIV in 1551. Transubstantiation was affirmed and the various Protestant theologies condemned. Communion, the presence of the undivided Christ under each species, the denial of the cup to the laity and eucharistic sacrifice, all had to wait until the Council was recalled for a third time in 1562.

The Breviary was revised in 1568 and the Missal in 1570. The liturgy that was produced at the end of the Council, however, was only a slightly revised version of that produced in Rome in 1474, but was promulgated as *the* liturgy of the universal Catholic Church.[75] In doing this, therefore, Pope Pius V did something that many popes and emperors had failed to do from the days of Charlemagne onwards: he stated that there was just one form of the Catholic Liturgy and removed, at a stroke, all the local and regional variations. It was only the religious orders, and those who could show that their liturgy had been in use for more than two centuries, who were allowed to maintain their own distinctive form of the rites. Milan and Lyons were among a very small number of dioceses that were exempt.[76] For the most part, however, and for the first time in the history of the liturgy, the whole Catholic Church had the same rite and this was celebrated, in Latin, with identical ceremonial throughout the Church, from Mexico City in the West to Manila in the East.

If this is the case, therefore, how can I argue that it was in Europe that the Catholic liturgy moved closer to the form of inculturation that had been attempted by the Jesuits, and crushed by the Pope, in China and elsewhere? The reason is relatively simple. What were fixed at the Council of Trent, and the texts that followed it, were the words and the actions of the liturgy. These remained practically unchanged for the next four hundred years till the Second Vatican Council in 1962.[77] The fixing of the words and the actions, however, still left a great deal of flexibility and variability in terms of the setting and the music of the liturgy. Following the Council of Trent there was something of a revival of the Catholic Church led from within Spain and the Austrian Empire. In both places the revival of the church was associated with, and went hand in hand with, a revival of the arts and the sciences. In Austria particularly the growth of the popularity of the Catholic Church was developing alongside a rapid transformation of the arts, particularly music, and a flowering of the sciences and associated

[75] A. Nocent, *La Célébration Eucharistique Avant et Après Saint Pie V.* Paris: Beauchesne, 1977, 44–5.
[76] C. Alzati, *Ambrosianum Mysterium: The Church of Milan and its Liturgical Tradition, vol. II.* Cambridge: Grove Books, 2000, 77–86.
[77] See pp. 219–20 below.

understandings of society.[78] The discourses of humanism were taking root in the Empire and this was affecting not just the sciences but also the arts and, more indirectly, the liturgy.

We only have to look, for example, at the position of Mozart in the late eighteenth century to see how far things had already developed. Wolfgang Amadeus Mozart, like most of his contemporaries, wrote music for the church as well as for the stage and for the courts of princes and emperors. It is his liturgical music, however, that is of particular interest here. The question of Mozart's own faith has been a matter of controversy in musical history.[79] He was associated, at least in part, with the Freemasons and had been heavily influenced by the ideas of the Enlightenment. We see throughout Mozart's stage works the discourses of humanism having free rein, often at the expense of the discourses of Christianity.[80] In relation to the liturgy, however, Mozart was still providing exactly what the church at the time was requesting. This was not, however, the traditional plainchant that had dominated the liturgical music of the Middle Ages. For Mozart and his contemporaries the request to write a mass setting was an opportunity to demonstrate their full musical talents. They had at their disposal, in the major cathedrals such as Salzburg, the full resources of a choir and orchestra and they were given a practically free hand to produce the kind of music that they wished to develop.

In order to understand where Mozart was coming from, however, we have to go back to the period immediately following the Council of Trent. The Council had tried to stop the development of what was considered 'secular' music within the mass. There was even an attempt to ban polyphony although the Emperor, Ferdinand I, objected to this. In the end polyphony was allowed so long as worldly forms were avoided and the words of the text could be heard.[81] In response to the reforms of the Council, Philip Neri began to draw to himself a community of men and boys in Rome who came together to pray, to discuss spiritual things and to sing.[82] As the group became established, an 'oratory' was built above the nave of San Girolamo. Here *oratoriani* gathered to hear Bible readings, sermons, and singing. Over time the music became more professional,

---

[78] For a study of the popular end of this revival see M. R. Forster, *Catholic Revival in the Age of the Baroque, Religious Identity in Southwest Germany, 1550–1750*. Cambridge: Cambridge University Press, 2001.

[79] R. W. Gutman, *Mozart, A Cultural Biography*. New York: Harcourt Brace, 1999.

[80] C. Wilson, *Notes on Mozart, 20 Crucial Works*. Edinburgh: St Andrew Press, 2003, 103–9.

[81] Westermeyer, *Te Deum*, 163.

[82] R. Addington, *The Idea of the Oratory*. London: Burns & Oates, 1966.

involving well-known musicians such as Giovanni Pierluigi da Palestrina and it was from this context that the oratorio was born.[83] The oratorio eventually allowed the boundaries between dramatic music, including the growing genre of the opera, and sacred music to merge into something that was neither fully liturgical nor strictly a concert. From the time of Palestrina, therefore, in the second half of the sixteenth century, the boundaries between dramatic music and liturgical music had begun to break down. By the end of the eighteenth century it was expected that a composer would produce a mass setting that allowed for the full dramatic range of soloists in just the same way as any contemporary opera. Mozart did not fail to respond and his masses, particularly the Requiem Mass, demonstrate this blurring of the boundaries in secular and sacred music to full effect.[84]

What had also changed, however, was the role that the music played within the liturgy. In the case of plainchant the music was subservient to the action of the rite. It fitted in between other elements and, while it might accompany processions and some other actions, it never encroached on the spoken elements of the rite. By the end of the eighteenth century, however, all this had changed; 'music [had] spread its gorgeous mantle over the whole mass, so that the other details of the rite scarcely had any significance'.[85] The worshipper would sit in the cathedral, surrounded by the baroque splendour of the architecture with the priest and his servers dwarfed by an enormous altar and reredos. Light would seep in through specially designed openings to provide the best dramatic effect among the clouds, the cherubs and the gilding of the decoration. The music would begin as the priest entered, often with the Kyrie; it would continue, over the spoken words, and move seamlessly through into the Gloria. It might have paused for a reading before the choir began the Creed, which would take the mass up to the offertory and the beginning of the eucharistic prayer. Having intoned the beginning of the prayer, the choir would begin the Sanctus and Benedictus while the prayer was being said, and then follow directly with the Agnus Dei as the priests received communion and began to leave.[86] The whole experience would have been one of waves of music, not accompanying the action as such, rather floating above it. Little

[83] Westermeyer, *Te Deum*, 237. [84] Wilson, *Notes on Mozart*, 116–20.
[85] J. Jungmann, *The Mass of the Roman Rite, Its Origins and Development (Missarum Sollemnia)*. New York, Benziger Brothers, 1959, 111.
[86] The Gradual, Alleluia, Sequence, Offertory and Communion may also have been sung by the choir between the fixed items on feasts and other major occasions. N. Sandon (ed.), *The Octave of the Nativity, Essays and Notes on Ten Liturgical Reconstructions for Christmas*. London: BBC, 1984, 23–7.

could be seen of the musicians, as they were housed in galleries. Clouds of incense and distance also made the clergy and their action difficult to follow. It was the architectural setting, therefore, and the music itself, that would have left the real impact on the minds of the congregation, not the actions of the liturgy. This, of course, would only have been the case for the very grandest of solemn high masses. However, with low masses being little more than a perfunctory rush through the words with a priest and a server, these would also have had little direct impact.

What this submerging of the liturgy in music allowed for was the growth of a new and very distinctive form of devotion that was once again, as with the music, saturated by the discourses of humanism. This was a series of devotions focused on the individual's relationship with God, Jesus or the saints and built around the emotional response of that individual to the experience of the rite. Devotions such as Benediction drew in music and drama to create an emotional experience, while the increasing devotions to Our Lady, the Passion and the Sacred Heart played on the emotional impact of these devotions on the individual. Devotion to the Sacred Heart, for example, had been developing within Carthusian and Jesuit devotions for almost a century before Marguerite-Marie Alacoque had a series of visions between 1673 and 1675, which fixed the shape and form of the devotion.[87] The feast itself, however, was only established in 1856. These forms of devotion, with their emphasis on the individual, on an emotional response from the individual, and on physical aspects of the human Jesus, indicate a direct application of certain principles within the discourses of humanism to the worshipping life of the people and were seen to be increasingly popular as these discourses of humanism grew within the population as a whole. They also show a much closer adaptation of the liturgy to the popular humanist discourses of Europe than was ever allowed in relation to the traditional discourses of China in the sixteenth and seventeenth centuries.

It was not only in Western Europe that the discourse of humanism was coming into contact with an ancient Christian tradition. In Russia the Patriarch Nikon and Tsar Alexis undertook a reform of the liturgy between 1654 and 1667. This was not nearly as substantial as that of the West, but substantial enough to force some members of the church to leave and to form the Old Believers.[88] These were members of the Russian Orthodox

[87] R. Jonas, *France and the Cult of the Sacred Heart, An Epic Tale for Modern Times.* Berkeley: University of California Press, 2000.
[88] See the account in P. Meyendorff, *Russia, Ritual and Reform, The Liturgical Reforms of Nikon in the Sixteenth Century.* Crestwood: St Vladimir's Seminary Press, 1991.

Church who refused to accept the Nikonian reforms and split off from the main body of the church, retreating often into remote areas of the country to avoid persecution and to maintain their beliefs and practices in a pristine fashion. What was interesting about Nikon's reforms, however, was that despite his claiming that they were based on a thorough review of the most ancient texts, they were, in fact, simply a Russian translation of the most recent Greek editions of the liturgy printed in Venice.[89] The primary purpose, it appears, was to bring the Russian church into line with contemporary Greek practice. Alexis was keen to establish Moscow as the inheritor of Rome and Constantinople, and himself as the true Christian Emperor. Moscow had recently been recognised as a patriarchate in its own right and the Tsar felt that it was important to recognise this by doing all things according to Greek practice. The emphasis in the Orthodox world on tradition, however, and the intimate relationship between liturgy and orthodoxy, meant that he had to pass the reforms off as being a revival of ancient practices. In the following century Peter, Catherine and other Tsars tried to take these reforms further in the hope of bringing Russia closer to the rest of Enlightenment Europe.[90] These reforms, however, were less successful than that of Nikon and ultimately failed to establish themselves.

ALL THE BEST TUNES

Having looked at the Catholic and Orthodox situation, I now wish to go back to the Reformation and trace some of the trends begun in the Reformation through to the end of the eighteenth century. In order to do this I want to place a particular emphasis on hymnody and music in worship during this period. To begin, however, I want to go backwards, into the fifteenth century, and to the reform tradition of Jan Hus in Bohemia.[91] Hus was among a number of reformers based at the University of Prague who developed the thought of the English reformer John Wycliffe. Among other things, these scholars called for a reform of the mass and other worship in the early years of the fifteenth century. Hus and his colleagues were convinced of the need for greater participation by the laity in the Eucharist and particularly in more regular reception of the elements of bread and wine. In order to facilitate this, they argued that the liturgy itself had to be in the local vernacular, in this case

---

[89] Ibid., 129.

[90] J. Cracraft, *The Church Reform of Peter the Great*. Stanford: Stanford University Press, 1971.

[91] D. R. Holeton, 'The Office of Jan Hus: An Unrecorded Antiphonary in the Metropolitan Library of Estergom', in J. N. Alexander (ed.), *Time and Community*. Washington: Pastoral Press, 1990, 137–52.

in Czech, and began to develop a devotional literature, mainly hymns, to accompany the worship. These reforms had some success, survived and flourished in Prague for almost twenty years, but were eventually condemned and squashed by the Catholic authorities with Hus himself being burned at the stake following the Council of Constance in 1415.[92] The Hussite tradition, however, lived on as a persecuted minority, particularly around the town of Tabor in southern Bohemia, eventually to become, through various twists and turns of history, the Moravian church.

The Moravians had a particular approach to music in worship that reflected Jan Hus's original dream of a form of liturgy that was accessible to all. The Hussites prepared liturgical music that drew on Catholic traditions, adapted Gregorian plainchant, and introduced a number of hymns based on local folk traditions.[93] The Moravians, by the sixteenth century, were a small, close-knit group who met for worship on a daily basis within which they sang in the vernacular up to thirty different hymns a day.[94] These traditions eventually came to influence Luther through the person of Michael Weisse, who made a number of visits to Wittenberg as Luther was preparing the German Mass. As we have seen, Luther was keen to develop the musical traditions of the church and supplemented these with hymns in the Moravian fashion and with chorales, that is longer, more established pieces of music setting words from the Bible that were relevant to particular times and seasons of the year.[95]

Lutheran traditions have always seen a positive role for music within worship, seeing it as complementing and supplementing the word. Luther himself even suggested that music provided a separate, but equally important, evangelistic tool alongside preaching.[96] Music therefore followed through from the Catholic to the Lutheran traditions with little change, apart from the increasing use of texts in the vernacular. As musical fashions changed, so Lutheran traditions adapted to them. The increasing influence of secular Italian genres such as cantata and opera had their impact on Lutheran musical traditions. These genres, combined with the great seventeenth- and eighteenth-century organ traditions of North and Central Germany, led to the undoubted peak of Lutheran liturgical music in the work of J. S. Bach and his family.[97] Bach brought the clarity of the tonal system to the developing choral tradition and added his own contributions

---

[92] See D. R. Holeton, *La Communion des Tout-Petits Enfants, Etude du Mouvement Eucharistique en Bohème vers le Fin du Moyen-Age*. Rome: Edizioni Liturgiche, 1989.
[93] Holeton, 'The Office of Jan Hus'.   [94] Westermeyer, *Te Deum*, 223.   [95] Ibid., 144–9.
[96] Matheson, *Imaginative World*, 25–6.
[97] R. A. Leaver, *The Liturgy and Music, A Study of the Use of the Hymn in Two Liturgical Traditions*. Bramcote: Grove Books, 1976, 18–19.

to the oratorio tradition in the two great Passions and much other music.[98] Here was a true mixing of sacred and secular traditions that was rooted firmly in the glory of God.

While Luther always embraced the musical tradition and saw it as essential to the preaching of the Gospel, other reform traditions, as we have seen, took a very different position. The most influential, among the widest range of Protestant churches, was that of Calvin, who restricted music within public worship to the unaccompanied singing of metrical psalms. This tradition was to influence the full range of Protestant churches over the next century and a half. Following on from the Reformation itself, in which Luther, Zwingli and Calvin all shared the view that any society should have only one true church and that all members of that society should by nature belong to that church, a number of other reformers were raising the possibility of gathered churches, or communities of Christians outside of society. These had their earliest expression in the various Anabaptist traditions of the Reformation itself.[99] Anabaptists shared a view that baptism could only be received by adults following a declaration of faith and insisted on the (re)baptism of all those who wished to join them. Many Anabaptist communities also rediscovered the gift of prophecy and maintained a millenarian stance over and against society at large. They were convinced of the need for worship to be free and open to the Spirit and on the whole banned any set forms of words or any singing in their worship. They drew for their inspiration largely from the Old Testament and even in a few scandalous examples advocated polygamy after the example of the Patriarchs.[100]

In practice many churches with a Calvinist tradition, as well as those deriving from the Anabaptists, the 'separatist' Puritans in England, and the Pilgrims who sailed for New England in September 1620, all shared a common view of the church as being a gathered community of believers bound together by worship and a godly life. Within these communities the big argument of the seventeenth century was whether the unaccompanied singing of psalms, as advocated by Calvin, should be allowed or not.[101] Most groups accepted the biblical warrant for singing, so the real discussion appears to have related to the place of set texts in worship. It would have been impossible to sing psalms if worship was believed to consist only

[98] Westermeyer, *Te Deum*, 240–1.   [99] See Lindberg, *European Reformations*, 199–228.
[100] R. Po-Chia Hsia, 'Münster and the Anabaptists', in R. Po-Chia Hsia (ed.), *The German People and the Reformation*. Ithaca: Cornell University Press, 1988, 51–70.
[101] Westermeyer, *Te Deum*, 179–98.

in the extemporary inspiration of those who took part. In some traditions the possibility of solo singing remained as the only viable option, but it appears that this rarely occurred. In practice churches either accepted the singing of metrical psalms or they rejected music in worship entirely. Many different editions of the psalms were produced throughout the seventeenth century, some closer to the original biblical texts than others, some set to more or less complicated music, but all designed for unaccompanied singing in public worship.

All these traditions, however, allowed for a far greater variety of music to be used for worship within the home, and it is important to note that it was not only public worship that was thought to be important at this time. The worship of the family gathered together as a mini-church of its own was an important site for worship throughout this period and across a number of different traditions.[102] Greater flexibility was clearly allowed in relation to music within the family, but it was in maintaining the regular daily prayer of the Christian community that the family came into its own. Throughout Protestant Europe and the New World families gathered at the beginning and end of each day to read from the Bible, to pray and to sing. This was a tradition in which women played a very important role and a tradition in which the regular worshipping life of the majority of the population was rooted.[103]

In the eighteenth century a new dispute arose among the Calvinist, Baptist and Independent churches. This came through the introduction of hymnody to supplement the singing of psalms. In many cases it appears that worship in these traditions, as among the Lutherans, the Anglicans and much of the Roman Catholic world, had become increasingly didactic and dry towards the end of the seventeenth and into the early years of the eighteenth century. Long and tortuous sermons dominated the worship and singing had slowed almost to a halt. In the New England colonies, by the 1680s, the practice of 'lining out' a hymn, whereby the minister or leader would sing a line followed by the congregation, along with the desire for inspired singing (that is without fixed tunes), had led to a situation where each note could last for seconds and the whole of a psalm could take twenty to thirty minutes to sing.[104] This was not inspiring worship and people were looking for ways to bring life and joy back into worship.

---

[102] See the many examples, primarily from America, in S. J. White, *A History of Women in Christian Worship*. London: SPCK, 2003.

[103] See A. S. Brown and D. D. Hall, 'Family Strategies and Religious Practice: Baptism and the Lord's Supper in Early New England', in D. D. Hall (ed.), *Lived Religion in America, Toward a History of Practice*. Princeton: Princeton University Press, 1997, 41–68.

[104] Westermeyer, *Te Deum*, 248.

In England Isaac Watts, at the age of sixteen and apparently fed up with the worship of his father's Congregational church, suggested that he could write something better. His father told him to go ahead, and, according to the story, the English hymn was born.[105] Watts wrote many hundred hymns between 1690 and his death in 1748, based on biblical and liturgical themes. Many people at first refused to accept them into worship as non-scriptural but slowly the fashion spread, both in England and in the American Colonies, and Watts's hymns became among the most widely sung compositions in the worship of the eighteenth century. A generation later, with a similar desire to inspire new life in worship, the Wesleys began to develop their own brand of hymnody and worship.

John and Charles Wesley had formed a 'Holy Club' for Christian living while at Oxford in the 1730s that was centred on regular communion (very unusual at this time), daily study of the Greek New Testament, fasting on Wednesday and Friday, and help for the sick and the poor. They were ordained into the Anglican Church and spent some time preaching in Georgia in the American South. On the way to America, John had become influenced by a group of Moravians and had been impressed by their musical traditions. Back in England he, and his brother Charles, began to gather people into classes for prayer, preaching and singing. John had already provided an edition of the Book of Common Prayer in 1748 for the churches he had founded in Georgia, known as *The Sunday Service of the Methodists,*[106] and when the English Methodists were eased out of the Anglican Church, a version of this book became the principal prayer book for the community. It was, however, the preaching service (often open-air) and the publication of *A Collection of Hymns for the Use of the People Called Methodists* in 1780 that came to distinguish Methodist worship, in all its various forms, for the next two hundred years.[107]

In New England the work of Watts had a profound effect on Jonathan Edwards, a minister at First Church, Northampton, Massachusetts. In 1742 Edwards led what has become known as the 'Great Awakening' in which much of the Colony was swept up into a religious revival.[108] An integral part of this revival was Edwards's own support for hymns, and through the awakening the practice of hymn-singing spread throughout New England

---

[105] Ibid., 202.
[106] J. White, *The Sunday Service of the Methodists in North America.* Nashville: United Methodist Publishing House, 1984.
[107] A. Burdon, *The Preaching Service – The Glory of the Methodists, A Study of the Piety, Ethos and Development of the Methodist Preaching Service.* Bramcote: Grove Books, 1991.
[108] F. Lambert, *Inventing the 'Great Awakening'.* Princeton: Princeton University Press, 1999.

and beyond. Much of this singing, in the churches, however, was still unaccompanied or was supported by a recorder and bass viol. The rise of the organ only really came later. Thomas Brattle had an imported organ in his home in Boston, and on his death in 1708 he left the organ to his Brattle Street Church. They refused it, but the organ was passed onto the Episcopalians, who became the first church in New England to have an organ installed.[109] Over the years the reed organ became the instrument of choice for chapels across the States and led to a major industry for such instruments based in Brattleboro, Vermont.[110]

A third tradition to come out of the Reformation owes more in musical terms to Zwingli's approach than to that of Luther or Calvin, although there is no direct link between Zwingli or his followers and the majority of these traditions. Zwingli, as we have seen, rejected music in worship, fundamentally, because he believed that worship should take place in the heart of each individual and this is where the true singing of praises to God should exist. The public assembly was not 'true worship' in this sense but rather an arena for the teaching and edification of the congregation to inspire them to true worship within their own context. This kind of thinking led a number of other Christian communities to develop their own particular traditions of worship often at odds with those around them.

The most well-known representatives of this approach are the Quakers, or Society of Friends. This was never a church as such, but rather a gathering of like-minded 'friends' who followed the example of George Fox. Fox was born in England in 1624 and went on to engage in a long and difficult religious search. This led him to emphasise the interior nature of religion and the importance of accepting God in the heart.[111] Along with a fervent pacifism and an active social conscience, the principal distinguishing feature of English Quakers is their form of worship. This consists of meeting in a plain unadorned room, usually sitting in a circle, in silence, waiting on the presence of God. If members of the community feel called to speak, or 'minister', to the congregation they are free to do so and the group will listen to them with care and respect. For much of the time, however, it is the communal gathering and prayerful silence that distinguishes the Quaker tradition. Like so many radical protestant groups, the

---

[109] Westermeyer, *Te Deum*, 257.
[110] D. G. Waring,. *Manufacturing the Muse.* Middletown: Wesleyan University Press, 2002.
[111] H. L. Ingle, *First Among Friends, George Fox and the Creation of Quakerism.* Oxford: Oxford University Press, 1994.

Quakers were severely persecuted in their early years but now hold a respected, if distinct, position within the Christian community.[112]

The Pietists in Germany developed a very similar approach, although coming from a very different background, their worship looked very different. In this case it was a rejection of the wordiness and intellectualisation of the Lutheran and Calvinist traditions that led Philip Jacob Spener in the later seventeenth century to encourage small groups of Christians to meet in each other's houses to pray together, to discuss the Bible and to edify one another. Once again the emphasis was on prayer in the heart and the individual relationship with God, although in this case 'simple and often sentimental hymns'[113] became a part of the worshipping tradition. By the early nineteenth century the worship of the Pietists became extremely subjective in its approach, placing ever greater emphasis on the heart over the mind and on emotional responses over intellectual reflection. Their music was of a highly emotional form and in many cases became indistinguishable from much contemporary non-religious music. As Paul Westermeyer puts it, 'here we have music not being pushed out of the church, but a whole frame of reference that quietly carried it out'.[114]

One expression of Pietism, however, was very distinctive and this was found particularly in America. In 1694 a community settled on the Wissahickon Creek near Philadelphia. This community was rooted in pietistic and millenarian mysticism. The community was committed to celibacy and lived and worshipped in a communal fashion. They were well known for their instrumental and musical tradition. The Wissahickon community did not outlast the first generation, but a similar community was founded in 1732 in Ephrata, Pennsylvania. Again, the members of this community were committed to celibacy and the men and women lived in separate communal houses. The centre of their life was in worship and work, with choir rehearsals lasting for four hours each night. Their singing was known for its contemplative and ethereal qualities.[115] A similar style of life was later taken up, in much the same area, by the Shakers. This group traced their roots to the religious visions of Mother Ann Lee, from Manchester in England. Owing to persecution in England the community fled to America in 1774, where they began to thrive. Once again the Shakers lived in agricultural communities in separate celibate houses of men and women. They became very well known for their furniture, their seed business and their very distinctive form of worship with simple, straightforward songs

[112] See P. Dandelion, *Liturgies of Quakerism*. Aldershot: Ashgate, 2004.
[113] Westermeyer, *Te Deum*, 229.   [114] Ibid., 230.   [115] Ibid., 260.

and complex, intricate dancing or 'shaking'. Because they were able to provide orphanage facilities for abandoned children they had a ready supply of new recruits but began to die out once the State began to take responsibility for such orphanages following the Civil War.[116] With the Shakers, however, we have probably reached the edge of what might be called Christian discourses in the eighteenth century and now I need to draw some of these themes together before going on to look at the last two centuries of Christian history.

THE POWER OF THE PRESS

One of the principal factors affecting worship during the period of the Reformation and Enlightenment has to be the invention of printing. In what I have said so far I have tended to downplay the importance of this invention. Others, I feel, have overplayed it, arguing that the Reformation and the Council of Trent could never have occurred without the invention of printing. While there is some truth to this theory – the idea that the attempt to impose one rite on the whole Catholic Church, for example, could only really be done through the distribution of printed texts – I also think that the situation is actually far more complex than this.[117]

Printing did not simply lead to the possibility of the reproduction of written material in large numbers. Like all changes in information technology, it also had other, probably unforeseen, consequences, particularly in the way in which people came to understand the 'text'. Alongside the increasing popularity of printed material came an increase in literacy and an increase in the use of texts in many different areas of life.[118] This was inevitable. Other consequences were not quite so clear. It could be argued, for example, that the various processes by which the humanist discourses began to develop and become influential were themselves a direct result of printing. Humanist discourses have, as one of their central elements, an emphasis on rationality. While it was perfectly possible to develop rational arguments within an oral or semi-literate culture, such as that of Ancient Greece or medieval Europe, the emphasis here was more on 'rhetoric',

---

[116] C. P. Anderson, 'Introduction' in *A Shaker Hymnal, A Facsimile Edition of the 1908 Hymnal of the Canterbury Shakers*. Woodstock: Overlook Press, 1990, iii–ix.

[117] Susan White points out that printing was invented some fifty years before the Reformation itself began to take hold. S. J. White, *Christian Worship and Technological Change*. Nashville: Abingdon Press, 1994, 45–7.

[118] M. U. Chrisman, 'Printing and the Evolution of Lay Culture in Strasbourg, 1480–1599', in Po-chia Hsia, *German People*, 74–101.

rather than 'rationality' as it came to be understood in the eighteenth and nineteenth centuries. Rationality is rooted in the ability to recall earlier steps of an argument and in the possibility of handling very large bodies of data. Both of these become increasingly possible with the invention of printing and it is the printed text, I would argue, that becomes central to the development of rationality along with all the humanist discourses that derive from that, including those which lead ultimately to atheism.

This clearly has an impact on worship. The textuality of worship is closer to that of poetry than that of rational argument. Many commentators have noted the fact that most of the Reformation liturgies, written after the invention of printing, are what they describe as 'didactic'; they are designed to teach us what we should know rather than simply expressing an eternal mystery.[119] This didacticism is itself a first step on the road to rationality and is only possible, week after week, service after service, because of the development of printing. The didactic nature of much Reformation worship, however, does not last, as the practice of worship actually militates against didacticism. Rationality comes back in with the development of the sermon, particularly in the eighteenth century. Sermons in London during this period could last up to an hour and, if the written examples are anything to go by, could be very convoluted and closely argued works of moral theology. Again, this desire to introduce the rational into the liturgy could only be a consequence of the taken-for-granted nature of textuality that produced contemporary works by David Hume, Adam Smith and others. We are sometimes told that people only went to these sermons because there was no other form of popular entertainment. I doubt this very much, both in relation to the historical record and as an explanation for attendance. People actually wanted this kind of rationality; they had come to expect it and thrived on it. Or at least they did until John Wesley came along with a far more emotional approach to preaching and found that, in actual fact, this was far more popular.

There are probably many other ways in which the drift towards rationality, and the textuality that underlay it, impacted on Christian worship. This is not the place to explore all of these impacts, as we need to move the discussion on to the nineteenth century and increasing globalisation of Christian worship. This is what we shall look at in the final chapter.

---

[119] See the references in Tripp, 'Protestantism and the Eucharist'.

CHAPTER 7

The globalisation of Christian worship, 1800–2000

INTRODUCTION: GLOBALISATION

This chapter represents the last two hundred years of Christian history with the spread of Christianity to every corner of the world. This is not to say that Christianity had never been an international, or even global, religion before; it simply recognises a new phase in its global spread. Part of this new phase simply acknowledges the extent of the global spread, but more importantly, and picking up ideas from previous chapters, it recognises a new relationship with other religious traditions and discourses. This puts the last two hundred years into a different context from much of what has gone before.

In talking about the way in which Christianity became global, and the impact that this had on worship, we must explore the idea of globalisation. Peter Beyer identifies four features of recent theories of globalisation that are specifically relevant to the discussions in this chapter.[1] The first is the importance of mass communication.[2] What is new about the world we now live in is that events and ideas can be spread around the world practically instantaneously and that developments in one part of the world, especially of an academic nature, inevitably affect developments in all other places. We are part of a single conversation, if not a single discourse. This can be seen, in terms of Christian worship, with the revisions of the liturgy that affected all the principal churches in the second half of the twentieth century. Although these had their roots in the nineteenth-century monastic revival in France, and the liturgical movement that grew out of it, the consequences were clearly global.

The second point that Beyer makes is that globalisation has inevitably led to a clash of cultures and identities.[3] It is no longer possible, within the context of global communication, to live in an isolated, sealed world.

[1] P. Beyer, *Religion and Globalization.* London: Sage, 1994.   [2] Ibid., 2.   [3] Ibid.

209

Peoples, cultures and discourses meet and interact with each other continuously. This can be destructive, as we see in the so-called war on terror, but it can also be extremely creative. One of the consequences of this, however, has been the growth in identity politics and the establishment of clear local identities based on the objectification of local cultures. In terms of Christian worship, the main context for this kind of globalisation has been in the debates over inculturation and the realisation that the worship developed and moulded for the Western churches is no longer relevant or applicable to many different parts of the world. The mainstream churches are being forced to take local cultures much more seriously and to see how their worship can be adapted to, or even transformed by, them.

Thirdly, Beyer stresses the way in which, alongside the expansion of local identities, globalisation has also led to the development of a burgeoning 'global culture'.[4] Beyer talks about this in eschatological terms, stressing that theorists argue that such a culture is coming, is on its way, but has not yet arrived. Such a culture is also seen to be part of the imperial or colonial roots of globalisation in the sense that it is essentially Western, even American, capitalist culture that is becoming the global norm. In this sense, alongside the growing strength of many local, more or less demotic, discourses, a new dominant discourse is emerging to encompass the whole world. That discourse, if the theorists are correct, is essentially and fundamentally 'humanist';[5] it is rooted in the rationalist and individualist discourses of Western capitalism. This is not the only 'global' discourse that is emerging, however; other, religious, discourses are also becoming global, and in Christian terms, that of the Pentecostal or Charismatic traditions is probably the most significant. There is no question that this is now a global discourse; it is much the same wherever it is to be found, at least in its underlying principles, and like all Christian discourses that we have explored, it is rooted in, and transmitted through, a distinctive form of worship.

Finally, Beyer presents the view that globalisation is something new, a product of the later part of the twentieth century, something that will fundamentally change the way in which all the peoples of the world see themselves and each other.[6] While in a strict sense this may be true, I want to take the concept of globalisation back at least four hundred years. In practice the final phase of the globalisation of Christianity began sometime in the fifteenth century with the expansion of the Spanish and Portuguese into South America, Africa, India and the Far East. It was, however, the

---

[4] Ibid., 9.   [5] See pp. 179–82 above.   [6] Beyer, *Globalization*, 7.

scramble for Africa in the nineteenth century that saw the peak of globalisation in the sense of a truly Christian discourse. This scramble was
essentially political, a movement of the colonial authorities for power
over natural resources. However, it went hand in hand with the expansion
of the missionary project in Europe and the two can never be fully
separated.[7]

Among the Catholic communities that had led the move into South
America, the responsibility for the expansion of the faith lay primarily with
the state and with the organs of the church, such as the Franciscans and the
Jesuits.[8] With the nineteenth-century expansion of the North European
empires, however, the missionary enterprise fell to voluntary societies,
often with the backing of the churches that supported them, but also in
obvious competition with each other, leading to fierce rivalry in the field.
The history of the missionary movement and its impact on worship will be
looked at in the third section of this chapter. All that needs to be noted here
is that the first wave of the missionary movement, from all the Protestant
Churches, followed the Catholic example that we have already looked at in
the previous chapter, in insisting that the liturgy and worship of the new
churches in other parts of the world should be identical to those of the
home churches in Northern Europe.[9] It was not until the beginning of the
twentieth century that ideas of inculturation began to re-emerge, and not
until the middle to the end of the century that they began to be implemented. This phase of globalisation, therefore, from the sixteenth to the
mid-twentieth century, was a phase in which the churches of Europe aimed
to reproduce themselves in essentially identical forms throughout the
world.

This, however, had its own impact on the discourses of the churches
themselves. In many ways the Catholic Church, by its very name, had
always seen itself in global terms. In practice, however, it had only ever
been the church of Western Europe. With the expansion of the church
through Spanish and Portuguese conquests, nothing really changed.
Certainly exciting things were happening in Latin America, in India and
in the Far East, but these had little or no impact on Rome, and the
hierarchy of the church remained European, or even Italian. The only
significant impact that the expansion of the Church into a truly global

---

[7] A. F. Walls, *The Missionary Movement in Christian History, Studies in the Transmission of Faith.*
Edinburgh: T. & T. Clark, 1996.
[8] J. Hemming, *Red Gold, The Conquest of the Brazilian Indians.* London: Macmillan, 1987.
[9] See pp. 192–5 above.

institution appears to have had is in the increasing centralisation of the Church itself in terms of its power structures. This is seen clearly in the decisions of the First Vatican Council in 1852, particularly in the proclamation of Papal infallibility. It can also be seen in the encyclicals of Pope Pius X at the turn of the twentieth century and, in a very different way, in the developments of the Second Vatican Council in the 1960s.[10] Vatican II was the first truly global gathering of the Catholic Church, but the driving force remained Europe, and to a lesser extent North America. Certainly the Council led to calls for the liturgy to be celebrated in the local language and for other 'loosening' of Papal authority, but this was never fully rolled out to the majority of the Church, and the pontificate of John Paul II has shown how even this can be used to increase the centralisation of the Vatican System.[11]

With the other churches a similar globalisation was occurring, noted primarily in the Missionary Conference in Edinburgh in 1910 and the subsequent growth of the World Council of Churches.[12] This expansion was also seen primarily from a European perspective, even when the Protestant churches of Europe were, in fact, declining rapidly in their home countries. Even by the end of the twentieth century with almost a hundred years of rapid global expansion and the development of many international institutions, global bodies such as the Anglican Lambeth Conference could still not really recognise that the real strength of the church now lay in the countries of Africa, Latin America and parts of Asia rather than in Europe.[13] The numerical profile of the church has changed dramatically while the institutional power structures remain almost identical with the position one hundred years earlier.

In terms of worship this is seen to be even more significant. Towards the end of the twentieth century all the mainline churches, both Catholic and Protestant, underwent a major revision of their worship. We will look at some of the main causes of this in the second section of this chapter. One of the principal driving forces, however, was the rise of scholarship, and the realisation within all the churches that liturgy had changed over the centuries and was therefore capable of changing yet again to meet new needs and new challenges. This scholarship existed in Europe and the United States, and it was driven largely by the needs of the churches in

[10] B. McSweeney, *Roman Catholicism, The Search for Relevance.* Oxford: Blackwell, 1980.
[11] See D. Torevell, *Losing the Sacred, Ritual, Modernity and Liturgical Reform.* Edinburgh: T. & T. Clark, 2000.
[12] Walls, *Missionary Movement.*
[13] Recent controversies over the consecration of openly gay bishops have only reinforced this view.

these regions. The focus of the scholarship began largely in Western medieval liturgy but soon settled on the patristic period as the 'golden age' of Christian worship.[14] This was an age at which there was felt to be some kind of uniformity of liturgy across all the Christian churches. However, this perspective was itself coloured by a Western viewpoint.[15] While this scholarship led to major, and important, changes to worship among all mainstream churches across the globe, the significant drivers were Western, and the liturgies that were adopted by the majority of the churches in Africa and elsewhere were of a distinctly European type. There was no real attempt to revise the liturgies of these areas in the light of local needs and understandings.

A good example of this was the development of the Rite of Christian Initiation of Adults in the Roman Catholic Church.[16] This was developed, in part, for the African church, where there were still thought to be significant numbers of potential adult converts, and was based on the fourth-century model of catechumenate and the elaborate baptismal liturgies that accompanied it.[17] In practice, however, it has proved most popular among the churches of Europe and America, where it has been used for people coming into the Catholic Church from other churches and for the renewal of Catholic life among current members. It has had little or no real impact on Africa or the other non-Western churches for which it was designed.

One of the major consequences of the globalisation of Christianity over the last four centuries has been the fact that Christianity has had to come into direct contact with other religions, another aspect of Beyer's clash of cultures. Once again we have to realise that this did not occur for the first time with the expansion of the Western church. Much of Eastern Christianity has been living within Islamic societies for many centuries and, as we saw in Chapter 5, the church in India has been part of a multi-religious context since its foundation.[18] Up to the end of the eighteenth century, however, the Christian relationship with other faiths had been relatively simple (the Chinese Rites controversy apart). Christianity either had to accommodate itself to a position where it existed as a minority religion within a society dominated by other faith traditions, or it was able

---

[14] See pp. 3–5 above.
[15] Very little account was taken of the development of Syrian and Egyptian liturgy at this stage. For a study of the Anglican academic tradition see C. Irvine (ed.), *They Shaped Our Worship, Essays on Anglican Liturgists*. London: SPCK, 1998.
[16] See C. J. Walsh, 'Adult Initiation and the Catholic Church', in D. A. Withey, *Adult Initiation*. Bramcote: Grove Books, 1989, 34–42.
[17] See pp. 55–6 above. [18] See pp. 154–8 above.

to see other faiths as the archetypal 'other', as Western Europe had long been doing with Islam and, in a different way, with Judaism. Both of these contexts forced Christians to assert their own tradition over and against the 'other' and instilled a kind of traditionalist Orthodox mentality. The change in the nineteenth century came, like that in liturgical thinking, through the development of scholarly research and the understanding of other religions as being like, or at least similar to, Christianity and so to be seen, potentially, as equals, even as alternative discourses. This was also part of the growing humanist discourses, with many of the scholars who took the view that all religions could be the same being largely antagonistic to religion per se.

In itself this has had little direct impact on Christian worship, apart from a few minor adaptations of the Indian churches to Hindu practices. What is probably ironic, given this changing relationship between Christianity and other faiths, is that the most frequently used form of worship in the world at the beginning of the twenty-first century belongs to a tradition that rejects out of hand any possibility of commonality between Christianity and other faiths and certainly would do nothing to adapt its worship to accommodate these other faiths, that is the worship of the Evangelical, Pentecostal and Charismatic churches. This worship, as we will see below, grew out of the Protestant tradition and rejects practically all of the traditions of Catholic and Orthodox worship that had developed over the previous nineteen centuries. It is also a form of worship that has spread rapidly throughout the world with little or no awareness of local traditions and what the Catholic Church refers to as 'inculturation'. Charismatic or Pentecostal worship is extremely confident in its expression of the uniqueness of Christianity and the rightness of its own brand of worship. It has become, unlike any other form of Christianity before it, the mark of a truly global church.

In order to explore the way in which globalisation has impacted on liturgy, therefore, I wish to pick out three contexts, from an infinite variety of possibilities. In many ways this is an arbitrary choice, but it is one that I hope will make the most relevant points in relation to globalisation. I will begin by looking at the situation in Western Europe and the revisions of the liturgies of the vast majority of the traditional denominations. I will then move on to look at the context in Tanzania and the questions raised by inculturation before, finally, coming to look at the growth of the worship of the Evangelical, Pentecostal and Charismatic churches. I will end with a summary of the ideas explored in this chapter as well as a reflection on the developments outlined in the book as a whole.

If we were to look at the worship of the typical Anglican parish church in England in 1900 and again in the year 2000 we would probably find a far more dramatic change in the worship of that church than in any other century, apart from the sixteenth. At the turn of the twentieth century the standard form of worship in most English parish churches was Mattins (with or without the Litany) in the morning and Evensong at night, with Communion celebrated for those who wanted to stay behind after Mattins maybe once a month (some churches may have celebrated an early morning Eucharist every Sunday but these would not be the majority). The priest would probably have worn a cassock with perhaps a surplice, scarf and hood. The hymns would have been from a few standard and well-known hymnbooks and would have been sung to the accompaniment of the organ, probably without a choir (although the popularity of the robed choir was growing in 1900). The congregation would have probably been dressed in their 'Sunday best' and children would have been expected to sit quietly during the service and then go to Sunday school in the afternoon. A large proportion of the congregation would have come to more than one service on the Sunday; and Sunday itself was seen as a special day on which no work was to be done and families, especially middle-class families, engaged in reading and other pious activities.

By the end of the twentieth century things were very different. The principal act of worship would probably have been a mid-morning eucharistic service. Evening worship had died out in the vast majority of churches and Mattins was almost unheard of (although some Evangelical churches still held services of the word as their normal Sunday morning fare). The popularity of vestments for the clergy, altar servers and choirs had grown through the century, and not only among those churches with a Catholic tradition. They had also begun to decline again towards the end of the century, to be replaced by more informal robes or ordinary clothing. In most churches the interior of the church had been reordered to enable the celebrant to face the people across the altar or table. Carpets might have been installed, along with chairs and other elements of modern furnishings and design. The singing would have included hymns, choruses and songs. These would sometimes be accompanied by an organ, but music groups were also popular, and in smaller congregations a taped accompaniment would be provided. The dress of the congregation, along with their posture and behaviour, would be far more informal and children would often leave for their own form of worship or instruction during the service. The worship itself would be in modern English and there would be far more involvement of the congregation at all stages in the rite. Everything looked, sounded and felt very different from the turn of the twentieth century.

It was not, of course, only the Anglican Church in England that saw this dramatic change. All the mainline churches, in most countries around the world, had undergone a similar dramatic reformation of their worship and much of it had, in fact, been undertaken in collaboration across the different churches. Only the Orthodox appeared untouched (although there are examples in the United States where even Orthodox churches have reformed their worship along similar lines). The Evangelical, Pentecostal and Charismatic churches had also been affected, but the changes here were very different and we will look at these in more detail below.[19]

In the Church of England perhaps one of the most popular intellectual and practical pivots around which this dramatic change revolved was what became known as the Parish Communion Movement.[20] This was inspired in the 1930s by the writings of Arthur Gabriel Hebert, a parish priest from Yorkshire and member of the Anglican Society of the Sacred Mission.[21] Hebert wrote a book, entitled *Liturgy and Society*,[22] and edited a further volume of papers on *The Parish Communion*[23] in which he and others with similar views laid out what were felt to be the most important principles of Christian worship. At the heart of these principles was the view that the Church was most fully itself in its eucharistic worship. This led to the drive to reinstate full participating communion as the principal service of the parish church. This has been attempted in different ways and in different churches throughout the history of Christian worship, as we have seen.[24] In the Church of England, however, the eucharist was either an occasional service for those who felt spiritually ready to take part, or a liturgy in which the priest and a select few of the congregation actually participated. Hebert, rooted in the Catholic tradition of the Church of England, saw the eucharist as the defining act of worship of the church, and the act of communion as essential to that worship. Therefore, he argued, the 'Parish Communion' should be placed at the centre of the corporate life

---

[19] See pp. 228–34 below.
[20] The formal name for the movement, or loose organisation, was 'Parish and People', but it is as the Parish Communion Movement that the organisation has come to be known. See C. Irvine, *Worship, Church and Society, An Exposition of the Work of Arthur Gabriel Hebert to Mark the Centenary of the Society of the Sacred Mission (Kelham) of Which he was a Member.* Norwich: Canterbury Press, 1993, 125.
[21] See Ibid.   [22] London: Faber, 1935.   [23] London: SPCK, 1937.
[24] See p. 191 and 200 above.

of the parish. Implicit in this understanding was the idea that worship should be seen as something essentially corporate, the act of the parish community as a whole, rather than an act of individual devotion. This represented a very significant change in thinking on the part of the Anglican Church at that time. The principles behind this revolution, however, did not originate with Hebert and can be traced back to the Liturgical Movement in continental Europe.

The Liturgical Movement had its roots in the revival of the Benedictine Communities in France in the middle of the nineteenth century. In particular Dom Prosper Gueranger founded the community of Solesmes specifically to encourage the development of a communal, worship-filled mode of religious life.[25] In developing the community Gueranger also developed the study of plainchant and the reintroduction of plainsong into the daily office. Liturgy was central to the life of the Solesmes community and it was the communal nature of this worship, focused in the singing of the chant, that typified the way in which that liturgy was to be understood. Towards the end of the century and into the early years of the twentieth century these principles were picked up among the Benedictine communities of Belgium and, mixed with the growing liturgical scholarship that was developing at this time, was made available for parishes.[26] Conferences and training sessions were held in order to help local congregations to rediscover the communal nature of their worship and hence to revive and renew their liturgical experiences.[27] The Liturgical Movement was rooted in solid scholarship and in practical application and became a very influential movement in Belgium, the Netherlands and parts of Germany. The Swedish Lutheran Church also became interested in the Movement through the work of Yngve Brilioth and through this link Hebert helped found the Parish Communion Movement in England with the same fundamental principles.[28]

While the founders and leaders of the Liturgical Movement were fully committed to the renewal and greater understanding of the liturgy, they never seriously considered the possibility of changing the texts themselves.[29] Liturgical revision as such was not a part of their original agenda. Forces for revision, however, were strong, both in England and in the

[25] L. Soltner, *Solesmes and Dom Gueranger, 1805–1875*. Orleans: Paraclete Press, 1995.
[26] J. Fenwick and B. Spinks, *Worship in Transition, The Twentieth Century Liturgical Movement*. Edinburgh: T. & T. Clark, 1995.
[27] B. Botte, *From Silence to Participation, An Insider's View of Liturgical Renewal*. Washington: Pastoral Press, 1988.
[28] Irvine, *Worship, Church and Society*, 49–50. [29] Botte, *From Silence*, 164.

Catholic and Protestant churches on the Continent. The Church of England had decided that it needed to revise its liturgy towards the end of the nineteenth century, partly because the actual practice of the majority of the churches no longer followed the liturgy as set, and partly because the extremes of the church, the Catholic and Evangelical wings of the Church of England were beginning to abandon the Book of Common Prayer for other texts, or none at all.[30] In order to maintain order it was felt that a judicious revision of the text would be appropriate. However, it proved almost impossible to come to any kind of consensus about the direction which that revision should take. The disputes went on until a final text was prepared and presented to the English Parliament, who had the final say in matters of reform owing to the established nature of the Church of England. The revised book was presented to Parliament in 1928 and was rejected by the House of Commons by 238 votes to 205. This was a significant blow to the Church and led to many changes over the next fifty years, most significantly in the relationship between the Church and Parliament.[31]

The revisions proposed in 1928 were, in hindsight, fairly minor. They consisted primarily of the reordering of parts of the text in the light of current liturgical scholarship.[32] No attempt to change the language of worship was being proposed at this time. It was, in effect, the 1928 version of the Prayer Book (technically illegal but permitted for use at the discretion of the bishop) that Hebert and the Parish Communion Movement took to be the norm.[33] Hebert, unlike many of the original members of the Liturgical Movement, had been closely involved in liturgical revision both in England and in South Africa.[34] Following the rejection of the 1928 Prayer Book, however, he was more concerned with renewal than with further revision.[35] The emphasis on renewal continued until the 1950s when the Church of England once again began the process of revision, having this time come to an agreement with Parliament to allow them to make changes so long as these changes remained as an 'alternative' to the Book of Common Prayer rather than superseding it.[36]

In the Roman Catholic Church there had also been minor revisions of certain elements of the liturgy through the twentieth century. In 1910 the

---

[30] R. C. D. Jasper, *The Development of the Anglican Liturgy, 1662–1980*. London: SPCK, 1989, 73–108.
[31] Ibid.   [32] For full details see ibid., 113–42.   [33] Irvine, *Worship, Church and Society*, 92.
[34] Hebert was one of the first to prepare a rite for the baptism of adults for the Church of the Province of South Africa in 1921. This included an adult catechumenate and a staged process of Christian formation. Ibid., 87–8.
[35] Ibid., 97.   [36] Jasper, *Anglican Liturgy*, 211–31.

Sacred Congregation for the Discipline of the Sacraments had set out principles for the renewal of baptism, confirmation and first communion in the Decree *Quam Singulari*. In this Decree the age of first communion was brought down to seven and so the order of the sacraments was changed with first communion coming before confirmation. This was in response to concerns within the church about the loss of members and the maintenance of order.[37] Pope Pius X also encouraged the active participation of the faithful in the liturgy, but little more of a practical nature was done officially at this time.[38] In May 1948 a Commission for Liturgical Reform was appointed within the Sacred Congregation of Rites and this worked on various texts, largely in secret, up to the setting up of the Second Vatican Council in the early 1960s.[39] In the 1950s this Commission, made up principally of liturgical scholars, proposed changes to the liturgy of Holy Week and corrected a number of the anomalies that had crept in over the centuries as services had been added and times changed for various different reasons. This gave the wider Catholic population the first clue that something was stirring in liturgical reform. A major congress in Assisi in 1956 also raised the vexed question of the use of Latin in the liturgy, and, while it failed to resolve the question, Pope Pius XII provided a strong encouragement to the reformers in his final address.[40] It was the announcement of the Second Vatican Council, however, by Pope John XXIII in 1959 that saw the beginning of the really radical revisions of the latter half of the century.

When the Second Vatican Council opened in 1962 the Scheme on the Liturgy was not very high on the agenda. As with the Council of Trent, and general Catholic thinking on worship and theology, it was assumed that four Schemata on doctrinal issues would be discussed first. These caused such confusion among the delegates that at the Second General Congregation it was agreed to raise liturgy to the top of the agenda.[41] Considerable work had already been undertaken on preparing the Scheme, building on the work of the Liturgical Movement and the previous Commission, and a certain amount of controversy still surrounded the subject, especially on the question of language.[42] The discussion on the liturgy in the Council, however, was much more measured and responsible than many people expected. What is more, it led to a radical rethinking of

---

[37] For a full analysis of this and its impact on first communion practice in England see S. P. McGrail, 'The Celebration of First Communion in Liverpool: A Lens to View the Structural Decline of the Roman Catholic Parish'. Dissertation submitted to the University of Birmingham, 2003.
[38] A. Bugnini, *The Reform of the Liturgy 1948–1975*. Collegeville, The Liturgical Press, 1990, 6.
[39] Ibid., 7–10. [40] Ibid., 12. [41] Ibid., 29. [42] Ibid., 14–28.

the very nature of the church, placing the emphasis, following the Liturgical Movement, on the corporate nature of the church, the church as a pilgrim people of God. The *Constitution on the Liturgy* that was produced as a consequence of the Council was one of the most far-reaching documents in the history of Christian worship, as it enabled a revolution in liturgical thinking and practice, not just within the Catholic Church but across all the mainline churches.[43] It 'enabled' the revolution rather than being itself the revolution because the proposals contained in the *Constitution* were not nearly as far-reaching as the practice that followed. In one of the most significant areas of change, for example, that of language, the *Constitution* simply allowed for a greater use of the vernacular where this was pastorally advantageous, such as in readings and hymns.[44] The consequence, however, was the translation of the liturgy into every language and the expectation that Catholic worship would, from the end of the 1960s forward, be conducted in the vernacular across the world.[45]

Language proved to be the most significant driving force behind liturgical revision across the churches, and the element of that revision that was both most controversial and most significant.[46] Following on from the discussions in the Catholic Church, the Anglicans and others began to update their language of worship from that of the sixteenth century to something approaching the theological vernacular of the late twentieth century.[47] Structures and forms of worship were also changed, as were theologies in areas such as baptism, or 'initiation' as it was rapidly becoming called.[48] In practical terms, however, it was the language question that drew most comment and had most impact on the ordinary church. Behind the change in language lay the desire, enshrined in the Liturgical Movement and the Parish Communion Movement, that the worship of the Church should be a truly corporate activity open and available to all. Exactly how this has been interpreted has itself changed over the last twenty years of the twentieth century, first with an emphasis on inclusive language,

---

[43] For a full text and contemporary commentary see J. D. Crichton, *The Church's Worship, Considerations on the Liturgical Constitution of the Second Vatican Council*. London: Geoffrey Chapman, 1966.

[44] Ibid., 19–20.

[45] See papers in P. C. Finn and J. M. Schellman (eds.), *Shaping English Liturgy*. Washington: The Pastoral Press, 1990.

[46] See K. F. Pecklers, *Dynamic Equivalence, The Living Language of Christian Worship*. Collegeville: Liturgical Press, 2003.

[47] For a view from the Church of England see M. Perham, 'The Language of Worship', in M. Perham (ed.), *Towards Liturgy 2000, Preparing for the Revision of the Alternative Service Book*. London: SPCK, 1989, 67–74.

[48] McGrail, 'First Communion'.

following the realisation that so much liturgical language is implicitly male,[49] and then through experiments with new and creative forms of language either towards the concrete use of language for children, the deaf and those uncomfortable with written text, or through increasingly poetic forms of language as the study of liturgical language itself has progressed.[50]

It was not just in England or Europe, however, that these changes and developments had an impact. All the mainline churches by the middle of the twentieth century were international churches with a global scope, even if the administrative, and in some cases the spiritual, heart of the churches remained in Europe. The initial moves and motivations for the Liturgical Movement, the Parish Communion Movement and the liturgical revisions all came from Europe. It was not long, however, before the American churches began to take up the initiative. Much of the translation of the Catholic rites and the principal voice in ecumenical English language committees such as the 'International Commission on English in the Liturgy' has been American.[51] In terms of the initiative for more radical revision, this has increasingly come from other parts of the world. In ecumenical collaboration, particularly in liturgical revision, India has taken the lead with the liturgy of the United Church of South India, produced in 1956, being one of the most influential texts of the century.[52] In other areas, such as inclusive language and the creative use of language in liturgy, the churches of New Zealand and Canada have taken a lead.[53] This drive for change has also been fully ecumenical, with Methodists and various Reformed traditions producing interesting and exciting liturgies of their own that both build on their specific traditions and can be seen to be moving in the corporate open and structured direction common to all the liturgical revision of the time.[54]

The changes in the official liturgies of the mainline churches, however, have been essentially a Western phenomenon. It has been commented that

[49] See the discussion in B. Wren, *What Language Shall I Borrow? God-Talk in Worship: A Male Response to Feminist Theology*. London: SCM Press, 1989.
[50] See the papers collected together in G. Ramshaw, *Worship: Searching for Language*. Washington: Pastoral Press, 1988. For a different perspective see C. Pickstock, 'Liturgy and Language: The Sacred Polis', in P. Bradshaw and B. Spinks (eds.), *Liturgy in Dialogue, Essays in Memory of Ronald Jasper*. London: SPCK, 1998, 115–37.
[51] F. R. McManus, 'ICEL: The First Years', in Finn and Schellman, *English Liturgy*, 433–59.
[52] T. S. Garrett, *Worship in the Church of South India*. London: Lutterworth Press, 1958.
[53] B. Peters, *The Anglican Eucharist in New Zealand, 1814–1989*. Bramcote: Grove Books, 1992 and W. R. Blott, *Blessing and Glory and Thanksgiving, The Growth of a Canadian Liturgy*. Toronto: Anglican Book Centre, 1998.
[54] N. Dixon, *Wonder, Love and Praise, A Companion to The Methodist Worship Book*. London: Epworth Press, 2003.

this in itself follows the development of modernism, and increasingly post-modernism, within Western culture.[55] It could be argued that as these liturgies have been exported in one form or another to the mainline churches of Africa, Asia and Latin America, the revisions have been a globalising influence within Christian worship. In part this is true. In practice, however, the liturgies adopted by many of the mainline denominations of Africa and Asia have been little more than translations of those being produced within Europe and America. These liturgies have not been taken to heart by the non-Western churches and there is still a strong sense that they and many of the issues that drove the revisions are anomalous within an African, Asian or Latin-American context.[56] One of the reasons for this may well be that the liturgies themselves were constructed as a direct response to the modernism of Europe and America, in an entirely humanistic discourse. If this is the case, recent scholarship on the variety of modernisms throughout the world, and particularly the exceptional nature of European modernism, would suggest that the situations that these liturgies were responding to are in themselves unique to the Western nations.[57] They could not possibly hope to appeal to, or relate to, the modernisms and discourses of the rest of the world. If this is true, then in a very real sense the revised liturgies are far from being a 'global' liturgy and to find the relationship between worship and globalisation we need to look elsewhere.

WORSHIPPING WITH LEPERS IN TANZANIA

In the early 1980s I spent nine months with the United Society for the Propagation of the Gospel, an Anglican missionary society, in Tanzania. While I was there I was offered the chance to travel to a remote spot on the Rufiji River where an elderly English priest was running a village for lepers. On the Sunday I joined Father Lamburn to go to the local church, a two-hour walk, and attended the eucharistic service for the villagers that he led. The church was packed with people, probably just over two hundred, and from beginning to end (with the exception of the sermon) the church was also full of music. The whole of the liturgy was in Swahili but kept to the basic Anglican pattern and it was easy to follow what was going on. Father

[55] Torevell, *Losing the Sacred*.
[56] P. Tovey, *Inculturation of Christian Worship, Exploring the Eucharist*. Aldershot: Ashgate, 2004.
[57] G. Davie, *Europe: The Exceptional Case, Parameters of Faith in the Modern World*. London: DLT, 2002.

Lamburn sang his parts of the service, including the eucharistic prayer and the gospel, to a traditional plainsong chant. The hymns were all taken from a Swahili translation of the English Hymnal, an Anglican hymnbook first published in the late nineteenth century. These hymns were all sung unaccompanied but were given much more rhythm and pace than I was used to at home. The congregational elements of the service, the Gloria, the Sanctus, the Benedictus etc., were all sung to traditional Swahili melodies in a responsorial style that is common to many different kinds of African singing. A cantor led the singing with a solo verse and the congregation replied in unison. This was accompanied by drums and other percussive instruments and built up through the canticles to a very high level of emotional intensity. The worship was a potent mixture of the African and the Anglican that lasted for almost two hours and it was an experience that I shall never forget.

In this worship we can also identify a number of the issues that are related to the spread of the Christian church into Africa and other parts of the world, and the consequences this has had for worship in many of these contexts. Christian mission in the nineteenth century was led by Europe and in many cases went hand in hand with the colonial expansion of the European empires.[58] Tanzania is, in fact, an interesting case study in this situation and has a complicated colonial history. The main European power to colonise the area known as Tanganyika was Germany from 1886 onwards.[59] Alongside the German colonial government there came Lutheran and Moravian missionaries and Benedictine monks from Bavaria.[60] These often took over mission stations set up by other societies throughout the country (with the Lutherans and Moravians tending to the North and the Benedictines moving into the South), and they brought their own form of worship and church organisation with them.[61]

The Germans, however, were removed from Tanganyika following the First World War and the country became a British Protectorate. There was never a significant influx of British colonial officers and settlers into Tanganyika, because it was never fully part of the British Empire. The Anglican missionary societies did move in, however, often across the

[58] E. Isichei, *A History of Christianity in Africa, From Antiquity to the Present.* Grand Rapids: Eerdmans, 1955, 74–93.
[59] J. Iliffe, *A Modern History of Tanganyika.* Cambridge: Cambridge University Press, 1979.
[60] Isichei, *History*, 86, 231. Meanwhile the Anglican bishop, William Tozer, had set up his main base on the island of Zanzibar and used this to develop missions in the south of the country. Ibid., 139.
[61] The Lutherans and Moravians took over from the London Mission Society and the Holy Ghost Fathers in the North. Iliffe, *Tanganyika*, 216–17.

borders from other British colonies in the area. The Universities Mission to Central Africa (UMCA) already had a cathedral on the Island of Zanzibar and moved up from the South where they had been working in Rhodesia and Nyasaland (Zimbabwe and Malawi), while the Church Missionary Society (CMS) moved down from Kenya and Uganda in the North.[62] Unfortunately for the Anglican Church in Tanganyika, these two missionary societies reflected very different traditions within the Anglican Church in England. UMCA was Catholic in orientation and placed a great emphasis on ritual and colour in worship, often developing a far more 'catholic' form of worship in the colonies than would ever have been allowed back home.[63] CMS, on the other hand, was Protestant and evangelical and brought a Protestant version of Prayer Book worship into the country. The English Hymnal was a Catholic Anglican production, and many elements of the worship of the Anglican Church in the South and East of what became Tanzania, even when I was there in the 1980s, maintained many of the traditions and practices of English Anglo-Catholic worship from the 1920s. In the North and West the Book of Common Prayer, along with Swahili translations of evangelical hymnbooks, was still the standard form of worship.

From the late 1940s onwards many of the countries in which the European missionaries had been working gained independence from their colonial rulers. This led to self-government in the political sphere, and to a similar call for self-government from the churches. Some denominations had been attempting to develop a local leadership, and local responsibilities for the mission churches, for some decades but this had not progressed very far by the 1950s. In most Protestant churches, however, the move to local leadership came soon after independence, and with this came a local control of worship, although this led to very little actual change in practice. It was in the Roman Catholic Church that the international drift towards local leadership was at its slowest. It was in the Catholic Church, however, that the first questions about the adaptation of worship to local cultures and customs began to emerge. I have already talked about the enabling consequences of the Second Vatican Council and the way in which the European churches took this as a sign that vernacular liturgy could become the norm.[64] In many non-Western countries the freedom that appeared to be offered by the *Constitution on the Liturgy* led to

---

[62] For a full description of the mission activity in Tanganyika before 1914 see ibid., 216–37.
[63] Isichei, *History*, 232.   [64] See pp. 220–1 above.

calls for far more drastic changes to reflect not just local languages, but local cultures and traditions.

In the backs of the minds of the priests who initiated the development of indigenous liturgies were the arguments that we have already witnessed in the context of the Chinese Rites Controversy.[65] Now, however, it appeared that the Vatican would at last look kindly on the kind of activities that the Jesuits were proposing in the sixteenth century and which were rejected out of hand by the Curia at the time. It was in Africa and India that the first moves towards what was to become known as 'inculturation' began.[66] In Africa the principal changes that were introduced in the name of inculturation were in the area of music and language. As with the worship I attended in Tanzania, local musical traditions were encouraged and elements of the rite were set to local forms and styles of music. This certainly provided a local feel for much of the worship but, with a few very notable exceptions, did not go very far in making the worship truly African. In Tanzania, in the late 1960s, the Catholic bishops asked students at the seminary to produce a possible rite for the church in Tanzania. The result combined African idioms, especially from a rural context, with elements of Tanzanian socialism to create some interesting prayers. The experiment, however, never got beyond the drafting stage.[67] It was in Zaire that the most extensive forms of inculturation of this kind were tried out, with a whole new mass being written in 1972 drawing on local melodies, local forms of poetry and language and local forms of dress, dance and symbolism.[68] The resulting liturgy began with a call to worship in the form of a call to the presence of the chief. It included an extensive confessional element and the eucharistic prayer was based on that of Hippolytus, although with extensive use of local imagery. The liturgy ended with dancing and the dismissal.[69] This rite was tolerated and performed widely within Zaire for a while but was eventually questioned by the Vatican as moving too far from the Latin original.

The attempts at inculturation in India were, in principle, much more far-reaching. Here, as in China in the sixteenth century, there was a far more literate culture into which the worship could be inculturated. The attempts at inculturation therefore went much further than simply adapting the music and language to local tastes. Attempts were made to

---

[65] See pp. 193–5 above.

[66] P. Tovey, *Inculturation: The Eucharist in Africa*. Bramcote: Grove Books, 1988. [67] Ibid., 32–33.

[68] L. N. Kalumba, 'The Zairian Rite: The Roman Missal for the Diocese of Zaire (Congo)', in K. Pecklers (ed.), *Liturgy in a Postmodern World*. London: Continuum, 2003, 92–8.

[69] For the full text see M. Thurian and G. Wainwright, *Baptism and Eucharist: Ecumenical Convergence in Celebration*. Grand Rapids: Eerdmans, 1983, 205–9.

incorporate Indian practices and organisations into the church.[70] This included certain forms of puja, or devotion to the gods (adapted to form a puja for Jesus or the saints), and the widespread use of Indian monastic forms, or Ashrams, for Christian religious orders. None of these adaptations was ever popular among the ordinary local Christians and they always tended to exist somewhat on the edge of the church. This has been true of many different attempts at inculturation. The local people, on the whole, have much preferred to stick to the forms of worship that the missionaries taught them and which they had come to understand as 'true' Christian worship. Having converted out of the local religious culture, often at great discomfort to themselves, they were not willing to accept elements of that culture back into their Christian worship. The old ways had been rejected as the way of the Devil and local people were not going to allow them to be reintroduced under other guises.

That said, some elements of the 'old ways' were maintained even in the most conservative of ex-mission churches. I remember, during my time in Tanzania, attending an exorcism following the morning service in an Anglican church. There was no official liturgy for exorcism within the Anglican Church of Tanzania and such rites were not popular in the Church of England. However, there was a need for such rites in Africa, where the driving out of evil spirits was an accepted part of everyday practice. I also attended a beautiful evening liturgy among the Maasai people after they had brought their cattle back to their pen in the middle of the African bush. These particular Maasai had been converted by Lutherans and inherited the need for an evening devotion from them. Apart from the reading from the Bible (which had to be done by my companion, an English doctor, as none of the Maasai could read) the whole act of worship consisted of Maasai songs adapted to Christian purposes. Finally, I was somewhat surprised to discover that the local Tanzanian parish priest, who acted as chaplain to the hospital where I was working, chose to take his baby son into the woods to a local healer for protective rites when the child was ill rather than bringing him to the hospital. This went further than simple 'inculturation' and came close to what is generally known as 'syncretism', that is the deliberate mixing of different religious discourses.[71]

---

[70] J. M. Brown and R. E. Frykenberg (eds.), *Christians, Cultural Interactions, and India's Religious Traditions*. Grand Rapids: Eerdmans, 2002.

[71] See R. Shaw and C. Stewart, 'Introduction: Problematizing Syncretism' and other papers, in C. Stewart and R. Shaw (eds.), *Syncretism/Anti-Syncretism, The Politics of Religious Synthesis*.

Beyond the mainline churches, many African Christians, and those of other ex-colonial countries, took things into their own hands in desperation at the slow pace of change in the missionary churches and, leaving these churches, founded their own churches with their own rites.[72] Some of the older and more conservative of these followed the essentially Protestant worship of the churches they had left. Most, however, included elements of prophecy, healing or exorcism from their local traditions and developed more clearly syncretistic rites. If I look at just one example, we can see the kind of worship that was involved. The Church of the Lord (Aladura) was founded when a lay catechist, Josiah Oshitelu, from the Anglican Church in Nigeria began to see visions in 1925 and was ejected from his Anglican congregation.[73] Josiah was a prophet who emphasised the importance of spiritual healing. This centrality of healing also had its impact on the worship of the new church. The rituals of the church are, in essence, Anglican, being based on the Book of Common Prayer. However, they have been so overlaid with local, biblical and prophetic elements that they are hardly recognisable in their current form. Fasting is a central feature of the church, as is confession accompanied by sprinkling with holy water. Hierarchy is also important and this is reflected in the worship through a range of coloured robes for the different levels of the hierarchy. Phillip Tovey comments that 'Church services are not as static as those of the mission parent. Besides kneeling there are prostrations, kissing the Bible, clapping, shouting, use of the sign of the cross, anointing, laying on of hands, the sprinkling of holy water, and usually at some point in the service there is dancing.'[74]

This form of worship, along with the range of influences that come together to form it, is typical of many of the independent churches of Africa although there will, of course, be local and doctrinal differences between the churches. The mainline churches rejected many of these independent churches for almost twenty years. However, towards the end of the twentieth century the older and more established of the indigenous churches were becoming accepted into ecumenical dialogue as local expressions of universal Christian norms. Their worship was seen as something positive, something to learn from rather than as something to condemn. In many cases, however, with the emphasis on healing and prophecy, the worship of these churches was

London: Routledge, 1994, 1–26. For another example of something that critics described as 'syncretism' in Tanzania see the development of the Jando initiation rites in the south of the country. I. Robertson, 'The Jando and Initiation in Southern Tanzania', in D. R. Holeton (ed.), *Liturgical Inculturation in the Anglican Communion, Including the York Statement 'Down to Earth Worship'*. Bramcote: Grove Books, 1990, 27–31.
[72] A. Hastings, *A History of African Christianity 1950–1975*. Cambridge: Cambridge university Press, 1979.
[73] Tovey, *Inculturation*, 17–23.   [74] Ibid., 19.

much closer to the fastest-growing form of worship in the twentieth century, that of Pentecostalism, and it is to this that I must turn next.

THE RISE OF THE CHARISMATIC

In the late 1820s a young woman from southern Scotland, Isabella Campbell, began to experience very strange phenomena. Following her death from consumption many people flocked to her house and to talk to her sister Mary. It was not long before Mary began to utter words in an incomprehensible language. Others in the region were also experiencing similar phenomena and this was attracting considerable attention both in Scotland and beyond. After much discussion and prayer it was agreed by those closely associated with the experiences that the phenomena that the young women were experiencing were the gifts of the Spirit as outlined in Paul's letter to the Corinthians. This experience led, along with other factors, to the founding of the Catholic Apostolic Church in Albury just outside London and the spread of 'charismatic' phenomena in the worship of the Church.[75] The Catholic Apostolics were firm believers in the second coming and saw these spiritual experiences as signs of the last days. Their leaders wrote to heads of government and church leaders to warn them of the things they were experiencing and they formed a group of twelve 'Apostles' to proclaim the message to the world. As the nineteenth century progressed the liturgy of the Catholic Apostolic Church became more and more elaborate, as the leaders engaged in detailed scholarship and drew on traditions from across the churches. Unfortunately for the church, however, it was believed that the Apostles were the only people who could ordain new ministers and when the last Apostle died in 1901 the ordained ministry of the church ceased to grow. The church itself entered a 'time of silence', slowly declined and will eventually die.[76]

In the early years of the twentieth century, in 1906, as the Catholic Apostolics entered their 'time of silence', an African-American preacher, William Joseph Seymour, was locked out of his church for preaching on the gifts of the Spirit. Seymour was put up by friends and supporters, and the subsequent group continued in prayer and Bible study until his host, Edward Lee, asked Seymour to lay hands on him. Lee immediately fell to the floor and began to speak in tongues. The community rented a small

---

[75] C. G. Flegg, *'Gathered Under Apostles', A Study of the Catholic Apostolic Church*. Oxford: Oxford University Press, 1992, 41–6.
[76] For a full and detailed study of the Catholic Apostolic Church see ibid.

abandoned church building on Azusa Street in a poor neighbourhood of Los Angeles, and people began to flock in to see what was happening.[77] Allan Anderson describes the meetings of the new congregation as follows: 'with sawdust-sprinkled floors and rough planks as benches, daily meetings commenced at about ten in the morning and usually lasted until late at night. They were completely spontaneous and usually emotional, without planned programmes or speakers. Singing in tongues and people falling to the ground "under the power" or "slain in the Spirit" were common phenomena.'[78] Racial integration and a significant role for women within the worship were particular features of the life of this and other subsequent fledgeling Pentecostal congregations in the States.

Meanwhile in Chile, in South America, similar phenomena were taking hold. In 1907, Willis Collins Hoover, a revivalist minister from the States, was in charge of the largest Methodist congregation in Chile, at Valparaiso.[79] He heard of the phenomena of gifts from friends in India and began to preach and pray for the gifts within his own congregation. The revival came in April 1909 when many different manifestations of the Spirit occurred at once; weeping, laughing, rolling on the floor, confession of sins, visions and singing and speaking in tongues. The people apparently made so much noise that the police were called and the press began to take an interest. The Methodist church eventually rejected these phenomena and asked Hoover to return to the States. He chose rather to leave the Methodist Church and to set up his own congregation. This led to further congregations and churches and ultimately to the rise of a significant Pentecostal population in Chile.[80]

Similar experiences happened at about the same time around the globe in Armenia, Wales, South Africa, and across much of the rest of South America.[81] This phenomenon was much more open than that experienced by the Catholic Apostolics and began to spread rapidly through the Protestant churches of the States, Latin America and across the world. It is a matter of dispute in the scholarly literature where these phenomena originated or what their ultimate roots were.[82] Some claim links to spirit possession in West Africa and among

---

[77] W. K. Kay, *Pentecostals in Britain*. Carlisle: Paternoster Press, 2000, 10–11.

[78] A. Anderson, *An Introduction to Pentecostalism, Global Charismatic Christianity*. Cambridge: Cambridge University Press, 2004, 39.

[79] Ibid., 64–9.

[80] E. L. Cleary, 'Latin American Pentecostalism', in M. W. Dempster, B. D. Klaus and D. Petersen, *The Globalization of Pentecostalism: A Religion Made to Travel*. Oxford: Regnum Books, 1999, 131–50.

[81] Ibid., 132.

[82] See W. J. Hollenweger, *The Pentecostals*. London: SCM, 1972 for a classic statement of these disputes, and for a more recent view see E. A. Wilson, 'They Crossed the Red Sea, Didn't They? Critical History and Pentecostal Beginnings', in Dempster et al., *Globalization*, 85–115.

slave populations in the American South. Others linked the phenomena with
the working-class situation of the congregations themselves and the need for
some kind of powerful expression of the power of God within these congregations. Whatever the origins actually were, the majority of the early Pentecostals,
like the Catholic Apostolic Church before them, saw the widespread nature of
the phenomena, along with their rapid growth, as a sign of the last days and the
imminence of the second coming.[83] Over the following century Pentecostalism
in many different forms began to spread very quickly and was to change the
nature of the church and its worship across many different continents. In
practice, revivals, and the spiritual phenomena that have accompanied them,
have tended to spread in waves, with each new outbreak being transferred from
church to church almost like an epidemic. These waves continued through the
twentieth century getting larger and larger and spreading further and further
with time. Each wave built on important aspects of the previous theologies and
practices, but also added something new. By the end of the century it was
possible to claim that South America was as much a Pentecostal continent as a
Catholic one,[84] and that Pentecostalism in South America was more authenti-
cally Latin American than the Catholic Church, with far more indigenous
leaders and a very distinctive style of worship.[85]

Towards the end of the twentieth century two of the most famous waves
of revival involved what became known as the 'Toronto Blessing' in North
America and Europe, and the growth of prosperity-orientated healing and
deliverance in Brazil. The Toronto Blessing was first experienced in a
church based in the airport at Toronto in Canada.[86] This congregation
was a part of an international body called the Vineyard Community with
its base in California. At first the phenomena were lauded as a true sign of
the spirit of God being poured out onto the church, and Christians from
around the world flocked to Toronto and the Airport Vineyard Church to
experience the phenomena for themselves and to carry them back to their
own churches. The phenomena were most often experienced as hysterical
laughter and the making of animal noises, typically the barking of a dog, by
those who were 'blessed'. This created considerable controversy in many
countries and in many churches. The Toronto Blessing rapidly spread
beyond the Vineyard churches and entered into the lives of many ordinary

[83] Wilson, 'Red Sea', 93–4.
[84] Cleary does note that the Catholic Church also saw a revival throughout South America as the
Pentecostal churches were growing, and so it was not the case that Pentecostalism grew at the
expense of the Catholic Church; both were part of a much wider movement. Cleary, 'Latin
American Pentecostalism'.
[85] Anderson, *Pentecostalism*, 63–82 and 6–7.   [86] Kay, *Pentecostals*, 93–106.

mainstream congregations, transforming their worship and their spirituality almost overnight. Eventually, by the mid 1990s, the phenomena were challenged by the Vineyard Community leadership and the Toronto church was censured by the fellowship. The phenomena had already begun to decline, but little more was heard of them after this time.

In 1977 a former state lottery official founded the Igreja Universal do Reino de Deus (Universal Church of the Kingdom of God) in Rio de Janeiro.[87] Bishop Edir Macedo went on to became one of the most controversial church leaders in modern Brazil by preaching a message of prosperity through healing and exorcisms. His church attracted many thousands of people, primarily from the poorer regions of Brazil, and emphasised mass exorcisms from Umbanda spirits and other dramatic displays of the power of the Spirit. People were encouraged to bring cash to church and to buy 'holy oils, anointed handkerchiefs, fig paste, water from the Jordan River and other sacred objects'[88] as aids to healing. Even different coloured flowers were used as part of the ritual world of the church. The 'Cathedral of Faith' in Rio de Janeiro seats 10,000 worshippers and is one of the largest church buildings in the world reflecting the incredible growth of Macedo's church. Despite the arrest and imprisonment of Macedo himself in 1992 the church has continued to grow, gaining an important international following across the world.

In order to understand the nature of these phenomena, and their spread, we need to step back and look at the context of the churches in which the majority of the phenomena took place. The churches of the radical reformation had grown over the centuries, particularly in the United States, and had stuck firmly to their belief in extempory worship 'led by the spirit'.[89] Not only was their worship free, and focused primarily on singing, Bible reading, preaching and open prayer; their organisation was also loose, focused primarily on the congregation. This led to regular division and the founding of new churches across both Europe and the United States. Some attempts were made to bring these disparate communities back together, such as the Methodist Union in Britain in 1932, but the history of these churches has generally been one of divisions and the multiplication of communities.[90] When these churches were transferred to Africa, Latin America and Asia through missionary activity the tendency to split and subdivide continued, with many indigenous churches separating from their missionary parents. The second context for understanding

---

[87] Anderson, *Pentecostalism*, 73–4.   [88] Ibid., 73.   [89] See pp. 202–3 above.
[90] For the impact of this on the Methodists, as one example, see Burdon, *Preaching Service*, 29–36.

Pentecostal worship was the series of 'revivals' on the American frontier in the nineteenth century. These were large open-air celebrations with camps set up in the wilderness attracting thousands of worshippers for days at a time, often from a very wide range of churches. These revival meetings were times of heightened spiritual awareness and emotion and the use of songs, emotive preaching and the giving of testimonies raised the emotional tension of the events to fever pitch.[91] Many healings and other phenomena happened at these meetings and the churches that sponsored them grew as a result. It is this freedom in worship, associated as it was in the revival meetings with a strong emotional or experiential element, and linked to the congregational form of church organisation, that formed the basic structure for Pentecostal worship. Music played a very significant role and, of course, varied considerably across the world, often combining a global rock idiom with local vernacular styles. At the heart of the worship, however, were the sermon and the power of the preacher.

Theologically many of the churches that developed these patterns of worship were essentially conservative and Bible-based.[92] The term 'fundamentalist' was developed from the title of a series of twelve books produced from 1910 onwards on the fundamentals of the faith, but it soon came to be used to refer to any group who took the scriptures literally and aimed to live their lives according to the dictates of the Gospel.[93] In practice there were many different interpretations of the Scriptures and it was the authority invested in the leader of the community and the principal preacher in each congregation that came to be seen as the mark of a fundamentalist congregation. While all the churches that claimed a reformed inheritance tended to encourage large meetings at which worship consisted primarily of singing, praising God, and preaching, only some of these churches began to experience and encourage the gifts of the Spirit such as speaking in tongues, healing or prophecy. It was perhaps these gifts, and their interpretation, that did more to divide these churches than any differences in attitudes to, or interpretation of, the Bible.

Loosely, the evangelical churches divided into two groups. There were those who remained focused on the scriptures, even if they encouraged spiritual gifts. These churches founded their authority on the Bible and always placed biblical truth above the revelations offered through the spiritual possession. Others, commonly referred to as Pentecostal, tipped

---

[91] Westermeyer, *Te Deum*, 263–70. [92] Anderson, *Pentecostalism*, 225–42.
[93] G. Kepel, *The Revenge of God: The Resurgence of Islam, Christianity and Judaism in the Modern World.* Cambridge: Polity Press, 1994, 105–6.

this balance further in the direction of the direct inspiration of the Spirit, such that the word spoken in worship often held more sway than the word of scripture. Of course, in practice, the churches involved in this form of worship formed a continuum with only those at each extreme rejecting completely the views of the others. Most maintained a balance between the authority of scripture and the authority of direct revelation in worship. What is more, most of those churches which were founded as a break away from a more traditional group tended to put more emphasis on spiritual inspiration in the first years of their life but gradually came closer to the traditional evangelical mainstream as time progressed. This certainly appears to be true of the churches founded by Willis Hoover in Chile. Within the range of churches that practised these forms of worship many different theologies prevailed. It was the worship, therefore, that was perhaps the most common factor, the core of the Pentecostal discourse.

Byron Klaus claims that 'Pentecostalism has been the quintessential indigenous religion, adapting readily to a variety of cultures'.[94] It is in part the very simplicity of this form of worship, rooted in preaching, the singing of songs or choruses, and the manifestation of the gifts of the Spirit, that has made this adaptation possible. It also has something to do with the sense of emotional release and power that can be experienced in this kind of worship, a power that relates as closely to experiences of spirit possession in Africa, as to poverty and oppression in Latin America, and to middle-class release in Europe and the United States. Finally it has something to do with the globalisation of capitalist cultures and the association that many of these churches, and their style of music and preaching, have with global humanist discourses and the commodification of faith. This is a church structure, and this is a form of worship, that is ideally suited to global culture, even if in some of its many manifestations it presents itself as virulently opposed to that culture. It has plenty of space for indigenous cultural expression, through forms of music and styles of preaching, which will change from Chicago to São Paulo to Cape Town to Seoul. However, the essence of the worship is not only the same but instantly recognisable by all those involved wherever in the world it originates, and the worship has no real space for 'inculturation' as understood in the previous section of this chapter. With the spread of Pentecostalism across the world, it would not be unfair to say that the Charismatic meeting, complete with 'worship time', powerful, emotive and biblical preaching, and the manifestation of

---

[94] B. D. Klaus, 'Pentecostalism as a Global Culture, An Introductory Overview', in Dempster et al., *Globalization*, 127–30, 127.

the Spirit in some dramatic form, is now the most common form of Christian worship in the contemporary world.

This position has been reflected in recent years by a series of studies from an essentially anthropological base into a number of different forms of Charismatic or Pentecostal worship. Harvey Cox and David Martin have produced classic studies of the Latin American church, relating that to the socio-cultural context in which it has flourished.[95] It has been widely recognised, however, that the study of Pentecostal worship as such cannot follow the normal patterns of liturgical study because it does not contain the kind of texts that liturgical scholars choose to focus on. There has had to be a different approach, therefore, to the study of this worship. Anthropology and ritual studies have provided an excellent way in and appear to be becoming increasingly common. In 1997, Thomas Csordas undertook a study of the Charismatic movement within the Catholic Church and drew on the work of Bourdieu and others to discuss the worship of the movement in relation to habitus, ritualisation and performance.[96] Daniel Albrecht's book *Rites in the Spirit* uses the concepts of 'ritual fields' and 'processual rites' to look at the macro and micro rites of the Pentecostal/Charismatic tradition.[97] Finally James Stevens published *Worship in the Spirit* in 2002, a study of Anglican Charismatic worship in England based on detailed ethnographic fieldwork.[98] What all these authors show is the importance of ritual, movement, space and sound to the worship of the Charismatic/Pentecostal tradition. They each demonstrate the importance of analysing this worship from a ritual studies perspective and, in so doing, open up the possibility of a much broader study of Christian worship in all traditions in the future. It is to this, therefore, that I must return in my conclusion.

THE MEAL AND THE SPIRIT REVISITED

In this chapter we have seen the development of the Parish Communion Movement as it developed out of the Liturgical Movement and the

---

[95] H. Cox, *Fire from Heaven: The Rise of Pentecostal Spirituality and the Reshaping of Religion in the Twenty-First Century.* London: Cassell, 1996 and D. Martin, *Tongues of Fire: The Explosion of Protestantism in Latin America.* Oxford: Blackwell, 1990.

[96] T. J. Csordas, *Language, Charisma, and Creativity, The Ritual Life of a Religious Movement.* Berkeley: University of California Press, 1977.

[97] D. E. Albrecht, *Rites in the Spirit, A Ritual Approach to Pentecostal/Charismatic Spirituality.* Sheffield: Sheffield Academic Press, 1999.

[98] J. H. S. Stevens, *Worship in the Spirit, Charismatic Worship in the Church of England.* Carlisle: Paternoster Press, 2002.

emphasis that this placed on the centrality of the eucharist. Towards the end of the twentieth century this had become so firmly established that in many of the mainline churches in the West the eucharist was the only form of worship that was celebrated and everybody who attended received communion. We have also noted the rise of the Charismatic traditions and the worship of the Pentecostal churches. Here the emphasis is less on the eucharist, which following in their Protestant traditions is less frequently held in these churches, and more on the gifts of the Spirit. This combination of the eucharist and the gifts of the Spirit takes us back immediately to the writing of Paul in his first letter to the Corinthians and his emphasis on the meal and the Spirit-filled worship. As we saw when we looked at this text in Chapter 1, there is some question as to whether the meal and the act of worship are parts of one single event or two separate occasions within the life of the Corinthian church.[99] Either way, it is clear that the Corinthians themselves engaged in both forms of worship. We could argue, therefore, that the history of Christian worship has gone full circle and that we have come back to our starting point with the emphasis on the sharing of the meal and the Spirit-filled assembly, neither of which have been of primary significance for much of the two thousand years in between. Such a suggestion, however, fails to recognise the very different situation of the church in the early years of the twenty-first century to that of thirty years after the death of Christ.

One of the most significant differences, which should be spotted immediately, is that those churches that put a primary emphasis on the shared meal of the eucharist are seldom those that place an emphasis on Spirit-filled worship, although there are notable exceptions.[100] The two traditions of meal and Spirit, while both being reinvigorated during the twentieth century, have yet to come together in any meaningful way. If or when they do, I believe that we will see something very significant within the church and the possibility of a new round of renewal and growth of faith and practice. This, however, is not the most significant difference between Paul's Corinth and the contemporary church.

What is also clear is that the social, cultural, and any other kind of context that we care to choose is immeasurably different. This is not simply a case of our being in a globalised world village while Paul was writing from the heart of an ancient Empire; it goes much further than this. Paul's Christians were a small struggling community on the margins of Corinthian society convinced that they were living in the last days. They

---

[99] See p. 30 above.   [100] See Stevens's 'St A' in *Worship in the Spirit*.

knew of other similar small marginal communities scattered throughout the Mediterranean world and even had minimal contacts with them. They were also aware of the presence of pagan and Jewish traditions surrounding them, many of which would have liked to see them destroyed. They were new and still struggling to develop a distinctive voice and a clear discourse of their own that would express their own experiences of God and the world around them. The church today, 2,000 years later, is a series of global institutions that express a bewildering variety of forms and theologies. Christianity has ceased to be the only dominant discourse of much of the globe, but it is still there, either as a lived memory or merged with other, humanist, discourses. The fact that for more than a thousand years Christianity did provide the dominant discourse for practically the whole of Europe, and much of the globe besides, has left its own mark on the church. There is in many parts of the old areas of dominance a sense of tiredness with the Christian discourses, a wanting to move on from them. Even in those areas where Christian discourses appear fresh and new they come with the baggage of colonialism or even neo-colonialism.[101] There is no way in which these two situations could ever be considered to be the same.

What is important, therefore, is that we must never fall into the trap of trying to go backwards. We cannot recreate the forms and the spontaneity of the Corinthian community. We cannot live within their particular set of discourses. Christians over the centuries have constantly tried to do this. As I said in my introduction, the nature of the Christian scriptures, and the place of those scriptures within the wider discourse, means that the temptation to look back, to try and cleanse ourselves and to go backwards, is always there.[102] It may be a temptation, and it is important to keep the scriptural discourses always before us, but it is a temptation that we have to avoid. The Christian communities of Corinth or Rome, or even Jerusalem, can never be recreated and we must not use history with this kind of nostalgic longing.

If we are not going to 'go back' therefore, what value does a study of the history of worship of this kind have? Do we want to say that there are lessons that we should learn from, mistakes that we have to avoid? To say this is probably only placing ourselves in a variation of the attempt to recreate some kind of golden age. What we consider to be mistakes, as well as what we consider to be 'golden', is an entirely subjective decision. It is

---

[101] The position of China, and perhaps post-Communist Russia, provide interesting exceptions to this.
[102] See pp. 22–3 above.

not possible to point to any stage of the history and say 'these Christians got it right, this is what all worship must look like'. As I have tried to show, the form and pattern of worship is rooted in the social and political situation of the church at each specific time and place. No time is like the present, and no time should be recreated. We can perhaps say that some events or activities in worship are not to our taste, or that they appeared to be too closely associated with naked political power or with something that we might want to call 'superstition', but this is also a subjective decision and we cannot say definitively that this rite was a mistake or that ceremony was wrong. We cannot look to history in any way but through our own spectacles, and that will inevitably distort all that we can see.

What then is the value of a history such as this? For me, the real value is to show the variety and diversity of Christian practice. It is the delight that is gained in seeing something new, something that I had not come across before, of seeing new approaches to old ritual problems, new possibilities, new rites and ceremonies, new theologies and new and often creative uses of well worn symbolisms. It is the sheer variety of ways in which Christians have worshipped over the centuries that draws me, both in the outward forms of the worship along with the art, music and spaces in which that worship took place, and in the underlying motivations for that worship. It is the realisation that within the basic framework of a single Christian discourse it is possible to construct worship that is appropriate to the small apocalyptic community in Corinth, the imperial rites of Byzantium and Charlemagne, the ascetical monastic traditions with their goal of perpetual worship, the different social and cultural situations of China, India and Ethiopia, the cosmological Christianity of Sarum and Kiev, the popular practical and pragmatic devotions of the ordinary people getting on with their everyday life, the radical social experiments of Anabaptists and the New England Pioneers, and the contemporary global technologies of the televangelist. All of these are 'Christian'. All of these draw on the same basic set of discourses. And yet all of these transform those discourses into something new and exciting.

More perhaps than these grand themes or trends in the history of Christian worship, it is also the small, the unique, the imaginative and creative, the forgotten that inspire me. It is here that we learn different things, new things about what it might mean to be Christian. It is here that we can tap into different kinds of tradition. There is the feminine imagery of God into the Syriac Odes of Solomon, the continuing tradition of animal sacrifice within the Armenian church, the dancing of the Ethiopian deacons before the ark, the ascetical traditions of the Celtic saints, the combination of Syriac and Chinese thought on a Nestorian tablet in Xian, the all-night feasting of Spanish peasants at the shrine of their saint, the joyful songs of the Moravians despite centuries of persecution and the absolute purity of Shaker music to accompany their celebratory dance. There is more, much more that could, and should, be discovered. However, even this glimpse shows the importance of seeing each of these situations not as part of some grand narrative of history, but in the glory of the specific, as a local expression of a response to God for his loving kindness in sending his only Son to die for us. Each of these particularities can and should be celebrated, and from each of these particularities we should learn once more to be creative in our own time and place.

This then, brings me back to the meal and the Spirit. I have already said that if these two could ever be successfully reunited then Christian worship could be launched again in a new round of renewal. These, however, are not the only elements from the last two thousand years that I personally would like to see renewed. The emphasis on charity, giving and the support of the poor and oppressed has always been close to the surface of Christian worship, even when it has been at its most imperial. The challenge of the poor should never be lost, and any form of worship that we think of as 'comfortable' should always cause us some level of concern. The language of sacrifice has almost gone from many contemporary discourses, often with good reason. It has often been the rich that have demanded sacrifices of the poor, men who have demanded sacrifices of women, the old who have demanded sacrifices of the young, and so on. However, the voluntary laying down of our lives, metaphorically or in reality, for God and for our friends is an important part of the Christian discourse, and one that sits at the heart of both the meal and the work of the Spirit at many periods of Christian history.

Aiden Kavanagh, in his book *On Liturgical Theology*, argues that many contemporary Western eucharistic services have become more like respectable suburban dinner parties than the inner-city butcher's slab on which the paschal lamb is sacrificed for all.[103] We have perhaps, he argues, focused on the wrong kind of meal, the meal that Paul was objecting to. In the same way, it is possible to argue that in many Western Pentecostal traditions, the reception and indwelling of the Spirit has more to do with what Paul Heelas has called the religion of 'well being' that is associated with the New Age and what 'feels good to me', rather than a Spirit that fires us to go out

---

[103] A. Kavanagh, *On Liturgical Theology, The Hale Memorial Lectures of Seabury-Western Theological College 1981*. New York: Pueblo, 1984.

and change the world whatever the cost.[104] I have noticed, in both England and the United States, an increasing sense of comfortableness and intimacy in contemporary worship that stretches across the traditions: carpets on the floor, a crèche for the children, powerpoint technology providing reassuring images, language that does not offend, and music aimed to speak to our emotions and calm us down.[105] This clearly reflects contemporary, global, society and the discourses of consumerism and individual well-being that dominate it, but is this truly Christian? Some people are now trying what is known in Britain as 'alternative worship', a post-modern approach to worship that does away with structure, hierarchy and all the usual reference points.[106] In practice, however, this only seems to take the current trends in the mixing of Christian and humanist discourses a few steps further, rather than producing anything very new.

While I am convinced that comfortableness and the illusion of intimacy is the gravest danger faced by contemporary Western liturgy, given what I have already said about there being no such thing as a wrong liturgy or a mistaken form of Christian worship, then, perhaps, we should simply see what the future brings, knowing only that it will probably be unlike anything that we have ever seen before. However, it is clear that there must come a point when any form of Christian worship verges on the edge of a truly Christian discourse and even appears to topple over. It is, I would suggest, the core of that discourse that must always be our guide for the future, whatever forms the worship of the church actually takes.

---

[104] P. Heelas, *The New Age Movement: The Celebration of Self and the Sacralization of Modernity.* Oxford: Blackwell, 1996.

[105] See the discussions of intimacy and conforming to contemporary social trends in J. H. S. Stevens, *Worship in the Spirit, Charismatic Worship in the Church of England.* Carlisle: Paternoster Press, 2002 and D. Torevell, *Losing the Sacred, Ritual, Modernity and Liturgical Reform.* Edinburgh: T. & T. Clark, 2000. One is evangelical and the other Catholic, but both highlight the dangers of intimacy and individualism to the contemporary church. Also see the discussion on pp. 20–1 above.

[106] M. Guest, ' "Alternative" Worship: Challenging the Boundaries of the Christian Faith', in E. Arweck and M. D. Stringer (eds.), *Theorizing Faith: The Insider/Outsider Problem in the Study of Ritual.* Birmingham: University of Birmingham Press, 2002, 35–56.

Bibliography

Addington, R. *The Idea of the Oratory.* London: Burns & Oates, 1966

Akeley, T. C. *Christian Initiation in Spain, c. 300–1100.* London: Darton, Longman & Todd, 1967

Albrecht, D. E. *Rites in the Spirit, A Ritual Approach to Pentecostal/Charismatic Spirituality.* Sheffield: Sheffield Academic Press, 1999

Alzati, C. *Ambrosianum Mysterium: The Church of Milan and its Liturgical Tradition,* 2 vols. Cambridge: Grove Books, 2000

Anderson, A. *An Introduction to Pentecostalism, Global Charismatic Christianity.* Cambridge: Cambridge University Press, 2004

Anderson, C. P. 'Introduction', in *A Shaker Hymnal, A Facsimile Edition of the 1908 Hymnal of the Canterbury Shakers.* Woodstock: Overlook Press, 1990, iii–ix

Arseniev, N. *Russian Piety.* London: Faith Press, 1964

Augustine, St. *Concerning the City of God, Against the Pagans.* Harmondsworth: Penguin, 1984

Bagnall, R. S. *Egypt in Late Antiquity.* Princeton: Princeton University Press, 1993

Bailey, T. *The Processions of Sarum and the Western Church.* Toronto: Pontifical Institute of Medieval Studies, 1971

Baldovin, J. F. 'The Urban Character of Christian Worship in Jerusalem, Rome and Constantinople from the Fourth to the Tenth Centuries: The Origins, Development and Meaning of Stational Liturgy'. Ph.D. dissertation, Yale University, 1982

  Liturgy in Ancient Jerusalem. Nottingham: Grove Books, 1989

  'The City as Church, the Church as City', reprinted in J. F. Baldovin, *Church and Renewal.* Washington: Pastoral Press, 1991

Banker, J. R. *Death in the Community: Memorialization and Confraternities in an Italian Commune in the Late Middle Ages.* Athens: University of Georgia Press, 1988

Barnard, L. W. *Justin Martyr: His Life and Thought.* Cambridge: Cambridge University Press, 1967

Barrett-Lennard, R. J. S. *The Sacramentary of Serapion of Thumis: A Text for Students, with Introduction, Translation and Commentary.* Nottingham: Grove Books, 1993

Barton, S. C. 'The Communal Dimensions of Earliest Christianity', in S. C. Barton, *Life Together, Family, Sexuality and Community in the New Testament and Today.* Edinburgh: T. & T. Clark, 2001, 85–116

'Christian Community in the Light of the Gospel of John', in S. C. Barton, *Life Together: Family, Sexuality and Community in the New Testament and Today.* Edinburgh: T. & T. Clark, 2001, 165–86

'Christian Community in the Light of 1 Corinthians', in S. C. Barton, *Life Together, Family, Sexuality and Community in the New Testament and Today.* Edinburgh: T. & T. Clark, 2001, 187–206

Baumann, G. *Contesting Culture, Discourses of Identity in Multi-Ethnic London.* Cambridge: Cambridge University Press, 1996

Baumstark, A. *Comparative Liturgy.* London: Mowbray, 1958

Baxter, P. *Sarum Use, The Development of a Medieval Code of Liturgy and Customs.* Salisbury: Sarum Script, 1994

Beattie, J. *Other Cultures: Aims, Methods and Achievements in Social Anthropology.* London: Routledge & Kegan Paul, 1964

Beckwith, R. T. *Daily and Weekly Worship: From Jewish to Christian.* Nottingham: Grove Books, 1987

'The Jewish Background to Christian Worship', in C. Jones et al. (eds.), *The Study of Liturgy.* London: SPCK, 1992, 68–80

Berger, T. *Women's Ways of Worship, Gender Analysis and Liturgical History.* Collegeville: Liturgical Press, 1999

Beyer, P. *Religion and Globalization.* London: Sage, 1994

Bishop, E. 'Holy Week Rites of Sarum, Hereford and Rouen Compared', in E. Bishop, *Liturgica Historica, Papers on the Liturgy and Religious Life of the Western Church.* Oxford: Oxford University Press, 1918, 276–300

Blond, G. 'Clement of Rome', in R. Johanny (ed.), *The Eucharist of the Early Christians.* New York: Pueblo, 1978, 24–47

Blott, W. R. *Blessing and Glory and Thanksgiving, The Growth of a Canadian Liturgy.* Toronto: Anglican Book Centre, 1998

Botte, B. *From Silence to Participation, An Insider's View of Liturgical Renewal.* Washington: Pastoral Press, 1988

Bourdieu, P. *Outline of a Theory of Practice.* Cambridge: Cambridge University Press, 1977

Bradshaw, P. F. *The Search for the Origins of Christian Worship, Sources and Methods for the Study of Early Liturgy.* 1st edn. London: SPCK, 1992

The Search for the Origins of Christian Worship, Sources and Methods for the Study of Early Liturgy. 2nd edn. London: SPCK, 2002

Bradshaw, P. F., M. E. Johnson and L. E. Phillips. *The Apostolic Tradition.* Minneapolis: Fortress Press, 2002

Bradshaw, P. F. (ed.). *The Canons of Hippolytus.* Nottingham: Grove Books, 1987

Brightman, F. E. 'The Sacramentary of Serapion', *Journal of Theological Studies,* 1 (1900), 88–113, 247–77

Brock, S. P. *The Luminous Eye, the Spiritual World Vision of St Ephrem.* Kalamazoo: Cistercian Publications, 1992

Brock, S. P. (ed.). *The Harp of the Spirit: Eighteen Poems of Saint Ephrem.* London: Fellowship of St Alban and St Sergius, 1983

242   *Bibliography*

Brown, A. S. and D. D. Hall. 'Family Strategies and Religious Practice: Baptism and the Lord's Supper in Early New England', in D. D. Hall (ed.), *Lived Religion in America, Toward a History of Practice*. Princeton: Princeton University Press, 1997, 41–68

Brown, J. M. and R. E. Frykenberg (eds.). *Christians, Cultural Interactions, and India's Religious Traditions*. Grand Rapids: Eerdmans, 2002

Brown, L. W. *The Indian Christians of St Thomas, An Account of the Ancient Syrian Church of Malabar*. Cambridge: Cambridge University Press, 1956

Brown, P. *The Cult of the Saints: Its Rise and Function in Latin Christianity*. Chicago: University of Chicago Press, 1981

Brown, R. E. and J. P. Meier. *Antioch and Rome, New Testament Cradles of Catholic Christianity*. London: Geoffrey Chapman, 1983

Bugnini, A. *The Reform of the Liturgy 1948–1975*. Collegeville: The Liturgical Press, 1990

Bulia, M. and M. Janjalia. *Mtskheta*. Tbilisi: Betania Centre, 2000

Burdon, A. *The Preaching Service – The Glory of the Methodists, A Study of the Piety, Ethos and Development of the Methodist Preaching Service*. Bramcote: Grove Books, 1991

Bynum, C. W. 'Women Mystics and Eucharistic Devotion in the Thirteenth Century', *Women's Studies*, 11 (1984), 179–84

  Holy Feast, Holy Fast, The Religious Significance of Food to Medieval Women. Berkeley: University of California Press, 1987

  The Resurrection of the Body in Western Christianity, 200–1336. New York: Columbia University Press, 1995

Cheremeteff, M. 'The Transformation of the Russian Sanctuary Barrier and the Role of Theophanes the Greek', in A. Leong (ed.), *The Millennium: Christianity and Russia (AD 988–1988)*. Crestwood: St Vladimir's Seminary Press, 1990, 107–24

Chilton, B. *A Feast of Meanings, Eucharistic Theologies from Jesus through Johannine Circles*. Leiden: Brill, 1994

Chow, J. K. *Patronage and Power: A Study of Social Networks in Corinth*. Sheffield: Sheffield Academic Press, 1992

Chrisman, M. U. 'Printing and the Evolution of Lay Culture in Strasbourg, 1480–1599', in R. Po-Chia Hsia (ed.), *The German People and the Reformation*. Ithaca: Cornell University Press, 1988, 74–101

Christian, W. A. *Local Religion in Sixteenth-Century Spain*. Princeton: Princeton University Press, 1981

Cleary, E. L. 'Latin American Pentecostalism', in M. W. Dempster, B. D. Klaus and D. Petersen, *The Globalization of Pentecostalism: A Religion Made to Travel*. Oxford: Regnum Books, 1999, 131–50

Clopper, L. *Drama, Play, and Game, English Festive Culture in the Medieval and Early Modern Period*. Chicago: University of Chicago Press, 2001

Cohen, A. P. *The Symbolic Construction of Community*. Chichester: Ellis Horwood, 1985

Cox, H. *Fire from Heaven: The Rise of Pentecostal Spirituality and the Reshaping of Religion in the Twenty-First Century*. London: Cassell, 1996

Cracraft, J. *The Church Reform of Peter the Great.* Stanford: Stanford University Press, 1971

Crehan, K. *Gramsci, Culture and Anthropology.* London: Pluto Press, 2002

Cross, S. H. *Medieval Russian Churches.* Cambridge, MA: Medieval Academy of America, 1949

Crum, R. J. and D. G. Wilkins. 'In the Defense of Florentine Republicanism: Saint Anne and Florentine Art, 1343–1575', in K. Ashley and P. Sheingorn (eds.), *Interpreting Cultural Symbols, Saint Anne in Later Medieval Society.* Athens: University of Georgia Press, 1990, 131–68

Csordas, T. J. *Language, Charisma, and Creativity, The Ritual Life of a Religious Movement.* Berkeley: University of California Press, 1997

Cuming, G. J. *A History of Anglican Liturgy.* London: Macmillan, 1969
   Hippolytus: A Text for Students with Introduction, Translation, Commentary and Notes. Nottingham: Grove Books, 1976
   Essays on Hippolytus. Nottingham: Grove Books, 1978

Dalby, M. *Anglican Missals and their Canons: 1549, Interim Rite and Roman.* Cambridge: Grove Books, 1998

Dandelion, P. *Liturgies of Quakerism.* Aldershot: Ashgate, 2004

Davie, G. *Europe: The Exceptional Case, Parameters of Faith in the Modern World.* London: DLT, 2002

Davies, J. G. *Pilgrimage Yesterday and Today, Why? Where? How?* London: SCM, 1988

Dawtry, A. 'The Decline of the Cult of Old English Saints in Post-Conquest England: A Case of Norman Prejudice or of Liturgical Reform?' in M. Dudley (ed.), *Like a Two-Edged Sword, The Word of God in Liturgy and History, Essays in Honour of Canon Donald Gray.* Norwich: The Canterbury Press, 1995, 61–8

Dempsey, C. G. *Kerala Christian Sainthood, Collisions of Culture and Worldview in South India.* Oxford: Oxford University Press, 2001

Dix, G. *The Shape of the Liturgy.* London: Adam & Charles Black, 1945

Dixon, N. *Wonder, Love and Praise, A Companion to The Methodist Worship Book.* London: Epworth Press, 2003

Dods, M., G. Reith and B. P. Pratten. *The Writings of Justin Martyr and Athenagoras.* Edinburgh: T. & T. Clark, 1867

Donaldson, C. *Martin of Tours, Parish-Priest, Mystic and Exorcist.* London: Routledge and Kegan Paul, 1980

Dowden, K. *European Paganism, The Realities of Cult from Antiquity to the Middle Ages.* London: Routledge, 2000

Duchesne, L. *Christian Worship: Its Origin and Evolution, A Study of the Latin Liturgy up to the Time of Charlemagne.* London: SPCK, 1904

Duffy, E. *The Stripping of the Altars, Traditional Religion in England c. 1400–c. 1580.* New Haven: Yale University Press, 1992

Dunn, J. D. G. *Baptism in the Holy Spirit: A Re-Examination of the New Testament Teaching on the Gift of the Spirit in Relation to Pentecostalism Today.* London: SCM, 1970
   Jesus and the Spirit: A Study of the Religious and Charismatic Experience of Jesus and the First Christians as Reflected in the New Testament. London: SCM, 1975

'Models of Christian Community in the New Testament', in D. Martin and P. Mullen (eds.), *Strange Gifts?* Oxford: Blackwell, 1984, 1–18

1 Corinthians. Sheffield: Sheffield Academic Press, 1999

Dunn, M. and L. K. Davidson. 'Bibliography of the Pilgrimage: State of the Art', in M. Dunn and L. K. Davidson (eds.), *The Pilgrimage to Compostela in the Middle Ages*. New York: Routledge, 1996, xxiii–xlviii

Dunn, M. and L. K. Davidson (eds.). *The Pilgrimage to Compostela in the Middle Ages*. New York: Routledge, 1996

Dunne, G. H. *Generation of Giants, The Story of the Jesuits in China in the Last Decades of the Ming Dynasty*. Notre Dame: University of Notre Dame Press, 1962

Eire, C. M. N. *War Against the Idols, The Reformation of Worship from Erasmus to Calvin*. Cambridge: Cambridge University Press, 1986

Engberg-Pederson, T. (ed.). *Paul Beyond the Judaism/Hellenism Divide*. Louisville: Westminster John Knox, 2001

Esler, P. *Community and Gospel in Luke-Acts: The Social and Political Motivations of Lucan Theology*. Cambridge: Cambridge University Press, 1987

Eusebius. *The History of the Church from Christ to Constantine*. Harmondsworth: Penguin, 1965

Evans, E. 'Introduction', in *Tertullian's Homily on Baptism: The Text Edited with an Introduction, Translation and Commentary*. London: SPCK, 1964, ix–xl

Tertullian's Homily on Baptism, The Text edited with an Introduction, Translation and Commentary. London: SPCK, 1964

Every, G. *Understanding Eastern Christianity*. London: SCM Press, 1980

Farmer, S. *Communities of St Martin, Legend and Ritual in Medieval Tours*. Ithaca: Cornell University Press, 1991

Fennell, J. *A History of the Russian Church to 1448*. London: Longmans, 1995

Fenwick, J. R. K. *'The Missing Oblation': The Contents of the Early Antiochene Anaphora*. Nottingham: Grove Books, 1989

'India, Syrian Christianity in the South', in K. Parry et al. (eds.), *The Blackwell Dictionary of Eastern Christianity*. Oxford: Blackwell, 2001, 251–6

Fenwick, J. R. K. and B. Spinks. *Worship in Transition, The Twentieth Century Liturgical Movement*. Edinburgh: T. & T. Clark 1995

Ferreiro, A. 'The Cult of the Saints and Divine Patronage in Gallaecia before Santiago', in M. Dunn and L. K. Davidson (eds.), *The Pilgrimage to Compestela in the Middle Ages*. New York: Routledge, 1996, 3–22

Finn, P. C. and J. M. Schellman (eds.). *Shaping English Liturgy, Studies in Honor of Archbishop Dennis Hurley*. Washington: The Pastoral Press, 1990

Finucane, R. C. *Miracles and Pilgrims, Popular Beliefs in Medieval England*. London: J. M. Dent & Sons, 1977

Fiorenza, E. S. *In Memory of Her, A Feminist Theological Reconstruction of Christian Origins*. London: SCM, 1983

Flegg, C. G. *'Gathered Under Apostles', A Study of the Catholic Apostolic Church*. Oxford: Oxford University Press, 1992

Forrester, D. and D. Murray (eds.). *Studies in the History of Worship in Scotland.* Edinburgh: T. & T. Clark, 1996

Forster, M. R. *Catholic Revival in the Age of the Baroque, Religious Identity in Southwest Germany, 1550–1750.* Cambridge: Cambridge University Press, 2001

Foucault, M. *The Archaeology of Knowledge.* London: Routledge, 1972
  Discipline and Punish, The Birth of the Prison. London: Penguin Books, 1977

Frere, W. H. *The Use of Sarum, vol I. The Sarum Customs as set forth in the Consuetudinary and Customary, The Original Texts edited from the Mss. With an Introduction and Index.* Cambridge: Cambridge University Press, 1898
  The Anaphora or Great Eucharistic Prayer, An Eirenical Study in Liturgical History. London: SPCK, 1938

Garrett, T. S. *Worship in the Church of South India.* London: Lutterworth Press, 1958

Gerrish, B. A. *Grace and Gratitude, The Eucharistic Theology of John Calvin.* Edinburgh: T. & T. Clark, 1993

Gibson, S. and J. E. Taylor. *Beneath the Church of the Holy Sepulchre, Jerusalem, The Archaeology and Early History of Traditional Golgotha.* London: Palestine Exploration Fund, 1994

Giddens, A. *Modernity and Self Identity; Self and Society in the Late Modern Age.* Cambridge: Polity Press, 1991

Giles, R. *Re-Pitching the Tent, Re-Ordering the Church Building for Worship and Mission in the New Millennium.* Norwich: Canterbury Press, 1996

Gramsci, A. *Selections from the Prison Notebooks.* London: Lawrence and Wishart, 1971

Grierson, R. 'Dreaming of Jerusalem', in R. Grierson (ed.), *African Zion, The Sacred Art of Ethiopia.* New Haven: Yale University Press, 1993, 5–17

Grierson, R. (ed.). *African Zion, The Sacred Art of Ethiopia.* New Haven: Yale University Press, 1993

Guest, M. '"Alternative" Worship: Challenging the Boundaries of the Christian Faith', in E. Arweck and M. D. Stringer (eds.), *Theorizing Faith: The Insider/Outsider Problem in the Study of Ritual.* Birmingham: University of Birmingham Press, 2002, 35–56

Gutman, R. W. *Mozart, A Cultural Biography.* New York: Harcourt Brace, 1999

Haenchen, E. *The Acts of the Apostles, A Commentary.* Oxford: Basil Blackwell, 1982

Haldon, J. F. *Byzantium in the Seventh Century, The Transformation of a Culture.* Cambridge: Cambridge University Press, 1990

Hall, B. *Humanists and Protestants, 1500–1900.* Edinburgh: T. & T. Clark, 1990

Hall, S. 'Cultural Studies and the Centre: Some Problematics and Problems', in S. Hall, D. Hobson, A. Lowe and P. Willis (eds.), *Culture, Media, Language.* London: Unwin Hyman, 1980, 15–47

Hanawalt, B. A. and K. L. Reyerson (eds.). *City and Spectacle in Medieval Europe.* Minneapolis: University of Minnesota Press, 1994

Harper, J. *The Forms and Orders of Western Liturgy from the Tenth to the Eighteenth Century, A Historical Introduction and Guide for Students and Musicians.* Oxford: Oxford University Press, 1991

Harrington, C. *Women in a Celtic Church, Ireland 450–1150*. Oxford: Oxford University Press, 2002

Hastings, A. *A History of African Christianity 1950–1975*. Cambridge: Cambridge University Press, 1979

Hebert, A. G. *Liturgy and Society*. London: Faber, 1935

Hebert, A. G. (ed.). *The Parish Communion*. London: SPCK, 1937

Heelas, P. *The New Age Movement: The Celebration of Self and the Sacralization of Modernity*. Oxford: Blackwell, 1996

Hemming, J. *Red Gold, The Conquest of the Brazilian Indians*. London: Macmillan, 1987

Henderson, J. 'The Flagellant Movement and Flagellant Confraternities in Central Italy, 1260–1400', *Studies in Church History*, 15 (1978), 147–60

Hertz, R. 'St Besse: A Study of an Alpine Cult', reprinted in S. Wilson (ed.), *Saints and their Cults, Studies in Religious Sociology, Folklore and History*. Cambridge: Cambridge University Press, 1983, 55–100

Holeton, D. R. *La Communion des Tout-Petits Enfants, Etude du Mouvement Eucharistique en Bohème vers le Fin du Moyen-Age*. Rome: Edizioni Liturgiche, 1989

'The Office of Jan Hus: An Unrecorded Antiphonary in the Metropolitan Library of Estergom', in J. N. Alexander (ed.), *Time and Community*. Washington: Pastoral Press, 1990, 137–52

Hollenweger, W. J. *The Pentecostals*. London: SCM, 1972

Hope, W. S. and E. G. C. F. Atchley. *English Liturgical Colours*. London: SPCK, 1918

Howell, C. 'From Trent to Vatican II', in C. Jones et al. (eds.), *The Study of Liturgy*. London: SPCK, 1992, 285–94

Humphrey, C. and J. Laidlaw. *The Archetypal Actions of Ritual, A Theory of Ritual Illustrated by the Jain Rite of Worship*. Oxford: Oxford University Press, 1994

Humphries, M. *Communities of the Blessed, Social Environment and Religious Change in Northern Italy, AD 200–400*. Oxford: Oxford University Press, 1999

Hunt, E. D. *Holy Land Pilgrimage in the Later Roman Empire AD 312–460*. Oxford: Oxford University Press, 1982

Hussey, J. M. *The Orthodox Church in the Byzantine Empire*. Oxford: Clarendon Press, 1986

Iliffe, J. *A Modern History of Tanganyika*. Cambridge: Cambridge University Press, 1979

Ingle, H. L. *First Among Friends, George Fox and the Creation of Quakerism*. Oxford: Oxford University Press, 1994

Ingold, T. *Evolution and Social Life*. Cambridge: Cambridge University Press, 1986

Irvine, C. *Worship, Church and Society, An Exposition of the Work of Arthur Gabriel Hebert to Mark the Centenary of the Society of the Sacred Mission (Kelham) of which he was a Member*. Norwich: Canterbury Press, 1993

Irvine, C. (ed.). *They Shaped Our Worship, Essays on Anglican Liturgists*. London: SPCK, 1998

Isichei, E. *A History of Christianity in Africa, From Antiquity to the Present*. Grand
 Rapids: Eerdmans, 1995
Jardine Grisbrooke, W. *The Liturgical Portions of the Apostolic Constitutions: A Text
 for Students*. Nottingham: Grove Books, 1990
Jasper, R. C. D. *The Development of the Anglican Liturgy, 1662–1980*. London:
 SPCK, 1989
Jasper, R. C. D. and G. J. Cuming (eds.). *Prayers of the Eucharist, Early and
 Reformed Texts*. Oxford: Oxford University Press, 1980
Jeremias, J. *The Eucharistic Words of Jesus*. London: SCM, 1966
Johanny, R. 'Ignatius of Antioch', in R. Johanny (ed.), *The Eucharist of the Early
 Christians*. New York: Pueblo, 1978, 48–70
Johnson, M. E. *Liturgy in Early Christian Egypt*. Nottingham: Grove Books, 1995
 The Rites of Christian Initiation, Their Evolution and Interpretation. Collegeville:
 Liturgical Press, 1999
Jonas, R. *France and the Cult of the Sacred Heart, An Epic Tale for Modern Times*.
 Berkeley: University of California Press, 2000
Joseph, G. 'India, Syrian Christian Community', in K. Parry et al. (eds.), *The
 Blackwell Dictionary of Eastern Christianity*. Oxford: Blackwell, 2001, 249
Jungmann, J. A. *The Mass of the Roman Rite, Its Origins and Development
 (Missarum Sollemnia)*. New York, Benziger Brothers, 1959
Kalumba, L. N. 'The Zairian Rite: The Roman Missal for the Diocese of Zaire
 (Congo)', in K. Pecklers (ed.), *Liturgy in a Postmodern World*. London:
 Continuum, 2003, 92–8
Karant-Nunn, S. G. *The Reformation of Ritual, An Interpretation of Early Modern
 Germany*. London: Routledge, 1997
Kavanagh, A. *On Liturgical Theology, The Hale Memorial Lectures of Seabury-
 Western Theological College 1981*. New York: Pueblo, 1984
Kay, W. K. *Pentecostals in Britain*. Carlisle: Paternoster Press, 2000
Keay, J. *India, a History*. London: Harper Collins, 2000
Kepel, G. *The Revenge of God: The Resurgence of Islam, Christianity and Judaism
 in the Modern World*. Cambridge: Polity Press, 1994
Klaus, B. D. 'Pentecostalism as a Global Culture, An Introductory Overview',
 in M. W. Dempster, B. D. Klaus and D. Petersen, *The Globalization of
 Pentecostalism: A Religion Made to Travel*. Oxford: Regnum Books,
 1999, 127–30
Koester, H. *Introduction to the New Testament, vol. II, History and Literature
 of Early Christianity*. New York: Walter de Gruyter, 1987
Kuefler, M. *The Manly Eunuch, Masculinity, Gender Ambiguity and Christian
 Ideology in Late Antiquity*. Chicago: University of Chicago Press, 2001
Lambert, F. *Inventing the 'Great Awakening'*. Princeton: Princeton University
 Press, 1999
Leaver, R. A. *The Liturgy and Music, A Study of the Use of the Hymn in Two
 Liturgical Traditions*. Bramcote: Grove Books, 1976
le Huray, P. *Music and the Reformation in England 1549–1660*. Cambridge:
 Cambridge University Press, 1978

Lerner, K. 'Georgia, Christian History of' in K. Parry et al. (eds.), *The Blackwell Dictionary of Eastern Christianity*. Oxford: Blackwell, 2001

Lewis, G. *Day of Shining Red, An Essay on Understanding Ritual*. Cambridge: Cambridge University Press, 1980

Lewis, I. M. *Ecstatic Religion, A Study of Shamanism and Spirit Possession*. London: Routledge, 1989

Lieu, S. N. C. *Manichaeism in Mesopotamia and the Roman East*. Leiden: Brill, 1994

Lindberg, C. *The European Reformations*. Oxford: Blackwell, 1996

Lossky, V. *The Mystical Theology of the Eastern Church*. Napierville: Allenson, 1957 *In the Image and Likeness of God*. London: Mowbray, 1974

Lüdemann, G. *Heretics, The Other Side of Early Christianity*. London: SCM, 1996

Lutz, C. and L. Abu-Lughod (eds.). *Language and the Politics of Emotion*. Cambridge: Cambridge University Press, 1990

Malina, B. J. *The New Testament World, Insights from Cultural Anthropology*. Louisville: Westminster John Knox, 2001

Mannion, M. F. 'Liturgy and the Present Crisis of Culture', *Worship*, 62:2 (1988), 98–123

Markus, R. *The End of Ancient Christianity*. Cambridge: Cambridge University Press, 1990

Marshall Lang, D. *Lives and Legends of the Georgian Saints*. London: George Allen & Unwin, 1956

Martin, D. *Tongues of Fire: The Explosion of Protestantism in Latin America*. Oxford: Blackwell, 1990

Matheson, P. *The Imaginative World of the Reformation*. Edinburgh: T. & T. Clark, 2000

McGrail, S. P. 'The Celebration of First Communion in Liverpool: A Lens to View the Structural Decline of the Roman Catholic Parish'. Ph.D. dissertation, University of Birmingham, 2003

McGuckin, J. A. 'Nestorius and the Political Factions of Fifth-Century Byzantium: Factors in His Personal Downfall', *Bulletin of the John Rylands University Library of Manchester*, 78: 3, 1996, 7–21

McManus, F. R. 'ICEL: The First Years', in P. C. Finn and J. M. Schellman (eds.), *Shaping English Liturgy, Studies in Honor of Archbishop Dennis Hurley*. Washington: The Pastoral Press, 1990, 433–59

McMullen, R. *Christianizing the Roman Empire*. New Haven: Yale University Press, 1984

McSweeney, B. *Roman Catholicism, The Search for Relevance*. Oxford: Blackwell, 1980

Meeks, W. *The First Urban Christians: The Social World of the Apostle Paul*. New Haven: Yale University Press, 1983

Méhat, A. 'Clement of Alexandria', in R. Johanny (ed.), *The Eucharist of the Early Christians*. New York: Pueblo, 1978, 99–131

Meissner, W. W. *Ignatius of Loyola, The Psychology of a Saint*. New Haven: Yale University Press, 1992

Mercier, J. *Art That Heals, The Image as Medicine in Ethiopia.* Munich: Prestel, 1997

Meyendorff, J. *The Orthodox Church, Its Past and its Role in the World Today.* Crestwood: St Vladimir's Seminary Press, 1981

Meyendorff, P. *Russia, Ritual and Reform, The Liturgical Reforms of Nikon in the Sixteenth Century.* Crestwood: St Vladimir's Seminary Press, 1991

Moorhead, J. *Ambrose: Church and Society in the Late Roman World.* London: Longman, 1999

Mosse, D. 'The Politics of Religious Synthesis: Roman Catholicism and Hindu Village Society in Tamil Nadu, India', in C. Stewart and R. Shaw (eds.), *Syncretism/Anti-Syncretism, The Politics of Religious Synthesis.* London. Routledge, 1994, 108–26

Moxnes, H. *The Economy of the Kingdom, Social Conflict and Economic Relations in Luke's Gospel.* Philadelphia: Fortress Press, 1988

Munro-Hay, S. *Aksum, An African Civilisation of Late Antiquity.* Edinburgh: Edinburgh University Press, 1991

Murphy-O'Connor, J. 'Pre-Constantinian Christian Jerusalem', in A. O'Mahony (ed.), *The Christian Heritage in the Holy Land.* London: Scorpion Cavendish, 1995, 13–21

Murray, R. *Symbols of Church and Kingdom, A Study in Early Syriac Tradition.* Cambridge: Cambridge University Press, 1975

Mytum, H. *The Origins of Early Christian Ireland.* London: Routledge, 1992

Neale, J. M. *Essays on Liturgiology and Church History.* London: Saunders, Otley & Co., 1863

Niederwimmer, K. *The Didache: A Commentary.* Minneapolis: Fortress Press, 1998

Nocent, A. *La Célébration Eucharistique Avant et Après Saint Pie V.* Paris: Beauchesne, 1977

O'Mahony, A. (ed.). *The Christian Heritage in the Holy Land.* London: Scorpion Cavendish, 1995

Palazzo, E. *A History of Liturgical Books from the Beginning to the Thirteenth Century.* Collegeville: Pueblo, 1998

Palmer, W. *Origines Liturgicae, or Antiquities of the English Ritual, and A Dissertation on Primitive Liturgies.* Oxford: Oxford University Press, 1832

Parker, D. C. *The Living Text of the Gospel.* Cambridge: Cambridge University Press, 1997

Parry, K. 'Images in the Church of the East: The Evidence from Central Asia and China', *Bulletin of the John Rylands University Library of Manchester*, 78:3 (1996), 143–62

Paxton, F. S. *Christianizing Death, The Creation of a Ritual Process in Early Medieval Europe.* Ithaca: Cornell University Press, 1990

Pecklers, K. F. *Dynamic Equivalence, The Living Language of Christian Worship.* Collegeville: Liturgical Press, 2003

Pedersen, K. S. 'The Qeddusan: The Ethiopian Christians of the Holy Land', in A. O'Mahony (ed.), *The Christian Heritage in the Holy Land.* London: Scorpion Cavendish, 1995, 129–48

Pellegrini, L. 'Female Religious Experience and Society in Thirteenth Century Italy', in S. Farmer and B. H. Rosenwein (eds.), *Monks and Nuns, Saints and Outcasts, Religion in Medieval Society, Essays in Honor of Lester K. Little*. Ithaca: Cornell University Press, 2000, 97–122

Perham, M. 'The Language of Worship', in M. Perham (ed.), *Towards Liturgy 2000, Preparing for the Revision of the Alternative Service Book*. London: SPCK, 1989, 67–74

Peters, B. *The Anglican Eucharist in New Zealand, 1814–1989*. Bramcote: Grove Books, 1992

Phillips, L. E. *The Ritual Kiss in Early Christian Worship*. Nottingham: Grove Books, 1996

Phillipson, D. W. *Ancient Ethiopia, Aksum: Its Antecedents and Descendants*. London: British Museum Press, 1998

Phythian-Adams, C. 'Ceremonies and the Citizen: The Communal Year at Coventry 1450–1550', in P. Clark and P. Slack (eds.), *Crisis and Order in the English Towns 1500–1700*. London: Routledge and Kegan Paul, 1972, 57–85

Pickstock, C. 'Liturgy and Language: The Sacred Polis', in P. Bradshaw and B. Spinks (eds.), *Liturgy in Dialogue, Essays in Memory of Ronald Jasper*. London: SPCK, 1993, 115–37

After Writing: On the Liturgical Consummation of Philosophy. Oxford: Blackwell, 1998

Po-Chia Hsia, R. 'Münster and the Anabaptists', in R. Po-Chia Hsia (ed.), *The German People and the Reformation*. Ithaca: Cornell University Press, 1988, 51–70

Poppe, A. 'The Building of the Church of St Sophia in Kiev', in A. Poppe, *The Rise of Christian Russia*. London: Variorum Reprints, 1982

Power, D. N. *Irenaeus of Lyons on Baptism and the Eucharist: Selected Texts with Introduction, Translation and Annotation*. Nottingham: Grove Books, 1991

Purcell, N. 'The Populace of Rome in Late Antiquity: Problems of Classification and Historical Description', in W. V. Harris (ed.), *The Transformations of Urbs Roma in Late Antiquity*. Portsmouth: Journal of Roman Archaeology, Supplement Series, 1999

Ramshaw, G. *Worship: Searching for Language*. Washington: Pastoral Press, 1988

Rankin, D. *Tertullian and the Church*. Cambridge: Cambridge University Press, 1995

Robbins, V. K. *The Tapestry of Early Christian Discourse, Rhetoric, Society and Ideology*. London: Routledge, 1996

Roberts, A. and J. Donaldson (eds.). *The Apostolic Fathers*. Edinburgh: T. & T. Clark, 1867

Roberts, C. H. *Manuscript, Society and Belief in Early Christian Egypt*. Oxford: Oxford University Press, 1979

Robertson, I. 'The Jando and Initiation in Southern Tanzania', in D. R. Holeton (ed.), *Liturgical Inculturation in the Anglican Communion, Including the York Statement 'Down to Earth Worship'*. Bramcote: Grove Books, 1990, 27–31

Robertson Smith, W. *Lectures on the Religion of the Semites.* London: A. & C. Black, 1907

Rordorf, W. 'The *Didache*', in R. Johanny (ed.), *The Eucharist of the Early Christians.* New York: Pueblo, 1978

Rosman, A. and P. G. Rubel. *The Tapestry of Culture: An Introduction to Cultural Anthropology.* New York: McGraw-Hill, 1995

Rubenson, S. 'The Egyptian Relations of Early Palestinian Monasticism', in A. O'Mahony (ed.), *The Christian Heritage in the Holy Land.* London: Scorpion Cavendish, 1995, 35–46

Rubin, M. *Corpus Christi, The Eucharist in Late Medieval Culture.* Cambridge: Cambridge University Press, 1991

Russell, J. C. *The Germanization of Early Medieval Christianity, A Sociohistorical Approach to Religious Transformation.* Oxford: Oxford University Press, 1994

Salzman, M. 'Christianization of Sacred Time and Sacred Space', in W. V. Harris (ed.), *The Transformations of Urbs Roma in Late Antiquity.* Portsmouth: Journal of Roman Archaeology, Supplement Series, 1999, 123–34

Sandon, N. (ed.). *The Octave of the Nativity, Essays and Notes on Ten Liturgical Reconstructions for Christmas.* London: BBC, 1984

Sawyer, D. F. *Women and Religion in the First Christian Centuries.* London: Routledge, 1996

Schoedel, W. R. *A Commentary on the Letters of Ignatius of Antioch.* Philadelphia: Fortress Press, 1985

Sennett, R. *The Fall of Public Man.* New York: Knopf, 1977

Shaw, R. and C. Stewart. 'Introduction: Problematizing Syncretism', in C. Stewart and R. Shaw (eds.), *Syncretism/Anti-Syncretism, The Politics of Religious Synthesis.* London: Routledge, 1994, 1–26

Skhirtladze, Z. *Desert Monasticism, Gareja and the Christian East: Papers from the International Symposium, Tbilisi University, September 2000.* Tbilisi: Gareja Studies Centre, 2001

Smith, D. E. *From Symposium to Eucharist, The Banquet in the Early Christian World.* Minneapolis: Fortress Press, 2003

Smith, J. Z. *To Take Place: Towards Theory in Ritual.* Chicago: University of Chicago Press, 1987

Soltner, L. *Solesmes and Dom Gueranger, 1805–1875.* Orleans: Paraclete Press, 1995

Sperry-White, G. *The Testamentum Domini: A Text for Students with Introduction, Translation and Notes.* Nottingham: Grove Books, 1991

Spinks, B. D. *Addai and Mari – The Anaphora of the Apostles: A Text for Students with Introduction, Translation and Commentary.* Nottingham: Grove Books, 1980

Stambaugh, J. and D. Balch. *The Social World of the First Christians.* London: SPCK, 1986

Stephens, W. P. *Zwingli, An Introduction to His Thought.* Oxford: Clarendon Press, 1992

Stevens, J. H. S. *Worship in the Spirit, Charismatic Worship in the Church of England.* Carlisle: Paternoster Press, 2002

Stevenson, K. *Nuptial Blessing, A Study of Christian Marriage Rites.* London: SPCK, 1982

 Covenant of Grace Renewed, A Vision of the Eucharist in the Seventeenth Century. London: DLT, 1994

Stoyanov, Y. *The Hidden Tradition in Europe, The Secret History of Medieval Christian Heresy.* London: Penguin, 1994

Stringer, M. D. 'Antiquities of an English Liturgist: William Palmer's Use of Origins in the Study of the English Liturgy', *Ephemerides Liturgicae,* 108 (1994), 146–56

 'Style Against Structure: The Legacy of John Mason Neale for Liturgical Scholarship', *Studia Liturgica,* 27:2 (1997), 235–45

 On the Perception of Worship, The Ethnography of Worship in Four Christian Congregations in Manchester. Birmingham: Birmingham University Press, 1999

 'Rethinking Animism: Thoughts from the Infancy of our Discipline', *Journal of the Royal Anthropological Institute,* N.S. 5:4 (1999), 541–56

 'Discourse and the Ethnographic Study of Sufi Worship: Some Practical Suggestions', in A. Zhelyazkova and J. Nielsen (eds.), *Ethnology of Sufi Orders: Theory and Practice.* Sofia: International Centre for Minority Studies and Intercultural Relations, 2001

Swanson, R. N. *Religion and Devotion in Europe, c. 1215 – c. 1515.* Cambridge: Cambridge University Press, 1995

Tachiaos, A.-E. N. *Cyril and Methodius of Thessalonica, The Acculturation of the Slavs.* Crestwood: St Vladimir's Seminary Press, 2001

Taft, R. F. 'The Structural Analysis of Liturgical Units: An Essay in Methodology', in R. Taft (ed.), *Beyond East and West, Problems in Liturgical Understanding.* Washington: Pastoral Press, 1984, 151–66

 'How Liturgies Grow: The Evolution of the Byzantine Divine Liturgy', in *Beyond East and West, Problems in Liturgical Understanding.* Washington: The Pastoral Press, 1984, 167–92

 The Liturgy of the Hours in East and West, the Origins of the Divine Office and its Meaning for Today. Collegeville: The Liturgical Press, 1986

 The Byzantine Rite, A Short History. Collegeville: Liturgical Press, 1992

 'In the Bridegroom's Absence: The Paschal Triduum in the Byzantine Church', in *Liturgy in Byzantium and Beyond.* Aldershot: Ashgate, 1995

 'The Liturgy of the Great Church: An Initial Synthesis of Structure and Interpretation on the Eve of Iconoclasm', in *Liturgy in Byzantium and Beyond.* Aldershot: Ashgate, 1995

 'The Armenian "Holy Sacrifice (*Surb Patarg*)" as a Mirror of Armenian Liturgical History', reprinted in *Divine Liturgies – Human Problems in Byzantium, Armenia, Syria and Palestine.* Aldershot: Ashgate, 2001

 'Women at Church in Byzantium: Where, When – and Why?' in *Divine Liturgies – Human Problems in Byzantium, Armenia, Syria and Palestine.* Aldershot: Ashgate, 2001

 'Liturgy in the Life and Mission of the Society of Jesus', in K. Pecklers (ed.), *Liturgy in a Postmodern World.* London: Continuum, 2003, 36–54

Talley, T. J. *The Origins of the Liturgical Year.* Collegeville: Liturgical Press, 1991

Teteriatnikov, N. 'The Role of the Devotional Image in the Religious Life of Pre-Mongol Rus', in W. C. Brumfield and M. M. Velimirovic (eds.), *Christianity and the Arts in Russia.* Cambridge: Cambridge University Press, 1991, 30–45

Theissen, G. *The First Followers of Jesus, A Sociological Analysis of the Earliest Christianity.* London: SCM, 1978

  The Social Setting of Pauline Christianity: Essays on Corinth. Philadelphia: Fortress Press, 1982

Thomas, D. (ed.). *Syrian Christians under Islam: The First Thousand Years.* Leiden: Brill, 2001

Thomas, J. P. *Private Religious Foundations in the Byzantine Empire.* Washington: Dumbarton Oaks Research Library and Collection, 1987

Thomson, R. W. 'Armenian Christianity', in K. Parry et al. (eds.), *The Blackwell Dictionary of Eastern Christianity.* Oxford: Blackwell, 2001, 54–59

Thornton, J. 'The Development of an African Catholic Church in the Kingdom of Kongo, 1491–1750', *Journal of African History,* 25 (1984), 147–67

Thurian, M. and G. Wainwright. *Baptism and Eucharist: Ecumenical Convergence in Celebration.* Grand Rapids: Eerdmans, 1983

Torevell, D. *Losing the Sacred, Ritual, Modernity and Liturgical Reform.* Edinburgh: T. & T. Clark, 2000

Tovey, P. *Inculturation: The Eucharist in Africa.* Bramcote: Grove Books, 1988

  Inculturation of Christian Worship, Exploring the Eucharist. Aldershot: Ashgate, 2004

Trevett, C. *A Study of Ignatius of Antioch in Syria and Asia.* Lewiston: Edward Mellen Press, 1992

  Montanism: Gender, Authority and the New Prophecy. Cambridge: Cambridge University Press, 1996

Tripp, D. H. 'Protestantism and the Eucharist', in C. Jones et al. (eds.), *The Study of Liturgy.* London: SPCK, 1992, 294–308

Tristram, E. W. *English Medieval Wall Painting, the Twelfth Century.* New York: Hacker Art Books, 1988

Trocmé, E. *The Passion as Liturgy, A Study of the Origins of the Passion Narratives in the Four Gospels.* London: SCM, 1983

Turner, D. *The Darkness of God, Negativity in Christian Mysticism.* Cambridge: Cambridge University Press, 1995

Tylor, E. *Primitive Culture: Researches into the Development of Mythology, Philosophy, Religion, Art and Custom.* London: John Murray, 1871

Van Gennep, A. *The Rites of Passage.* London: Routledge & Kegan Paul, 1960

Vladyshevskaia, T. 'On the Links between Music and Icon Painting in Medieval Rus', in W. C. Brumfield and M. M. Velimirovic (eds.), *Christianity and the Arts in Russia.* Cambridge: Cambridge University Press, 1991, 14–29

Vogel, C. *Medieval Liturgy, An Introduction to the Sources.* Washington: Pastoral Press, 1986

Wagner, R. *The Invention of Culture.* Chicago: University of Chicago Press, 1981

Wakefield, G. S. *An Outline of Christian Worship.* Edinburgh: T. & T. Clark, 1998

Walker, P. W. L. *Holy City, Holy Places? Christian Attitudes to Jerusalem and the Holy Land in the Fourth Century.* Oxford: Oxford University Press, 1990

'Jerusalem and the Holy Land in the Fourth Century', in A. O'Mahony (ed.), *The Christian Heritage of the Holy Land.* London: Scorpion Cavendish, 1995, 22–34

Wallace-Hadrill, J. M. *The Barbarian West 400–1000.* Oxford: Blackwell, 1985

Walls, A. F. *The Missionary Movement in Christian History, Studies in the Transmission of Faith.* Edinburgh: T. & T. Clark, 1996

Walsh, C. J. 'Adult Initiation and the Catholic Church', in D. A. Withey, *Adult Initiation.* Bramcote: Grove Books, 1989, 34–42

Waring, D. G. *Manufacturing the Muse.* Middletown: Wesleyan University Press, 2002

Warren, F. E. *The Liturgy and Ritual of the Celtic Church.* Oxford: Oxford University Press, 1881

The Sarum Missal in English. London: A. R. Mowbray & Co., 1913

Werbner, R. 'Introduction', in R. Werbner (ed.), *Regional Cults.* London: Academic Press, 1977

Westermeyer, P. *Te Deum, The Church and Music.* Minneapolis: Fortress Press, 1998

White, J. F. *The Sunday Service of the Methodists in North America.* Nashville: United Methodist Publishing House, 1984

A Brief History of Christian Worship. Nashville: Abingdon Press, 1993

White, S. J. *Christian Worship and Technological Change.* Nashville: Abingdon Press, 1994

A History of Women in Christian Worship. London: SPCK, 2003

Wilkinson, J. *Egeria's Travels.* Warminster: Aris & Phillips, 1999

Williams, A. V. 'Zoroastrians and Christians in Sasanian Iran', *Bulletin of the John Rylands University Library of Manchester,* 78:3 (1996), 37–54

Willis, G. G. *Further Essays in Early Roman Liturgy.* London: SPCK, 1968

Wilmart, A., E. A. Lowe and H. A. Wilson. *The Bobbio Missal (Ms Paris. Lat. 13246), Notes and Studies.* London: Harrison and Sons Ltd., 1924

Wilson, C. *Notes on Mozart, 20 Crucial Works.* Edinburgh: St Andrew Press, 2003

Wilson, E. A. 'They Crossed the Red Sea, Didn't They? Critical History and Pentecostal Beginnings', in M. W. Dempster, B. D. Klaus and D. Petersen, *The Globalization of Pentecostalism: A Religion Made to Travel.* Oxford: Regnum Books, 1999, 85–115

Winkler, G. *Studies in Early Christian Liturgy and Its Context.* Aldershot: Ashgate, 1997

'Armenian Liturgy', in K. Parry et al. (eds.), *The Blackwell Dictionary of Eastern Christianity.* Oxford: Blackwell, 2001, 60–2

Withey, D. A. *Catholic Worship, An Introduction to Liturgy.* Bury St Edmunds: Kevin Mayhew, 1990

Woolfenden, G. *Daily Prayer in Christian Spain, A Study of the Mozarabic Office.* London: SPCK, 2000

Wren, B. *What Language Shall I Borrow? God-Talk in Worship: A Male Response to Feminist Theology.* London: SCM Press, 1989

Wybrew, H. *The Orthodox Liturgy: The Development of the Eucharistic Liturgy in the Byzantine Rite.* Crestwood: St Vladimir's Seminary Press, 1989

Yarnold, E. *The Awe-Inspiring Rites of Initiation, The Origins of the RCIA.* Edinburgh: T. & T. Clark, 1994

Yelverton, E. E. *An Archbishop of the Reformation, Laurentius Petri Nericius, Archbishop of Uppsala, 1531–73, A Study of His Liturgical Projects.* London: Epworth Press, 1958

Zetterholm, M. *The Formation of Christianity in Antioch, A Social-Scientific Approach to the Separation Between Judaism and Christianity.* London: Routledge, 2003

Index